Books by Jack Mendelsohn

WHY I AM A UNITARIAN

GOD, ALLAH, AND JU JU

WHY I AM A UNITARIAN UNIVERSALIST

THE FOREST CALLS BACK

THE MARTYRS

CHANNING
The Reluctant Radical

CHANNING

William Ellery Channing in 1811
(Engraved by Cheney after a portrait
by Washington Allston)

Channing
The Reluctant
Radical

A Biography by
JACK MENDELSOHN

Little, Brown and Company · Boston · Toronto

LIBRARY OF CONGRESS CATALOG CARD NO. 75–161863

FIRST EDITION
T11/71

Published simultaneously in Canada
by Little, Brown & Company (Canada) Limited

PRINTED IN THE UNITED STATES OF AMERICA

To Joan

Author's Note

RESPONSIBILITY for the defects of this book is wholly mine. Its merits are a different matter. These I heartily share with Richard Myers, a cherished friend who happens also to be a gifted historian, researcher, and student of Channing. By the labors of Richard Myers, a mountain of basic data materialized before me. He checked my source notes, wrote many of the foot-notes, selected the pictorial illustrations, and created the index. In addition, he worked closely with Llewellyn Howland III, my Little, Brown editor, in sustained, constructive criticism of the text. My respect and affection for both men is equaled only by my gratitude. Together, we three share a conviction that Channing merits one of the front rooms in the house of history, that he moved far ahead of his time as an unromantic anticipator of a serious modernism, that he struggled, with unique combinations of genius, hope, and realism, to release the human spirit from melancholy, cloistered religion, to fill it with inner spirituality and strong feeling, and to turn it loose on the secular frontiers of thought and action.

JACK MENDELSOHN

Illustrations
(Between pages 106–116)

CHANNING

The Return of
William Ellery Channing

CHANNING DIED IN 1842, and has periodically been recovered. This is not unusual with historical figures of genuine distinction. There is often an unaccountable oscillation in the repute of a genius. "Sometimes," as Conrad Wright has written, "the revival of interest in someone long neglected may be accounted for by the discovery of a mass of research material stored away in a forgotten attic, or by the release of such material, previously kept under restriction by the man himself or by his family. Sometimes a man's message may make more sense to one generation than it did to those preceding it."[1]

There are no great new finds of documents or manuscripts to explain the successive rediscoveries of Channing. Staggering amounts of material have always been available. Each time interest in Channing has quickened, there have been veins to be freshly mined, but not because they were newly available. They were already at hand, buried in the mass. Actually, the vital bulk of Channing documentation is his own. He was a fantastically prolific writer. His hand worked compulsively in tandem with his mind. He was a fanatical scribbler of every thought that crossed his brain. Channing *was* exactly what, in millions of his scrawled words, he seemed to be. There is no mysterious man behind the man.

Yet there is a mystery, or, at least, an enigma.

Each time Channing returns, he does so in response to someone's need to reconceive him, to rediscover him as real and believable. Poor old John Pierpont (1785–1866) — Unitarian clergyman, poet, reformer, great-grandson of James Pierpont,

3

grandfather of J. Pierpont Morgan, and beloved friend of Channing. Taken as a divinity student under Channing's sheltering wing, Pierpont lived as much to merit Channing's fraternal commendation as that of his own conscience. When Pierpont flirted with professional disaster by attacking the "rumsellers" who were among the leading members of his own congregation, Channing put his enormous prestige solidly at Pierpont's back. When Channing died, Pierpont tried to utter what his revered colleague's friendship had meant through the years: Dr. Channing, while he lived, was like the sun on Pierpont's meridian; shedding the light of his mind upon Pierpont's world, waking it to a moral life by the truths that he taught, and warming it by the fervor of his own spirit.[2]

Years later, Pierpont's failing mind was assaulted by a devious medium named J. V. Mansfield, a promoter of spiritualism. Mansfield convinced Pierpont that by not throwing prestige and support to the spiritualist cause, he was distressing his departed friend Channing. Pierpont was not so far gone that he neglected to demand "proof," which the calculating Mansfield was more than happy to fabricate. He urged Pierpont to address a letter to Channing on "the other side." With so competent an amanuensis as Mansfield acting in Channing's behalf, an answer was swiftly forthcoming. It urged Pierpont to take to the hustings as spiritualism's messenger. For a doddering Pierpont, in the twilight of his life, Channing had indeed returned — unexpectedly, but in response to a need. A battle-weary Pierpont laced on his boots and hit the Lyceum trail in behalf of spiritualism, the old fire once again in his eye.[3]

Fortunately, the serial rediscoveries of Channing have generally been of a more solid nature. Though significant *new* information has not been a major factor, there are interesting tidbits. It has not occurred to scholars that the monumental genius of Max Weber might have been instructed, perhaps even aroused, by Channing. Yet it was, as both Weber's mother and wife were ready to attest, if anyone had been interested. Writing to his mother from Strasbourg on July 8, 1884, Weber mused: " . . . my sole preoccupation during my time in the army infirmary was some philosophy and in addition the reading of a

4

small volume of Channing's writings. The latter, which Aunt Ida was kind enough to lend me, was of especially great interest to me, because Channing bases his views on exceptionally lofty sentiments — sentiments which in their own way are unassailable. His view of what constitutes the essence of religion is highly original and often grand in its scope, albeit scarcely Christian. [Channing would have been appalled at this. Most emphatically did he consider himself to be a Christian. Still, he would have understood Weber's subtle meaning.] It is combined with an uncommonly attractive personality, which makes this somewhat older contemporary and fellow countryman of Theodore Parker an even more appealing figure than the latter. In any case he is a considerably more universal one, if only because he is not always passionately concerned with finding answers to those theoretical questions of religion and philosophy which were so important to Parker. *This is the first time in many years that I can recall anything of a religious nature having aroused in me a more than objective interest, and I do not think the time I spent getting acquainted with this great religious phenomenon was wasted."*[4] (Italics mine.)

Weber's discovery, forty-two years after Channing's death, typifies the enigma. In 1880, the one hundredth anniversary of Channing's birth, elaborate public celebrations sprang up throughout the United States, in Great Britain, Ireland, and Europe. Enthusiastic tributes flowed from Asia. New York's Henry W. Bellows, D.D., in a fervent memorial discourse in Channing's hometown, Newport, sounded what was literally a worldwide note: "Of Channing, we do not say that he *was*, but he *is*, a burning and shining light; and the season has not gone by, it has not even reached its meridian, when the Church and the world are willing to rejoice in his light."[5]

Sydney Ahlstrom, one of the canniest of contemporary religious historians, could still be exhilarated in 1957 by the 1880 phenomenon: "During half of the nineteenth century, Channing was probably the most influential American religious thinker being heard abroad; and he reached beyond Britain to the Continent where Jonathan Edwards, for example, had remained virtually unknown. This American prophet, moreover, was not

5

merely read. Men of great intellectual stature had their ways of thinking changed. His words wrought conversions."[6]

The Channing who fashioned "conversions" in the 1830's, was virtually forgotten by the 1870's. By the 1880's he was back in circulation again. With a new century, he suffered another eclipse. As a sickening world became obsessed with its psychic wounds, Channing was brusquely reshuffled downward. This fluctuation is explicable. Ours was becoming an existentially tormented age, in which, according to Alexander Cowie, we were "compulsively drawn toward the darker spirits, choosing Lucifer after the Fall."[7]

We were hell-bent, says Cowie, to reject those whom we believed to be "naively innocent of experience." We were drawn toward those who had "seen the serpent in Eden, . . . been initiated into the knowledge of good and evil"; particularly those who were "probers of guilt and possessors of a 'tragic vision.' "[8]

Who could expect to find Channing in that dismal scene? Anyone as serene and buoyant as he, had to be out of it. Where were his nightmare fantasies, his tortured despair, his cancerous sense of impending doom? So, if he was noticed at all, it was as a harmless old fellow, a pleasant enough but abominably innocent chap, who had a tiresome lot to say which was simply irrelevant to the tangled, tormented human condition.

Yet there is another return of Channing, another gathering process of rediscovery and reconception. Emerging from the shadows in which he was all but smothered (much as he was wont to smother himself in scarfs and cloaks against the chill Boston wind), Channing is again radiating his strange compelling power. One wonders if a portion of his recurring power is not in the primitive paradox of weakness and smallness combined with boundless force. For Channing was physically small and weak. He was an invalid, barely five feet tall. He had to be soaking wet to weigh one hundred pounds. Throughout his forty-year professional career, he was a physical ruin. But he lived a magnificently affirmative life. It is just possible, then, that this latest return of Channing says something about a growing wish for an upbeat impulse in the midst of our existential bedevilments. Channing found curing answers, not for his dyspepsia and deafness and numerous other bodily maladies, but for the spirit of life. He found, pronounced, and lived a reverberating *yes*.

Yet Channing spent his seasons in hell. He was tormented by the evils which are the bane of all generations — the classical evils, both inward and outward. He lifted himself through and over them, never pretending that they were not there. If this is a reason for our latest rediscovery of him, it is a strong one. Channing did not overcome his chronic illnesses, he lived in spite of them. He did not "come to terms" with moral evil, he let it storm his consciousness, and fought back. He is recalled as serene. Such he was, but not accidentally. He struggled for his serenity. He won it. He is remembered as happy. Indeed, as his life wore on, his body ever subject to more pains, more aches, he awoke mornings a progressively happier man. But this did not come to pass as a gift of his genes. He won happiness by repudiating contentment. More than a century before Sartre, he was aware of what it meant to bear the "condemnation" of human freedom. He knew that he was free, and he knew the terrors of being free. He fronted the terrors and endured. No, he did more than endure. He rejoiced.

The troubles that plagued Channing's personal life were substantial. As a youngster he watched his mother struggle in genteel but real poverty to feed and clothe a large family. Though wiry and muscular enough as a boy to defend himself, he was shaken to the roots of his young being by the brutality of teachers to pupils, larger student to smaller student. Occupying British troops had left much of his home town of Newport a sorry, stripped-down shambles. He fell in love early with his schoolmate Ruth Gibbs, remained in love with her for what seemed an eternity before his personal circumstances permitted a relatively late marriage.

The two years he spent in Richmond, after his Harvard graduation, were a nightmare of postadolescent fantasies, devastating loneliness, feverish Luther-like wrestlings with inner demons. These two desperately unhappy years, undertaken to help, as best he could, his family's harsh financial circumstances, permanently broke his health.

Death, in its most jolting fashion, stalked through his life. His

7

father suddenly died when he was thirteen. Two of his own children were snatched from him, one while he and his wife were traveling in Europe — a crushing situation. Of the many protégés he acquired, none reached deeper inside him than the brilliant German émigré, Charles Follen, who suffered a horrifying death by fire while sailing from New York to Boston. And then, in a move of pulverizing insensitivity, Channing's own church refused his request for a memorial service. Follen was an early abolitionist. Channing saw at the time that "suffering comes to us through and from our whole nature. It cannot be winked out of sight. It cannot be thrust into a subordinate place in the picture of human life. . . . It is, to not a few, the most vivid recollection of life."[9]

And there was more for Channing to bear. Ruth, the woman he had waited so long for, was, almost from the beginning of their marriage, a victim of punishing arthritis. His son, in an unanticipated adolescent rebellion, shattered for a time the family's morale. Channing's sister, especially cherished, died. The brother he had been closest to died also, leaving a son in Channing's care.

Through all of these ordeals, he faced, in his professional life, a deepening crisis. The congregation at Federal Street, for which he had poured out his energies, was made up in part of men who steadily soured on their celebrated pastor's involvement in social and political issues. When some of his most prominent parishioners began cutting him as they passed in the street, Channing knew at firsthand the pang of failure. He had preached his heart out to reach just such men as these, to move them to what he called "cheerful, vigorous, beneficent *action* of each for all." Instead, behind his back, they croaked that he had become a locofoco. To his face, there was deliberate and open insult. But, unlike Emerson and Ripley, Channing did not resign his pastorate. A stranger to the pedestrian griefs of life? Sheltered from the slings and arrows? Hardly.

True, harsh circumstances and sorrows do not of themselves a philosopher make, so there remains the very legitimate question about Channing. Did he make to all of this a coherent response? Amazingly so, I would answer. If you would learn what a man

8

is, Channing reasoned, it is not enough to dissect his mind, and analyze separately the thoughts and feelings which serially march through him. "The question is, what thoughts and feelings predominate, stand out most distinctly, and give a hue and impulse to the common actions of his mind? What are his great ideas?"[10] Channing knew that for him there was a reigning idea — a high God-intoxicated estimate of human nature. He knew also the perils of such an idea. "The truth is, that a man, who looks through the present disguises and humbling circumstances of human nature, and speaks with earnestness of what it was made for and what it may become, is commonly set down by men of the world as a romancer, and, what is far worse, by the religious as a minister to human pride, perhaps as exalting man against God."[11] Channing matched his reverence for the human soul with a tragic sense worthy of it, in the eye of which "man is such a mote in the creation, his imperfections and sins are so prominent in his history, the changes of his life are so sudden, so awful, he vanishes into such darkness, the mystery of the tomb is so fearful, all his outward possessions are so fleeting, the earth which he treads on so insecure, and all surrounding nature subject to such fearful revolutions, that the reflective and sensitive mind is prone to see nothingness inscribed on the human being."[12] It was because of these darker visions, not in bland disavowal of them, that Channing asserted the greatness of the soul. To probe the means of his triumph is, surely, reason enough for rediscovering him in our existentially tormented age.

Given the accumulating realities of his development, he might easily have become a determinist, like Edwards, or a resigned absurditarian. The point is that he did not shy away from the powerful realities driving in that direction. Nor did he neglect the never-ending battle that pits necessity against free will. "Life is made up of necessary and free forces," he wrote to Elizabeth Peabody, "and it is a great question which of these prevails in our history. . . . It is a superficial philosophy which dismisses this subject with saying 'man rows, but destiny steers.' The question is, whether our *rowing* springs from destiny; whether this be fate-bound or free? If the latter, then the faithful rower wins the race of life, no matter how steered."[13]

9

Easy cures, bland promises, spiritual tranquilizers — for these Channing could muster scorn, or as close to scorn as he could get. One does not annul by artificial means one's profound ignorance of the soul. "But I *do* catch a *glimpse*," he wrote, " . . . I can bear the burden of the infinite mystery."[14] He could find no empirical proof for freedom of the will, but was delighted to report, after painstaking study of Jonathan Edwards's Promethean tomes, that Edwards had failed to find empirical proof against it. Channing added wryly that if Edwards had succeeded in establishing that men's actions were fixed links in a chain of destiny, "it would be one of the most pernicious books ever issued from our press."[15] In an affirmation symbolic of his certainty that free will and necessity coexist, Channing buoyantly dismissed Edwards's contrary effort as "a demonstration which no man believes, which the whole consciousness contradicts."[16] In this fashion Channing confirmed for himself the reality of hope, then radiated it outward, as a fountainhead, to Emerson, to Parker, to Ripley. Obviously, each of them might have come independently to the notion that freedom and fate cohabit man's reality, but the fact is that they heard it first and foremost from Channing. They rode Channing's arrow.

That the Emersons, Parkers, and Ripleys did not simply ape him, but were soon firing darts of their own, was exactly what he wished. Channing wanted people to listen hard to what he had to say. He was certain enough of his own ground. But he disclaimed imitators. Nothing discouraged him more, he said, than those "looking out for some beaten path."[17] Frankly aware of his charismatic power, Channing confided to Elizabeth Peabody how it pained him to be told that he had preached an eloquent sermon. "If I had touched the depths of spiritual energy, my hearers would not express admiration for my words."[18] What Channing wanted others to find was their own motivation. No one could take another's voyage of the spirit. Eloquence, charisma — these in themselves could be anodynes for petty egos, leading to the nursing rather than the giving of self. If people were to learn their moral powers, they had to be movers, not mimics. They had to discover for themselves that the self-giving life was a far cry from the self-insisting life.

All of this, Channing, with his flowing mind, his great, luminous eyes, his wasted body, searched for in the abyss of his own soul. He hungered for others to do the same. "There *is* such a thing," he promised, "as a serene, immovable conviction."[19] He could vouch for it. And he believed that the conviction of man's worth had the power to revolutionize society, to "create relations among men not dreamed of at the present day."[20] Knowing the desert places in self, and the hideous places in society, he girded himself to assault both.

This is why the current recovery of Channing makes sense. He speaks to our need. In the midst of our emancipated identity-seeking, fed up with a theology that labors our all-too-obvious limitations, weary with guilt, sin, and pride and our celebration of human pathology, we welcome one who stared into the void and found meaning. We had forgotten that Channing was such a man, so bemused were we by the plaster in which his earlier hagiographers had cast him.

Throughout the first half of the twentieth century, Channing's denigration was complete. The scholarly and popular worlds treated him with massive indifference. John White Chadwick's sprightly biography in 1903 was the last consequential effort to recover him. Thirty-six blank years followed. Only then did an intellectual historian — Herbert W. Schneider — take a tentative peek; he was impressed enough by what he found to venture that Channing might well have been the "American Schleiermacher."[21] Since no one was particularly interested in Schleiermacher, Schneider's lavish estimate was ignored. But attention was paid to Schneider's scouting of Channing as a primary synthesizer of the American mind. Channing, said Schneider, took eighteenth-century Christian piety, republicanism and rationalism, and kneaded them into a powerful, new, "native" liberalism.

In 1942 the English scholar Anne Holt rushed into print with a thin volume marking the centenary of Channing's death.[22] It was a pity that she felt pressed by the anniversary, and even more a pity that she did not later take time to broaden her approach. Appreciative but unawed, she found a warmly human and fallible Channing behind the marble bust.

In 1952 Robert Leet Patterson, an erudite theologian, reported on his heroic plunge into the formidable oceans of Channing's writings.[23] He found what others, like Bellows, had earlier hinted at — that Channing was capable of startlingly original theological thought. Carried away, Patterson was convinced that Channing's *Via Affirmativa,* his doctrine of the "essential sameness" of God and man, was like nothing else in the history of Christian speculation.

Three years later, David P. Edgell provided a fresh, lucid portrait of Channing's personality, mind, and leadership.[24] The syrup of adulation is squeezed from it. Channing's equivocations are permitted in fetching humanness. The documentation, as far as it goes, is admirable. But whether from lack of time or money, Edgell leaves us hankering for wider dimensions of his subject. To Edgell's enduring credit, he discerns that one of the most memorable marks of Channing's appeal was his capacity to bear the ambiguity of confusing and contradictory issues, to perceive more deeply than the masses of people, to put forward a broader and better synthesized range of passionate commitments than other intellectual leaders, and yet to retain the confidence of both.

Amidst an outcropping of scholarly articles and doctoral dissertations on various facets of Channing lore, two traditional biographies then surfaced: Arthur W. Brown's in 1956,[25] and Madeleine Hooke Rice's in 1961.[26] The merit of both is that they weave new highlights into Chadwick's basic fabric. Their importance is in further ordering and shaping the materials by which our desire to *know* the man may yet be satisfied. The enigma persists. If we are to penetrate it in terms of our own needs, there is much to do.

The freedom Channing staked his life on is at the root of the modern spiritual crisis. So we must, as Ahlstrom has testified, "attempt to reconceive Channing's milieu, the society and culture of which he was a part."[27] It was in that setting, after all, that Channing willed himself to bear the awesome dimensions of freedom.

Realization that there are not just two worlds, the sacred and the profane, but as many worlds as there are human modes of apprehending them, has fronted us with the necessity of grounding religion, if it is to be grounded anywhere, in the human condition — exactly where Channing placed it. So, having recreated the aura in which Channing developed, we must concentrate on Channing's indelible self-identification as a minister of religion, a prophet and reformer of the moral life. This was the core of his being, the authentic matter-of-factness of his life, the uncompromised center of his soul. If he has something to say to us, he must speak as he was. And we in turn must discover, if the search is to be worth the effort, that Channing landed where we find ourselves today, not trying to solve outmoded theological riddles, but with the necessity of starting with the human situation, perceiving its multitude of possibilities, and questing simultaneously for more adequate standards of religious action, for greater personal maturity, for sharper social relevance. The test of Channing's germaneness is whether or not he saw in a multiplex reality that religious action is not less but more demanding than ever.

In any case, I am satisfied that we are pointed in the right direction in believing that if the Channing renaissance is to be advanced, the basis of Channing's claim on people must be eagerly explored.

ONE

Pathways to a Life Style

I

How a Poor Boy from Newport Got to Harvard and Beyond

WILLIAM ELLERY CHANNING, who was distinguished by an extraordinary sanity and a clearly defined scale of values, was born in a town and territory distinguished for packing "more bizarre and incredible history per square foot than any other state in the Union."[1]

Newport, his birthplace, was haven to both Captain Kidd, pirate, and Anne Hutchinson, heretic. Rhode Island was the first settlement in the new world to foster religious liberty, yet for a century was a high-volume trader in black flesh, with Newport itself acknowledged to be one of the world's busiest slave ports.

A year and a half earlier than the Boston Tea Party, Rhode Island's sons of liberty brazenly burned the *Gaspee*. A month before any other colony — on May 4, 1776 — Rhode Islanders declared their independence from Great Britain. Yet, these same Rhode Islanders were the last of the original thirteen to ratify the Constitution of the United States.

Two of the towering eighteenth-century religious figures, Stiles and Hopkins, were simultaneously at work in Newport, along with twenty-two rum distilleries. The remarkable Bishop Berkeley, in residence in Newport, epitomized the handsome port's culture, while Godfrey Malbone, Newport's richest man, epitomized its materialism.*

---

* Colonel George Washington, twenty-four, visited Godfrey Malbone's elaborate home in 1756. An exemplary guest, he left behind, in Virginia currency, a generous tip for the Malbone servants, and an equal amount for a bowl he broke. Not long afterward, the Malbones were about to seat their guests at a dinner party when the house caught fire. Malbone, cursing but

In 1779, Newport's events were a mixture of the historic, the absurd, the personal. A large British force, after three years of vengeful occupation, departed, leaving once prosperous Newport a wreck. Edward Brinley, a twenty-one-year-old native, accidentally shot a ramrod clean through his own body. The ramrod was found at the foot of an apple tree thirty yards away. Brinley lived into his nineties.[2] Lucy Ellery Channing, wife of William Channing, became pregnant with her third child.

On April 7, 1780, the child, William Ellery Channing, was born. "The most splendid child I ever saw," one of the relatives remembered. His birthplace, however, was not then so splendid. The ravages of revolution had reduced the population from twenty-two thousand to less than four thousand. British troops, with a fanatical concern for firewood, had defoliated the landscape and chopped up the furnishings of most public buildings, including the pews of the Channing family church, which they used as a billet.

The Reverend Dr. Ezra Stiles, soon to be Yale's president, made a pastoral visit to his Newport flock. He preached. He baptized the infant son of his friends, William and Lucy Channing. He recorded in his diary in minute detail the desolation of Newport and the desecration of his church. There was a broader bleakness as well. A large quantity of clothing and muskets that Lafayette had persuaded the French to make for Washington's army never reached America's shores because Franklin could not find the merchant ships to load them or the warships to escort them. A Rhode Island colonel, writing to his state government begging for clothing, said his men were called "the naked regiment."

For contrast, Lafayette arrived. Short months after William Ellery Channing's birth, Rochambeau's French expeditionary force, sixty-seven thousand strong, marched into Newport. If Washington, without sea power, could not yet figure out how to use his allies, at least they were on hand, a promise of a turning tide.

---

undismayed, declared, "If I have lost my house there is no reason why I should lose my dinner." A table was set in the garden and the courses served while the house burned to the ground.

Meanwhile, at a deeper level, thoughts of a cotton gin were germinating in a man's mind; spinning and weaving machines were being dreamed of. From them would spring an industrial revolution, a burst of population, a radical anachronization of slavery. Soon, in England, a paper-making machine would be invented to use the flood of rags to be generated by textile machines. Expansion of the printing and publishing industries was inevitable. Indeed, a whole chain of revolutionary developments was forming. With printed material cheap, literacy, for the first time in human history, could be dramatically extended. Every conceivable area of human interaction would be affected.

William Ellery Channing learned to crawl, to walk, then to run, as a new nation and a new age emerged. Famous and fifty-six, he looked back on his earliest years as "a critical, perilous season."[3] His endowments, however, were impressive.

The first Channings, of solid middle-class English stock, came to Newport from Newton Abbot, in Devonshire, at the dawn of the eighteenth century. Their coat of arms, a cluster of three moors' heads, linked them to the Canning family, which would produce one of England's strongest foreign ministers. It also traced their descent from the Canyngeses of Bristol, powerful fifteenth-century merchant princes, restorers of the church of St. Mary Redcliffe.

Young William Ellery Channing automatically acquired propriety and status, but not property. That would come with marriage. His father, a devoted promoter of America's liberation, was not a *social* revolutionist. He saw little problem in slavery. He treated slaves well. He produced ten children, but no wealth. He abounded in respectability and public involvement, so much so that he saw less of his children than they desired. He worked hard and long to feed the many mouths in his School Street household. He died suddenly, with no money in the bank. Among his personal friends and dinner guests had been Washington, Jay, and other prominent Federalist figures of his time. One of them, Asher Robbins, U.S. Senator from Rhode Island, makes him stilted but real.

"Mr. Channing," Robbins wrote, "was very well read in the law, especially in the forms of pleading; law cases were his favorite reading, even for amusement. He had a large library, and one very well selected.

"He interested himself much in state politics, and his office was the central point of rendezvous, where the leading men congregated for their consultations.

"He was very popular in the State, was attorney-general and district attorney at the same time, and held both offices at the time of his death.

"His manner of speaking at the bar was rapid, vehement, and impressive; never studied, nor exactly methodical in his pleadings; but he always came well prepared as to matter and authority. He had an extensive practice, attended all the courts regularly, and was considered, for several years before his death, as the leading counsel of the State.

"In person, he was of middle stature, well made, erect, and of open countenance; he was lively and pleasant in his conversation, and much disposed to social intercourse; he was hospitable and kind-hearted. His agreeable manner was one great source of his general popularity.

"In dress, he was not remarkable for any particular; it was always proper and becoming, though not an object of much attention with him; the color was commonly black; indeed, I do not recollect ever to have seen him in any other.

"His temper was remarkably good, as were his manners, mild, liberal, generous; his habits were also correct, temperate, industrious, mindful and observant of all the duties and proprieties of life."[4]

William Channing's celebrated father-in-law, a Declaration of Independence signer given to no idle echoes, matched the Robbins tribute. His son-in-law, he attested, was "beloved and respected." To the poor and needy, "his table and his purse were always open." His religious sentiments were "liberal," his political sentiments were displayed "in a warm attachment to the rights of mankind." As a husband and father, he was "tender . . . beloved and respected."[5]

Young Channing recalled his father as "the delight of the circle in which he moved. I well remember the benignity of his countenance and voice." At the same time, "he was a strict disciplinarian at home, and, according to the mistaken notions of that time, kept me at too great a distance from him." Still the father shared much with the son. He took him often to court, and when, finally, in 1790, the Rhode Island state convention ratified the Constitution, ten-year-old William was there, savoring his father's "boundless exultation." There were certain paternal dynamics the son remembered with special feeling: the father's lack of "sensibility to the evil" of slavery; the father's "peculiar abhorrence" of profanity — no small matter in a community noted for its colorful blasphemies.[6]

The mother, Lucy Ellery, was, like the son, short and elastic, keen, candid, and assertive. From her spirited father, she received energy, judgment, and a charm of romance. She was strong. She could be chillingly severe with pretension and fraud. She laughed discriminatingly but with zest.

"The most remarkable trait in my mother's character," Channing later wrote, "was the . . . simplicity of her mind. . . . She had the firmness to see the truth, to speak it, to act upon it. She was direct in judgment and conversation . . . I cannot recall one word or action betraying the slightest insincerity. She had keen insight into character. She was not to be imposed upon by others, and, what is rarer, she practiced no imposition on her own mind. She saw things, persons, events, as they were, and spoke of them by their right names. Her partialities did not blind her, even to her own children. Her love was without illusion."[7]

Young William found growing up something of a struggle. Slight, muscular, and agile, he was popular. Yet he could not later look back to his childhood with nostalgia. The discipline at Mr. Rogers's school was unapologetically harsh. No child was to be lost for want of proper flogging. The boys tormented one another. He could wrestle with the best of them, but was strangely moved when one of his schoolmates threw his body over a downed youngster being pounded by several others, and the violence suddenly, eerily drained away. He developed early a horror and contempt for physical violence, but was also aware within himself of an unnatural lack of physical fear.

There was something about power that fascinated him. His

playmates, with reason, called him "Little King Pepin," after the diminutive father of Charlemagne, ruler of the Franks. Still he fled repeatedly to the meadows and beaches, an unaccountable sense of isolation upon him.

But after everything else has been said about William Ellery Channing, a final judgment has to be that he was a man of faith. People of faith are certain that some part of what is given them is free. They are driven hard to explore what it means to exercise that freedom. They need spaces beyond the self to peer into because the future fascinates and commands them. They feel an obligation to it, a duty. When calamity comes, they stand. They face up to calamity, or injustice — whatever. They draw the despairing together and speak to them of what they can do. Not so much what they *must* do, but what they *can* do. A man has to know the part of him that is free, in order to be a person of faith. Channing's first taste of such freedom, as he later said, came as he roamed alone over Newport's fields and shores. ". . . Amid this glorious nature, that love of liberty sprang up which has gained strength within me to this hour."[8]

Also, a man of faith has to learn somehow that the true depths are to be found in what people *mean* by what they say. Channing's biographers have, in this respect, generally missed the significance of the most classical story of his childhood. Elizabeth Peabody was a notable exception.[9]

According to Miss Peabody's notes, Channing himself often told the story. "When I was quite young," he would say, "I heard a sermon from an itinerant preacher, which roused in me the first doubt of human veracity. I was taken by my father in a chaise to a meeting, to which he went to hear a famous preacher of the revival kind. My father, I think, took me rather to give me the drive, and relieve my mother of the care of me, than with any expectation of my attending to the sermon. But I could not choose but attend; for the preacher made such a terrific picture of the lost condition of the human race rushing into hell . . . that it filled my imagination with horror. It must have been done with some artistic skill, I think, for it vanquished the preacher's own imagination, so that in very moving tones he besought his hearers to flee from the wrath to come into the arms of Jesus, who was described as wounded and bleeding at the hand of the inexorable God, who exacted from him the uttermost penalty due to a world of sinners."

Channing recalled that a small war was going on inside himself when the sermon ended. There was a knot of terror along with a streak of skepticism. But the skepticism was crushed, leaving only the terror, when, as they climbed back into the chaise, he heard his father say to a friend, "Sound doctrine that! Leaves no rag of self-righteousness to wrap the sinner in!"

He was certain that on the way home his father would say something about the family's personal plans for "fleeing the wrath to come." But to the boy's bewilderment, the father began to whistle! Yet on reaching the house, when Mrs. Channing asked if the preacher had been a disappointment, Mr. Channing answered: "No; he is a strong man."

They sat down to supper, which was eaten with not a word to indicate the extraordinary danger suggested by the sermon. After supper, the father took his pipe and a newspaper, sat down before the fire, removed his shoes, and began calmly to read. Young William was transfixed by a shaft of insight. *Not,* as is usually assumed, in the form of distrust "of the emotional ardors of religion" (Chadwick's phrase).[10] But in the necessity of withholding judgment upon what people say until one is able to divine by their actions what they *mean.*

Men of faith, because they are men of faith and hold the future so dear, must avoid squandering their precious freedom on phantoms. This, as Channing mused toward the end of his life, was the only form of caution he consciously indulged. But this form, he took most seriously. "I mean not to justify myself," he wrote in a letter to Elizabeth Peabody, "but I ought to say that I have had but one form of 'caution,' so far as I know myself. I have never hesitated to say clearly and strongly what I was persuaded was *true.* But I have not 'dared' to send forth opinions around which doubts and objections lingered in my own mind. I hold a *clear conviction of truth* to be essential to a religious teacher, and I reprobate as well as dread the teaching of that which we have not thought on calmly and seriously, or which on being examined has opened on us problems, perplexities, and difficulties, rendering much reflection needful in order to our speaking with deliberate consciousness of truth. The want of reverence for truth manifest in the rash teaching of our times shocks me greatly. I owe the little which I am to the conscientiousness with which I have listened to objections springing up in my own mind to what I have inclined and sometimes thirsted to believe; and I have attained through this to a serenity of faith."

The roots of Channing's ultimate repudiation of Calvinistic theology were grounded not in such messages of doom as he and his father heard. He was learning to build his liberal faith on the *actions* of which human nature, in its likeness to God, is capable. *That* is where one finds the true meaning of what is said, not in words themselves. The crucial figure in the familiar anecdote was not the evangelist; it was his father, whose words affirmed the dark horror of the sermon, but whose actions signaled something else.

Channing's boyhood was a pulsing, creative time. Americans, newly conscious of their independent identity, were proud of a remarkable all-American horse named Justin Morgan. They were also too stubborn to change their drinking habits in favor of the wines pressed upon them by the French. A republican culture was springing up, contrary to John Adams's dour forecast. Noah Webster, a young Hartford schoolmaster, declared: "America must be as independent in *literature* as she is in politics, as famous for *arts* as for *arms.*" To show the way, Webster ground out in quick succession his celebrated blue-backed speller, his first American reader, his famous *American Dictionary* — all dedicated to Americanizing the King's English. The Reverend Jedidiah Morse, eventually to be Channing's antagonist in the Unitarian controversy, put in print when Channing was a nine-year-old schoolboy the first edition of his *Geography Made Easy*. Phillis Wheatley, black poetess — a former slave freed by her Boston owner — was the girl wonder of the day.

At the Channing table in 1786, we may suppose there was anxious talk about Daniel Shays's "rebellion" in Massachusetts, about mobs of angry farmers storming Berkshire courthouses, and the mob in Concord, which was demanding relief from unpayable debts and taxes. The Rhode Island assembly avoided riot and insurrection by offending against sound Federalist finance. In its wisdom and mercy, it provided that if a creditor refused to accept the state's nearly worthless paper currency at par, the debtor could discharge his obligation simply by depositing the script with the nearest judge. According to Samuel Eliot Morison, "the reverse of the usual situation took place — harassed creditors were pursued by implacable debtors eager to tender a wad of depreciated paper for the full value of their debt. Rather than sell goods for worthless paper, merchants shut up shop, hid their stock, or loaded it on a vessel and escaped to New York or the West Indies."[11]

The Channings and their relatives were torn. They were staunch Federalists, part of the commercial, social, and political elite. But they held strong republican sentiments as well, and decent sympathies for the less favored. William was introduced early to the paradoxes of self-government.

From France came word of the Bastille. William's father relished the news that France was following in America's footsteps. When the report arrived that the French had declared themselves a republic and decreed war "against all kings," there was near-hysterical enthusiasm, even in sophisticated Newport. Soon, the French Revolution, by guillotining Louis XVI, by declaring war on Great Britain and Spain, by installing the Girondin party in power, by attacking religion, became one of the most combustible issues in American politics, and in Channing's reach toward identity.

In the making of Channing's mind, or that of any other privileged New England boy of his time, piety was a brooding, permeating force. Dr. Ezra Stiles took leave from the Channing family's church, Second Congregational on Clarke Street, a few years before young William's birth. For the first six years of his life, the family attended the First Congregational church on Mill Street, meetinghouse of the formidable Dr. Samuel Hopkins, pupil and friend of Jonathan Edwards, chief spokesman for what Channing was later to call "the stern and appalling theology" of Hopkinsian Calvinists.

Hopkins, like Stiles, had been driven by the British occupation from Newport. In 1780 he returned to stay, finding his congregation reduced in number and bedraggled in spirit. Channing's recollections were blunt. He sat with his parents and listened to Hopkins, he said, "with no profit." He found the Hopkins pulpit style "singularly unattractive."[12] As a young man, Channing would come to respect and admire Hopkins the man, Hopkins the scourge of slavery, Hopkins the tower of principle. But he never altered his impression of Hopkins the lugubrious pulpiteer: "His delivery in the pulpit was the worst I ever met with. Such tones never came from any human voice within my hearing. He was the very ideal of bad delivery . . . the matter . . . often as uninviting as the manner."[13]

By 1786, Second Congregational had a new pastor, the Reverend William Patton, and the Channing family returned to it. Though Channing spent most of his childhood worship hours there, he was apparently unaffected by Patton. When he reflected on these early years, his thoughts centered on Stiles and Hopkins; and on Rachel De Gilder, the family's housekeeper and confidante. A powerful and maternal woman of marked cheerfulness, Mrs. De Gilder spoke often to young William of the pearls of religious wisdom she received from Mr. Eddy, her Baptist minister, who was later known as a Unitarian. Between Rachel De Gilder and grandfather William Ellery, an amateur religious scholar, the sensitive boy found much to mull over in the realms of piety. He recalled that as a child he was "quite a theologian, though I hated to hear my elders chop logic, according to the fashion of that controversial time."[14]

The prevalence of terror in preaching, logic chopping in theology, the insufferably dull weekly drill of assembly catechism — intermingled with Newport's fabled profanity, high life, and hard drinking — gave rise, as Channing remembered, "to ludicrous stories among the boys."[15] He was taking it all in, wondering what it all meant.

Meanwhile, schooling for the most part was a necessity to be suffered. Young William was bright enough, but he preferred the waterfront, the lonely beach, kite flying, quoits, gardening — almost anything — to the classroom. His Boston ministerial colleague of future years, Joseph Stevens Buckminster, was then a Portsmouth, New Hampshire, boy of four, but already proficient in Latin and Greek. Far from precocious, Channing required extra Latin tutoring from a clerk in his father's office.

Not unreasonably, Channing associated formal instruction with an early schoolmistress, a whalelike woman who wore two sets of eyeglasses on her ample nose, and whose confidence in the redemptive power of the rod was consummate. There was further trauma in his next institution of learning, the dame school of Mrs. Sayre and her daughter Betsy, which he attended, according to family custom, in a threadbare calico smock that prudent Mrs. Channing imposed upon each of her sons in turn as they reached the appropriate size.[16] Finally, his preparation for college was begun at the respected school of Mr. Rogers, where, to a reputable extent, Channing bloomed. Several of the enrolled students were Southern boys, sent by their prominent families to profit from New England learning, among them the celebrated painter-poet of later years, Washington Allston. Indeed, Channing and Allston became lifelong friends. There was also William's Newport cousin, Ruth Gibbs, immune both as a girl and a very rich one from the more violent rigors of Mr. Rogers's discipline. William would marry her eventually, and he, at least, believed that the idea burrowed into his thoughts as he watched her go AWOL from the school and skip down the street, taunting through the window those she left behind.

By the time William was twelve, his parents decreed that he had exhausted Newport's educational opportunities. He was dispatched to New London, Connecticut, to ready himself for Harvard with his uncle Henry Channing, a distinguished divine of liberal reputation, who had earlier broken his tutorial relationship with Yale in a doctrinal dispute.

It was sadly early for a childhood to end. Young William had not even learned to swim, and never did. Mrs. Channing, for whatever reason, was phobic about her boys swimming unless accompanied by an adult. But there were no adults to accompany them. William's brothers went swimming anyway, and took their lumps. Obedient William did not. The punishment he could have taken. Disregard for his mother's wishes was beyond him.

So, off to New London he went, just in time to be caught in the swirl of a religious revival. These were the years of such popular uprisings of piety in New England. New London was in the grip of one that strongly moved Uncle Henry, who in turn passed along to his impressionable nephew a lasting enthusiasm for religion. In the future, Channing would pinpoint this as the beginning of his decided interest in the spiritual life.

It is difficult, from his printed sermons, to measure Henry Channing's theological views precisely. He was deeply impressed by the new spiritual interest aroused in his flock by the New London revival. On the other hand, it is significant that at a later date he left his pulpit in a controversy involving his hearty support of the Reverend John Sherman of Mansfield, Connecticut. Sherman's troubles sprang from an anti-Trinitarian tract he published in 1805: *One God in One Person Only*. It is likely that Henry Channing, during young William's influential years with him, was an Arminian — that is, believed that men are born with the capacity both for good and evil; that they can respond to the impulse toward virtue as well as the temptation toward sin; and that life is a process of testing and discipline by which, with the aid God extends to all, the enslavement to sin may little by little be overcome. The Arminian declaration of human competence contrasts with the assertion of Calvinism that the inborn talent of human nature is for sin alone, that God has decreed eternal bliss to some and eternal torment to others, and that salvation comes as the undeserved gift of God's Holy Spirit.

In terms of Channing's later development, the distinction between what he probably heard from Uncle Henry and what he most assuredly heard from Dr. Hopkins is important. Local historians agree that despite the dour Calvinism of Connecticut, Henry Channing was at least leaning in the Arminian direction, possibly from the very outset of his career. One who knew him well, his great-nephew William Henry Channing, adds another note. He says that Henry Channing "preserved a spirit free and bright, cheerful in hope and utterly intolerant of bigotry."[17] These traits were to become high, universal virtues in Channing's subsequent outlook, but first there was to be an adolescent anguish.

On September 21, 1793, midway in Channing's stay at Uncle Henry's, his father unexpectedly and suddenly died. The cause is obscure, but the effect on William, immediate and long-term, was not. Overnight, he had to gird himself to be a man. Was he ready?

Francis, his older brother, then a junior at Harvard, and William, with their widowed mother and the seven other children, followed the coffin through the streets of Newport to the burying ground. Overnight an advantaged, independent family found itself in chilling financial straits. William Channing, for all his honors and undertakings, had laid up little property. There was a house, but not much more. It was clear that at the earliest possible moment Francis and William would have to come to the support of the family. But in the best New England tradition, high aims were to be maintained in the midst of refined poverty. Francis returned to Harvard; William to New London for another year of college preparation. He was admitted to Harvard College in 1794.

Letters from Uncle Henry suggest the seriousness that his father's death had fastened on him. "Your aunt loves you tenderly," one letter stated, "and often expresses her feelings while recounting your affectionate respect and attention. Never did you excite one painful emotion in our breasts. . . . We never can forget such a nephew, or rather such a son. . . . Without flattery, I can only say that your progress was more the result of your assiduity than of my attention. . . . We know that your situation and your genius justify us in forming the most flattering ideas of the future eminence of our nephew."

It was not unusual then for wellborn boys of only fourteen to enter Harvard, but how did a *poor* wellborn boy manage it? His family's position must be remembered. The Channing household was extremely well connected. Mrs. Channing's sister, for example, was married to Francis Dana, chief justice of Massachusetts, whose "country seat" was one of Cambridge's most stately homes. Being a member of New England's birthright aristocracy was as natural to Channing, and as uncomplicated, as putting on his socks. There was no question whatever that he would attend college, with funds to be found in the mysterious ways familiar to such extended families as his. To lighten the financial burden, he would live at Unce Francis Dana's home.

What kind of youth was it, who prepared for the journey from Newport to Cambridge? His body, though bantam-size, was sound. In temperament, he was self-contained, but amiable and well mannered. His mind, though unprecocious, was thorough and inquiring. He had grown up in a fond but essentially dispassionate family atmosphere, permeated with *noblesse oblige*. He was not a rebel. Years would pass before the contradictions in his family would strike home — cherishing political liberty, but profoundly suspicious of anything that smacked of "leveling" the social classes; loving freedom, but strangely unperturbed by slavery as a social issue, or by the thriving Newport rum trade through which the "peculiar institution" expanded. True, the Channings had always treated their slaves humanely and had liberated them after the revolution, and favored Rhode Island's emancipation edict. But it was a personal matter, not a problem of principle. Then there was the French Revolution — splendid as long as it seemed to be a carbon copy of the American revolt, but a stench in the nostrils of decent men when it took its own radical course.

The intimate family life that harbored and hid these paradoxes patterned Channing's later unique trait of coupling castigation of moral evils with a direct, compassionate appeal to evildoers. Those he loved best in the world, his family, were party to some of the world's malignancies. Were not other evildoers like his own father? He could never take the fateful step — as a Garrison or Parker did — of throwing the evil and the evildoer into the same bag, and smiting them simultaneously hip and thigh. Whether this made him a greater or lesser man in his own time is perhaps an insoluble conundrum. That mankind might still do well to ponder his basic approach, is self-evident.

Harvard in 1794 was vastly different from its present leviathan state. There were two dormitories, and two other buildings, one a chapel. A president, three professors, and several young tutors constituted the faculty. Total enrollment was one hundred and seventy-three. The gap between students and faculty was a yawning chasm. In Chadwick's words, "The Jews had more dealings with the Samaritans than the students with the president and the professors and their families in a social way."[18] Outwardly, deportment was strictly regulated. "All the undergraduates," the sumptuary regulations read, "shall be clothed in coats of blue gray, or dark blue. And no student shall appear within the limits of the college or town of Cambridge in a coat of any other color, unless he shall have on a night gown, or in stormy or cold weather an outside garment over his coat. . . . Nor shall a surtout or any other outside garment of any other color than a blue gray or a dark blue be substituted for the uniform coat. . . . But the students are permitted to wear black gowns, in which they may appear on all public occasions. No part of their garments shall be of silk; nor shall they wear gold or silver lace, cord or edging upon their hats, waistcoats or any other parts of their clothing. And whosoever shall violate any of these regulations shall be fined a sum of not less than 80 cents, nor more than one dollar and sixty cents for each offense; and if anyone persist in such violation he shall be subject to higher censures."[19]

Channing, living comfortably in his uncle's mansion, was spared the rigors of meals at commons: breakfast, a biscuit and butter, washed down by a tin cup of unsettled coffee; lunch, a pound of boiled meat, two potatoes, and a pewter mug of cider; supper, bread and diluted milk.[20]

Joseph Story, who joined Channing's class in 1795, recorded the dreary undergraduate curriculum: "In Greek," he recalled, "we studied Xenophon's Anabasis, and a few books of the Iliad; in Latin, Sallust and a few books of Livy; in Mathematics, Saunderson's Algebra, and a work on Arithmetic; in Natural Philosophy, Enright's Natural Philosophy and Ferguson's Astronomy; in Rhetoric, an abridgment of Blair's lectures, and the article on Rhetoric in the 'Preceptor'; in Metaphysics, Watts's Logic, and Locke on the Human Understanding; in History, Millot's Elements; in Theology, Doddridge's Lectures; in Grammatical Studies, Lowth's Grammar."[21]

Judge Story forgot to mention that official Harvard responded to widespread rumors of student atheism, moral experimentalism, and resistance to authority, by thrusting on each boy a personal copy of *Apology for the Bible,* Bishop Watson's onslaught against Tom Paine's *Age of Reason.*[22] Channing remembered the college as "never in a worse state" than when he entered it: "The French Revolution had diseased the imagination and unsettled the understanding of men everywhere. The old foundations of social order, loyalty, tradition, habit, reverence for antiquity, were everywhere shaken, if not subverted. The authority of the past was gone."[23] But if Harvard became for a time a cesspool of infidelity due to the French mania, there was little evidence of it either in his activities or those of his fellow students.

The Harvard hierarchy, in tune with the Yankee ruling class of clergy, merchant, and squire, joined Washington, Adams, and Hamilton in storming against French Jacobinism and its Jeffersonian apologists, and the students lockstepped behind. During his senior year, Channing composed a passionate memorial of support to President Adams in his resistance to French insolence and intrigue, which was signed by virtually the entire student body. Adams, in reply, wrote: "Your youthful blood has boiled and it ought to boil."[24]

Aside from being more straitlaced, Channing was a typical Harvard student of his time. In politics, he was an ardent Federalist; in religion, neither a dogmatist nor a skeptic. His charging-list at the college library[25] reveals no flirtations with evangelical orthodoxy, or mockery. Hopkins, Edwards, and Voltaire were not among his borrowings. He was attracted to English and Scottish rationalists, some of them Socinian in outlook. He read John Leland, Thomas Belsham, Joseph Priestley. He was even bold enough to take on Hume, perhaps because from Richard Price he had learned that the sensory psychology of Locke did not inevitably funnel into the skepticism of Hume. Thomas Reid taught him a similar lesson. A unique impact came from his reading of Hutcheson under the willows near Judge Dana's. Suddenly he was seized by mystical feelings of joy and peace and love as his eye followed Hutcheson's assertions of man's capacity for unselfish affection. Channing claimed that there burst upon him at that moment a view of the dignity of human nature which would ever after be "the master light of all his seeing."[26] He was so moved that he "longed to die; as if heaven alone could give room for the exercise of such emotion." Instead he sensibly sat down and wrote a love letter to Ruth Gibbs. Channing, in later years, enjoyed telling the story in Ruth's presence. He would put his hand on her arm, and say, "But I never got courage to send the letter, and have it yet."[27]

In Adam Ferguson's *Essay on Civil Society,* also read under the willows, Channing found enthusiasm for social progress, and for the idea that a quest for moral perfection is crucial to ethical practice. A creative melding of Hutcheson and Ferguson is unmistakable in his maturer point of view, as is the influence of Price, whom Franklin revered and Burke reproved. Price, by Channing's hindsight, "saved" him from Locke's sensationalist psychology and opened vivid anticipations of transcendentalism. "He gave me the doctrine of ideas," Channing told Elizabeth Peabody in 1840. "That book profoundly moulded my philosophy into the form it has always retained."[28]

It delighted him near the end of his life to discover in Jouffroy's *Ethics* that Price, in translation, produced a much greater impression in Germany than in England, and was a pioneer mover of the German mind in transcendental directions.

A Shakespeare revival burst on Harvard during Channing's days there, awakening dramatic inner tensions that would give his future preaching a compelling power. The varied and sustained force of Shakespeare's style provided a model for Channing's student attempts at composition. He worked hard then and always to give his producutions a glow of racy, flowing Shakespearean life.

Channing's surface temperament was like that of the mature man: almost too equable to be true. He excelled academically, but in such an unselfconscious way as to fend off jealousy. His need for dissipation was nil, yet he was unobtrusive in his rectitude. Except for a circle of choice friends, he was standoffish; still his conciliatory nature earned him general esteem. In Judge Story's words, "The little strifes, and jealousies, and rivalries of college life . . . scarcely reached him. . . . I do not believe that he had a single personal enemy during that whole period."[29]

Channing was, however, anything but the prig he might have been. "Though small in stature, his person at that time was" — according to Washington Allston — "rather muscular than slender; I should think it was even athletic, from the manner in which he prolonged the contests with heavier antagonists, in the wrestling matches that were then common among the students. And for animal spirits he was . . . remarkable . . . ; amounting occasionally to unrestrained hilarity, but never passing the bounds of propriety. I well remember his *laugh*, which could not have been heartier without being obstreperous."[30]

He was in great demand. The Speaking Club elected him president. Phi Beta Kappa tapped him in his junior year. Adelphi bestowed membership, as did Hasty Pudding and Porcellian. He was easily the campus's most eligible young man, yet he drank not so much as a drop of wine. Was there anything he wanted that was denied him? Were there those who wanted him whom he denied? If so, there is no indication. Whatever the morals of other students, he was content with his own. He had no money to waste, but was placid about it. His mother might have been hovering at his elbow, so acceptable to him were her expectations. A time of turmoil approached, but the closest he came in college to fretting about what he did or didn't yearn for concerned choice of a profession. In lively correspondence with his grandfather Ellery, he sent up and shot down trial balloons about law and medicine, finally settling on divinity as the ideal interweaving of dominant threads in the texture of his life. He was entranced by the life of reason. At the same time, he longed to know God beyond reason. He would devote the rest of his years to embracing the inherent ambiguity of these themes. He began at the unlikely age of seventeen an exhaustive scrutiny of the evidences for Christianity, finding, as he put it, *"for what I was made."*[31]

If his personal life was singularly free of anxiety, he could still be exercised politically. His classmates named him commencement orator, the ultimate recognition. The terrain, however, was tricky. The previous year's class had created a minor tempest by declaiming against Jeffersonians. Though Federalist to the core, the faculty wanted no embarrassing repetition. Channing was told candidly that he could orate to his heart's content, *nonpolitically*. His free speech instincts were offended. His classmates were incensed. One of them, in dead earnestness, wrote: "William, should you be deprived of a degree for not performing at commencement, every friend of liberty must consider it as a glorious sacrifice on the altar of your country."[32] In fact, Channing had decided to risk loss of his degree rather than accept the faculty's muzzle. President Willard, convinced that he was dealing with a bluff, first accepted Channing's resignation as class orator, then grew nervous, and finally sought a negotiated settlement. Channing conciliated, partly at the urging of his brother Francis, partly in premonition of his lifelong bias against wrangling. He wrote and delivered an oration on "The Present Age," in which he concisely dramatized both his free speech position and his Shakespearean bent. Referring to the French Revolution, he said, "But that I am forbid, I could a tale unfold, which would harrow up your souls."[33]

Simultaneously saving his honor and his degree, Channing, in 1798, rang down the curtain on his undergraduate career, and hurried back to his mother's house in Newport. A friend and classmate did not fare as well. Arthur Walter, unpersuaded by the compromise offered to Channing, refused to participate in the commencement's scientific conference. His degree was withheld.

On the surface, then, it was a singularly serene eighteen-year-old who returned to his Newport family; deeper down, however, there was turbulence. William Ellery Channing knew that his goal was the ministry, but he was profoundly in the dark about reaching it. The money situation was serious. Relatives had already been generous enough. He wanted to support himself, and make some contribution to his mother's exchequer. Restless and unsettled, he wandered as in earlier years along the beach, seeking solace. His emotions were erratic. They must be controlled.

They must *always* be controlled. He scribbled a tense letter to his classmate William Shaw: "I am either borne to heaven on 'rapture's wing of fire,' or else I am plunged into the depths of despair. How different from my situation at college! There I had friends to fly to, when the world looked gloomy. . . . Here I brood over melancholy."[34]

Shaw, who was familiar with the supercharged nature of his friend's inner life, but whose own cool temperament had gained him an appointment as President John Adams's private secretary, must have blinked when he read Channing's feverish closing lines. "Yes, Shaw, I shall be a minister, a shepherd of the flock of Jesus, a reformer of a vicious, and an instructor of an ignorant world. I look forward to a better country, and, while journeying toward it myself, I wish to lead others the same way. I know that you revere religion; and I wish that in your political career you would sometimes look beyond the strife, crimes, and intrigues of nations, to the harmony and blessedness of the Christian society in another state. We shall take different courses in life; but we shall meet in the grave. We shall bow before the same tribunal, and, I trust, shall rejoice for ever in the same heaven, and join in the same celebration of Almighty love. You will think I have grown quite ministerial, but, believe me, I cherished the same sentiments in college as I do now. In my view, religion is but another name for happiness, and I am most cheerful when I am most religious."[35]

This volcanic expression must be contrasted with another of William's letters to illuminate the complex relationship of his feelings and controls. At about the same time, writing to his uncle Henry in New London, he sounded like a different person: "It has always been a favorite wish of my heart to support myself. Bitter is the bread of dependence. All I had a right to expect from my friends was an education. This I have obtained, and I trust that Heaven will smile on my exertions."[36]

Heaven's smile materialized quickly enough in the form of David Meade Randolph, Esq., of Richmond, who was visiting in Newport, and took a liking to Channing. The Randolphs and some of their Virginia neighbors needed a tutor for their chil-

36

dren.* William quickly accepted, and in October traveled with his employer to Moldavia, the Randolph estate.

Channing's first reaction to life in Richmond was wide-eyed. The Randolphs were Old Dominion aristocrats: cordial, elegant, sophisticated, and philosophical. The wife, Mary, a cousin of Thomas Jefferson, was proud of her direct descent from Pocahontas. In future years, her brother would be governor of Virginia, and another cousin, Robert E. Lee, would lead the Confederate forces. She was thirty-six when Channing joined the Randolph household. Upon her death in 1828, she was the first person ever to be buried at Arlington, the Custis-Lee estate, which later became Arlington National Cemetery.

Channing was entranced by the Randolphs and their circle. David Randolph, who was United States marshal for Virginia, kept constant open house for the most celebrated personalities of the South, among them Chief Justice John Marshall, whom Channing thought one of the most impressive human beings he had ever met.†

The young man's jaw dropped as he heard the political talk from these affluent, cultured people. Federalism was the only respectable political topic in Newport and Cambridge. But 1798 was a year of great political ferment in the nation, and many Virginians fumed against Adams and the "Federalist Reign of Terror" embodied in the Alien and Sedition Acts. Madison and Jefferson, in their startling Virginia and Kentucky resolves, openly declared the acts to be unconstitutional. Something was happening in American life, something having to do with popular feelings and expanding forces, that Channing, in his New England setting, had not previously sensed. Among these fasci-

* It was not unusual for prominent Southerners summering in Newport to make such arrangements for private tutoring.

† Like Marshall, David Meade Randolph (1760–1830) was a staunch Virginian Federalist. Appointed marshal by Washington, he did not resign after Thomas Jefferson's election as President, and was removed from office. Shortly thereafter his fortunes declined and he was forced to sell his Richmond home. Jefferson's daughter, Martha Jefferson Randolph, reported to her father on January 2, 1808, that David Randolph had no property to pay his debts. (Edwin Morris Betts and James Adam Bear, Jr., eds., *The Family Letters of Thomas Jefferson* [Columbia, Mo.: University of Missouri Press, 1966], p. 318. See also pp. 57, 122.)

nating Virginians, he felt it and responded. And history itself was helping. Federalist hawks, busily drumming up enthusiasm for a *real* war with France, would have to settle for a petering-out *quasi* war. Domestically, the chosen Federalist basis for managing the explosive energies of the revolution, a conservative oligarchy of the wealthy and gifted, was giving way to headier visions of democracy. Channing's time in Virginia compassed the very years, 1798–1800, in which the Federalist rubrics of quality and privilege were yielding to suppressed, deep-rooted popular aspirations. Spending those years in Virginia rather than in New England probably proofed him against becoming just another Proper Bostonian.

His letters provide tracings of his new environment's seductive course. At first, he poured out homesickness to his mother: "I am far from your social fireside. I am neither a sharer in your joys, nor the object of your fond attentions."[37] But self-pity soon dissolved in the spell he described to his brother Francis, now practicing law in Newport. Richmond men, he wrote in wonder, used one another's first names! "They address each other . . . with the same familiarity and frankness which they used to do when they were boys. How different from our Northern manners! There avarice and ceremony at the age of twenty graft the coldness and unfeelingness of age on the disinterested ardor of youth."[38]

To Shaw, the budding Federalist politician, he confessed without apology the excitement he felt in his new Southern acquaintances, in spite of their grievous faults: "I blush for my own people, when I compare the selfish prudence of a Yankee with the generous confidence of a Virginian. Here I find great vices, but greater virtues than I left behind me. . . . They *love money less* than we do. . . . Their patriotism is not tied to their purse-strings. Could I only take from the Virginians their *sensuality* and their *slaves*, I should think them the greatest people in the world."[39]

In a flood of correspondence with Shaw, he sketched the changes in his thought. He could no longer see France as a threat to America. He was heretic enough to believe that France's pacific professions to Ambassador Gerry were sincere evidence of France's own critical situation. He was adamantly opposed to Adams's call for a larger standing army. Knowing Shaw's close contact with the President, he wrote: "You may call me Jacobin, if you please, but I am *not* for enlarging our *standing army*. I wish there was nothing of the kind. It is the engine which has beat down the walls of liberty in all ages; . . . You do not know what an enthusiast I have grown for *liberty*."[40]

With an edge, considering Shaw's delicate position, Channing wrote: "I blush when I think of the Alien and Sedition laws. . . . They were worse than useless."[41] When word of Nelson's naval defeat of the French came, Channing cautioned Shaw against exultation, reminding him that it would be no automatic boon to have an aggressive Britain rise from the ruins of an aggressive France. He also wanted it understood that, despite his deepening liberalism, he was gratified that "odium . . . everywhere attached to the name of Jacobin . . . even in Democratic Virginia."[42]

Channing's lofty overview of public affairs and national policy was created in Virginia, never really to change. He would be guided by sober reflection rather than personal or partisan prejudice. He would insist on the widest possible perspective. He would measure political institutions by their responsibility to improve and elevate human nature. He would judge issues in terms of how minds could be enlightened, hearts dignified, and wills purified. The vigilant manysidedness worked out in his nineteenth and twentieth years was to be a consistent theme through the decades of his public life. There were also firm conclusions: War, even in its mildest forms, was horrible; the worship of money was a pestilence; to suppress free expression was foolish and wicked.[43]

In addition, his Virginia experience sharpened his perceptions of slavery. The sight of slavery nauseated him, but he pressed his advantage as a member of the Randolph household to make all the firsthand observations he could. The slave quarters of neighboring plantations were open to him, and the Randolphs seemed to go out of their way to let him wander about freely among their slaves, visiting their shacks, distributing their rations. On one occasion, while they were away, they left him in charge. The Randolphs were not defensive about their involvement in the peculiar institution. Rather, it disgusted them, as it did most of their friends. Yet they felt trapped by it, almost helpless. After his return from Virginia, Channing continued to correspond with the Randolphs. In one of their letters, they wrote of a threatened insurrection in Richmond.* "Such is our boasted land of freedom," Mary Randolph sighed; and David Randolph added, "This is a small tornado of liberty."[44]

It was almost as if Virginia slaveholders were as anguished as the slaves, and Channing could see that the problem was not a simple one. Young and callow as he was, however, he was still a human being thinking — thinking as hard as he possibly could. There was no doubt in his mind that salvery did terrible things to slaveholders, especially the more sensitive ones. But the overriding evil was slavery itself, and beneath slavery the money-grubbing that sustained it. Virginia had righteously voted for the abolition of the foreign slave trade, but then became the profitable breeding pen for the cotton-growing areas farther south. Yes, the consciences of Virginians suffered, but what was that compared to the cotton boom inspired by Eli Whitney's machine? Channing grasped the nettle exactly as he always would: slavery was detestable primarily because it struck at what was of God *in the slave* — his moral freedom. In a letter, he spelled it out: "Man, when forced to substitute the will of another for his own, ceases to be a moral agent; his title to the name of man is extinguished, he becomes a mere machine in the hands of his oppressor. No empire is so valuable as the empire of one's self."[45]

He granted that the influence of slavery on the whites was *almost* as fatal as on the blacks, but what his analysis lacked, what he failed to probe, either in the Virginia slaveholders or himself, was the unquestioned assumption of their own superior-

* The insurrection actually took place on August 30, 1800, under the leadership of the slave Gabriel Prosser. It was aborted by a violent storm and by the action of the state militia, which had been alerted by two slave informers. However, Gabriel reportedly had said he would save Mrs. David Meade Randolph and make her his queen because she knew so much about cooking! Mrs. Randolph was the author of a popular cookbook. (Cf. Mary Newton Stanard, *Richmond: Its People and Its Story* [Philadelphia: J. B. Lippincott Co., 1923], p. 84.)

ity on the part of whites. Indeed, he shared it, and would be sharing it still in 1831, when the Virgnia House Assembly began its historic debate on slavery. Condemnation of slavery was unanimous, from slaveholders and non-slaveholders alike. Equally unanimous, however, was the conviction that blacks and whites could not live in the same community *as equals*. In the end, the only action the assembly took was to intensify repression of free Negroes.[46]

It was to be a stubborn weakness of Channing's abhorrence of slavery that he failed for so long to recognize the white racist block over which the Virginia assemblymen stumbled.

France and slavery were not the only forces engaging his interest. Channing was a schoolmaster, charged with taming the energies of twelve boys who lacerated his conscience. Was he too hard on them, or not hard enough? He refused to cane them, but he postured and intimidated. A slave woman came to complain about damage done by the boys to her garden and fence. When she saw how tiny Channing was, she threw up her hands and told him that if he tried to do anything about it, the boys would toss him through a window. He was inclined to agree.

He was also pursuing, on his own, a heroic course of reading. He blazed through numerous biographies. He tackled Hume again, but decided to set Gibbon aside until later. Voltaire — some of his historical works at least — was now acceptable. In a letter to Shaw, Channing explained that he was reading history "as a politician and a moralist," and felt differently about it than in his college days. "I shall found my opinions of government on what I see to be the effects of different systems, and not just on idle speculation."[47] He was looking for broad views of human affairs; he was fed up with authors who rode hobbies. He gained "considerable advantage" from Priestley's lectures, a point of view he would later qualify. He was stirred by Mrs. Wollstonecraft, by her husband Godwin, and by Rousseau. Of course, he disapproved of Mrs. Wollstonecraft's irregular liaison with Gilbert Imlay before she met Godwin, but he thought her letters the best he ever read: "superior to Sterne's." Paying her the highest compliment he could think of, he called her *Rights of*

Women a "masculine performance."[48] Of Rousseau's *La Nouvelle Héloïse,* he exclaimed, "What a writer!" He warmly recommended Godwin's *Caleb Williams* to Shaw. Then, as if the melancholy thought had just struck him, he bemoaned that all three, Mrs. Wollstonecraft, Godwin, and Rousseau, were Deists!

No Deism for him. No orthodox Calvinism either. By poring over the Scriptures, seeking what he called "the uncorrupted doctrines" taught by Jesus, he was embracing the Christian cause more fervently than ever, but with a special slant supplied by Adam Ferguson, the Edinburgh transmitter of Montesquieu. Above all, he admired Ferguson's *Essay on the History of Civil Society,* an out-and-out alternative to the orthodox doctrine of the Fall. Ferguson taught that regeneration came not by eternal decrees, but by gradual degrees. Portents of Darwin! The quest for moral perfection, he said, was a *process,* not a covenant. Channing felt that he was reading his own pent-up thoughts.

Ferguson's developmental psychology was significant enough in Channing's maturer outlook to deserve a summary. Ferguson believed that there are three levels of human motivation. First, a purely animal reaction, which he called instinctive self-preservation. Self-love, Ferguson insisted, was not involved; in fact, didn't exist. The second level, he termed "love or interest" directed toward objects. Men are capable, he taught, of sacrificing even their lives for objects that arouse their love and interest sufficiently. The third level, and ultimate motive in human conduct, he labeled "moral sentiment." Its highest form, a persistent dedication to social good, was, according to Ferguson, practically equivalent to the love of God.[49]

Channing, in the years ahead, would repeatedly Christianize, embroider, embellish, and vivify these seminal secular ideas. His mind in Richmond was steadily sifting out dominant thoughts and feelings. Struck as he was by Godwin and Ferguson, he could accept neither their mechanistic conception of the universe, nor their humbling of the emotional side of man's nature in deference to reason. He was his own man, and no one else's sloganeer.

When he drove off the deep end for a communistic scheme of society, as he did during his second year in Richmond, he was experiencing only what many young idealists of his time felt.

But he rhapsodized with such animation that his family and friends back home wondered if he was becoming deranged. There was more cause for their concern than they realized, though not because William dreamed for a time of rejecting private property forever and signing on as spiritual mentor to a utopian-minded group of Scottish immigrants. His brother Francis was cruelly close to the heart of things when, meaning to chastise William for his wild-eyed social theories, he wrote: "You know nothing of yourself . . . you are the baby of your emotions, and dandled by them without any chance of being weaned."[50]

Actually, Channing was doing an extraordinary job of putting a foundation under his ultimate moral system. He had already identified his pillar principles: start with what man finds within his own nature; take hold of what is there, especially that unique mark of kinship with God, *mind;* labor ceaselessly for the mind's improvement in knowledge and virtue; convince men that their precious dignity, because they are parts of God's great whole, depends upon their toil for the good of all; believe that man is not born to vegetate as a self-centered, avaricious wretch, but to grow and glow with benevolence, sympathy, humanity, understanding.

He implored his friends Shaw and Walter to join him in a lifelong crusade to "beat down with the irresistible engines of truth those strong ramparts consolidated by time, within which avarice, ignorance, and selfishness have intrenched themselves. We will plant the standards of virtue and science on the ruins, and lay the foundation of a fair fabric of human happiness to endure as long as time."[51]

There was nothing woolly about Channing's system. Ingenuous, perhaps, but not fuddled. He went in a straight mental line from his premises to his prescriptions to his goals. But William was having a ghastly time with himself. He did, after all, have a young man's body, and it tormented him with its yearnings. Sexual fantasies, coupled with the exhaustion of driving himself in his teaching and reading, left him in despair as to his "virtue." Guilt snaked in, bringing with it a touch of madness. He struggled to fight off the inner demons. But with no opportunity to curb them either in creative work or human relationships, he

43

began to exorcise them through self-destruction. He drove himself harder in his teaching, and turned his ten-by-fifteen-foot room into an anchorite's cell.

Exaggerating his poverty, he refused to buy himself new clothing, then used his tacky appearance as an excuse for no longer socializing with the Randolphs and their provocative guests. Night after night, until two, three, or four in the morning, he forced his blurring eyes to probe the written page by candlelight. At odd moments, he broke into uncontrollable sobbing. He took to sleeping on the hard floor without blankets. He denied himself sufficient food. He punished the flesh as the only answer he knew to his "shameful" passions. If, as with Luther, a visible devil had appeared in the gloom of his cell, he, like Luther, might have driven it off with a well-aimed inkwell. But Channing's devil stayed inside, where its price for surrender was William's health.

The biological basis for such damaged physiques as Channing's is better known now through the work of contemporary medical researchers. The anxiety, stress, and exhaustion Channing tried to wrestle with alone, without help or guidance, take a terrible toll of the adrenal glands and weaken the entire human organism. It is not really a mystery that Channing's lasting physical wretchedness was pervasive rather than specific. The cost of winning the victory he sought was enormous. But he would never again lose control of the heat in his blood. Instead, it would serve *his* aims. In the last year of his life, he placed his written seal on the Richmond experience: "If I ever struggled with my whole soul for purity, truth, and goodness, it was there. There, amidst sore trials, the great question . . . was settled within me, whether I would be the victim of passion . . . or the free child and servant of God."[52]

Channing understandably looked to Richmond as the scene of a germinal experience. He disliked the traditional concept of conversion, insisting that if the word had to be used, his whole life must be seen as a process of conversion. At Richmond, there was, however, a "change of heart." He "felt the influences of the Holy Spirit."[53] But not enough of the "influences" to spring him from his obsession with frugality.

44

In July 1800, twenty-one months after his arrival in Richmond, he set sail for Newport on the cheapest ship he could find: a damp, leaky, miserable little coaling sloop which was captained and manned by drunks. The food was foul and the weather wretched. The ship, after running aground, heaved and groaned until the next tide lifted it, and Channing heaved and groaned along with it.

The family was stunned by this pallid shadow of the compact, sturdy young man they had sent off to Richmond. But there were depths in him that could not otherwise have been. His eyes were larger, or at least seemed to be, and glowed with the powerful stuff of his nature, which he had brought under control. Obviously, he could not have been the same man if that wild stock had discharged itself in other ways in Richmond. He might have been greater or lesser, but not the same.

Channing now had two teaching stints to his credit: a brief one in Lancaster, Massachusetts, during an undergraduate summer, and the more substantial experience in Richmond. Like Emerson later, he judged himself a failure as a pedagogue. The Randolphs, however, had a brighter view, and sent their son to Newport to be tutored by William, along with the youngest Channing boy, Edward. William also took on responsibility for supervising the education of his three sisters. He was delighted to be at home, seemed to carry his teaching duties lightly, and made avid use of the town's Redwood Library, which was still something of the wreck the British had left it. But it was quiet, usually empty except for William, and had most of the books he needed at the time.

When Francis took advantage of his return to seek a more substantial law career in Cambridge, Channing accepted the head-of-household duties cheerfully enough, yet he was also aware of spasms of irritability and sternness. He attributed the traits to inheritance, and went solemnly to work to bring them under full control before he became a minister.

He was now old enough, he decided, to approach Dr. Hopkins on a man-to-man basis. The whimsical impressions of his boyhood quickly dissolved in his recognition of the celebrated theologian's monumental integrity and intellectual force. The old man was by no means an embodiment of gloom and despair. The Hopkinsian theology, Channing felt, was for the most part as unsavory as he remembered it from his childhood, but the man was something else again. And there was one facet of the theology, excitingly harmonious with the man himself, which Channing liked very much. As Channing told it, Hopkins "maintained that all holiness, all moral excellence, consists in benevolence, or disinterested devotion to the greatest good; that this is the character of God; that love is the only principle of the divine administration."[54]

The notion that Hopkins was a major theological influence on the early Channing is to this extent correct. Yet beyond this, the assumption crumbles. Channing was a great one to sort out the nourishment he wished from the nourishment he wished not. His delight in Hutcheson during college days had prepared him for Dr. Hopkins's noble doctrine of moral selflessness, and he embraced it gratefully. Still, he insisted on developing the idea in a non-Calvinist way. He could not and would not accept Hopkins's derivative willingness to be damned for the glory of God, or his insistence on absolute predestination. Channing's reason was explicit. He found these ideas to be "utterly irreconcilable with human freedom."[55]

What captivated William was the astonishing consistency with which the old man *lived* his doctrine of disinterested benevolence. With respect to money — Hopkins regularly gave away what little he had, as fast as he got it; with respect to sleep — he trained himself to get along on four hours a night, to leave more time for study; with respect to slavery — he didn't care whose ears among the South-sympathizing Newport gentry he singed.

Channing kept a tight rein on himself. He went to church and to monthly prayer meetings to hear either Dr. Patton or Dr. Hopkins, and was fascinated, as in earlier years, by what he called Hopkins's "untunable . . . cracked bell" voice.[56] Much of how *not* to preach he learned from his aged friend. Befitting his lifetime championing of temperance, William faithfully avoided the laymen's after-service gatherings at taverns, where sermons were washed down with generous quantities of flip, rum toddies, and whiskey. In fact, he avoided all social life but that of the family circle, in apparent determination not to risk again the fleshly tingles aroused by the parties on the Randolph veranda. His habits of solitariness, seclusion, introspection, and self-searching were jelling to an alarming degree. Once again he turned daily to his beloved shoreline for a renewed sense of freedom and strength. "No spot on earth has helped to form me so much as that beach," he remembered. "There I lifted up my voice in praise amidst the tempest. There, softened by beauty, I poured out my thanksgiving and contrite confessions. There . . . with the mighty power around me, I became conscious of power within."[57] Channing was more of a pagan than he realized.

William's twenty-first birthday came as the country recovered from a slashing national election. In the fashion of the day, the contending presidential candidates, John Adams and Thomas Jefferson, like proper Olympians, refrained from making speeches or issuing statements. But their partisans blew up a nasty storm of abuse and accusation through newspapers, hand-bills, pamphlets, and public meetings. Jefferson was pictured as Jacobin, atheist, and French agent; Adams as an autocrat and lackey of the British crown. The voting was close. The electors, stuck in a glue pot of indecision, threw the election to the House of Representatives, which went through thirty-five deadlocked ballots. Not until February 17, 1801, did Jefferson emerge the winner, a fortunate result since the popular vote had given his party a substantial majority in the congressional races.

For Channing, it was a confusing time. His admiration for Adams was deeply imbedded, but positive feelings for Jefferson had crept in during Richmond days. He could not help responding to Jefferson's healing plea in his first inaugural address: "We are all Republicans — we are all Federalists." Hopkins, on the other hand, was a Federalist with no nonsense about being also a Republican. His one deacon, virtually his last remaining male church member, had openly embraced the Jeffersonian heresy. Hopkins decided that he must risk losing his church's only officer rather than let such flagrant error go unrebuked. Channing's impulse was to back away from politics, and he followed it. With his unique ability to wave a wand over his will, he simply put the distractions of government and history and all of his attached prejudices aside for the time being, in favor of having, as he worded it, "a few important truths impressed deeply on my mind."[58]

As the Harvard commencement exercises of July 15, 1801, approached, Channing found himself deep in a personal shell. Thirty-one of the forty-eight members of his graduating class were to receive their Master of Arts degrees. Not that this represented a stupendous accomplishment. Little formal study was involved. The gossipy assessment of candidacy for a Harvard M.A. at the time was keeping out of jail and paying five dollars. The master's degree was traditionally taken three years after the bachelor's. No work in residence was required. Candidates were expected to return to Cambridge sufficiently in advance of commencement to discuss a philosophical problem or give a sample sermon, to turn in a synopsis of arts, and to respond to a general academic question prepared, printed, and distributed beforehand.[59]

For a combination of reasons — finances, health, tutoring responsibilities, general reluctance — Channing remained isolated in Newport while most of his intimates of undergraduate days became Masters of Arts. His absence did not go unnoticed; indeed, it created enough of a stir that by December news was on its way to him of his election to the office of regent in Harvard University. The job was a plum, proposed by President Willard himself. A regent was expected to keep an eye on students living in the dormitory where he himself had quarters. There was a modest stipend, a freshman to do accounts and errands, and free run of the college library. In addition, divinity studies could be pursued under the tutelage of Tappan and Willard.

William spent the Christmas season with his family, then journeyed to Cambridge for the first time in nearly four years. While his brother Francis had grown used to the change in William's appearance and manner, only Washington Allston, among his college friends, was fully aware of the Richmond ravages. The shock for others was recorded by Daniel White, his companion of Hasty Pudding days: "Instead of the firm, elastic step and animated manner . . . he appeared . . . debilitated by ill health, and was more remarkable than formerly for gentleness, and a serious air and tone of conversation. . . . I began to feel in his company . . . a mingled affection and respect, approaching to awe, which the presence of no other man ever inspired in the same degree."[60] The Channing spiritual *presence* — ever after a source of his public power and personal despair — had materialized.

Harvard Yard was a warmer and more welcoming hearth for ministerial aspirations than Richmond or Newport. While Channing wrestled with demons and tutored children at the Randolph home on Richmond's Main Street, organized religion tottered. Deism flourished throughout Virginia, virtually emptying its churches. In one of his letters, Channing lamented: "Christianity is here breathing its last. I cannot find a friend with whom I can even converse on religious subjects."[61] There were no more than three decently supported houses of worship in all of the state, only one of which, St. John's Episcopal, was in Richmond, and that so far from the center of town it was used for public worship solely on holy days. On ordinary Sundays, Presbyterian and Episcopalian clergymen alternately preached to sparse congregations in the hall of the House of Delegates at the Capitol.

That Deism's "natural religion" and "reign of reason" was but a thin veneer showed up eleven years after Channing left Richmond. A raging fire at a packed performance in the Richmond theatre on December 11, 1811, took the lives of seventy-two people. The diaster set off a religious revival. Richmond citizens expiated their sense of guilt by building a second Episcopal church on the theatre site. A Roman Catholic parish and a Presbyterian church were hastily organized. Baptist and Methodist meetinghouses prospered.

Nor was the desultory state of Hopkins's congregation in Newport entirely attributable to the old man's wretched preaching. Newport people could not possibly have been as bad as Hopkins described them in his "Farewell to the World" — "dissolute, vicious, erroneous and ignorant" — but they lacked certainly a universal zeal for the practice of organized Christianity.

At Harvard, however, Deism and apathy had skilled opposition. Professor David Tappan and President Joseph Willard were "moderate" men theologically, and eminently respected, practicing Christian clergymen. Tappan, the more benign of the two, fell quickly into an earnest relationship with William. Admired as a preacher, he also met one of Channing's primary personal requirements: he was remarkably impartial in his doctrinal views, and devoted to the principle that students should be urged to judge for themselves. Willard might have been equally tolerant, but Channing was disinclined to penetrate the president's forbidding exterior. It is significant that at his ordination William chose Tappan rather than the more prestigious Willard to preach the sermon.

At Harvard, Channing's faith in a possible future for the church was revived. Though he continued to read avidly, he became even more interested in writing down the ideas that flooded his mind. He honed his unique talent for pushing a train of thought with his pen. He polished his highly personal method of noting on paper every association his brain discharged when confronted with an idea. Every application, contradiction, objection, and qualification was recorded. Appropriate general principles were scribbled next; then possible conclusions; until finally a whole series of major and minor branches emerged, dividing and subdividing. It was an astonishingly methodical performance, but never a mechanical one. It expressed his refreshing combination of order and spontaneity. Like a composer, he took a theme — human nature, God, society, the church, human relationships — and sent his mind and pen in hot pursuit of variations.

A monitory soliloquy, written to himself about himself as a student, illustrates. "It is easy to read, but hard to think," Channing muses. "Without thinking, we cannot make the sentiments of others our own. Thinking alone adopts them into our family. It is my misfortune, that I have read much, but have reflected little. Let me reverse this order.

"I prefer strength of impression to superficial knowledge, however extensive.

50

"We are very apt to think we have ideas, when we have only words. We mistake synonymes for definitions. I have often found rich ideas by analyzing words, particularly when they are metaphorical. . . .

"I often find my mind confused; a thousand indistinct ideas distract it. In such cases, it would be best to snap the chain of thought at once. . . . There are periods, when the mind is indisposed to serious study, when it sympathizes with a suffering body, when its tone is destroyed, and its powers require relaxation. But we should distinguish natural infirmity from that indolence which grows by indulgence, and which one vigorous exertion would drive away. . . . Do I not too often apologize for indolence, by attributing it to bodily indisposition? . . .

"It is always best to think first for ourselves on any subject, and then to have recourse to others for the correction or improvement of our own sentiments. . . . Let me observe before perusing the opinions of observers. We check original thought by first learning how and what to think from others. The strength of others should be called in only to assist our weakness, not to prevent the exertion of our own powers. . . . Truth received on authority, or acquired without labor, makes but a feeble impression.

"I was born for action. My object is to do good in the world by promoting the cause of religion, as well as to advance myself in religion. A life of constant action and unwearied exertion excludes universal knowledge. The improvement of the heart is infinitely more important than enlargement of the understanding. I hope for immortality in heaven, not immortal fame on earth. I therefore wish to have a few important truths impressed deeply on my mind, rather than to be lost in that chaos of universal knowledge which has hitherto distracted me. Knowledge is only a means. Let me not make it the end. Abstruse speculation on useless subjects will but waste my time. . . .

"I should endeavor to form my mode of preaching, as well as of thinking, on the Scriptures. Every sect has its *cant*, and there is danger of being blindly led by it. Let me strive to discover the errors of the party or sect to which I belong. Indiscriminate approbation is a sure step to error. Adherence to *principles*, and not to *men*, should separate me from all *parties.*"[62]

Channing may never again have looked at these private musings, but they were the map he followed for the next forty years. At any point in his career, those wanting to know what made him tick could have found out by reviewing his Harvard memo to self. It was all there, including a life "born for action," but continually damped by "infirmity." He had so sooner scribbled these notes than he was writing to his grandfather Ellery of "a kind of stupefaction . . . a weight of dullness" that oppressed him. "I am hemmed in," he moaned. "I am fettered. Like Enceladus, I groan under the mountain."[63]

His grandfather was crusty enough not to lament with him, and it was just as well, for as Channing himself recognized, an emotional hypochondria was one of his gravest temptations. There were enough genuine infirmities without that! William found that he could break a morbid spell by linking up with Francis for a hike through the woods of Mount Auburn or a climb to the top of Prospect Hill.

As he rounded out his theological studies, he became a member "in full communion" of the Rev. Dr. Abiel Holmes's First Church of Christ in Cambridge, a comfortable congregation of moderate Calvinist bent. He composed a strangely bland and unimaginative statement of faith (one of his "moods" was apparently on him), which combined Hopkins's disinterested benevolence with an Arian view of Jesus as neither wholly God nor wholly man, but a unique, preexistent Son, only less eternal and less infinite than the Father. On a later occasion, Channing looked back to this time and remembered that he "verged toward Calvinism, for ill health and depression gave me a dark view of things." But the doctrine of the Trinity held him back: "When I was studying my profession, and religion was the subject of deepest personal concern with me, I followed Doddridge through his 'Rise and Progress' till he brought me to a prayer to Jesus Christ. There I stopped, and wrote to a friend that my spiritual guide was gone where I could not follow him. I was never in any sense a Trinitarian."[64]

Along with being awarded his Master of Arts degree by

Harvard, Channing had to face the Ministers' Association for his license to preach. He was determined not to be drawn into controversy, and apparently succeeded. The assembled clergymen either fell victim to the Channing spiritual aura, or had other pressing business to conduct. He read his sermon and fielded just one loaded question, that from liberal Dr. Stearns of Lincoln: "Did Mr. Channing believe that God was the author of sin?" His negative answer apparently satisfied. As an "approbated minister of Christ" he preached his first sermon on October 24, 1802, at Medford. His friend Daniel White was in the congregation, and was charmed by William's style. Channing's host minister, the Rev. Dr. Osgood, decided there and then that a young preacher "of extraordinary gifts" had appeared on the horizon.

This first sermon was on the text, "Silver and gold have I none, but such as I have give I unto you." It was an existential message, often repeated in the months and years ahead, always after changes that traced his passage from a more florid to a simpler style. He spoke in it, with feeling, of the wretchedness we experience when we let fretfulness and anger poison our relations with others. He even anticipated Theodore Parker's South Boston heresy of 1841, in a quite different context of course, saying: "Perhaps Christ when on earth won the hearts of publicans and sinners more by his gentle manners and offices of kindness, when he ate and drank with them, than by exhibiting his miracles." Channing had no intention of disavowing miracles then or ever. But he did have what, for him, was his point of points: more than miracles or money, human beings need sympathy and love![65]

Flushed with success, Channing returned to Newport as something of a town hero, and was immediately invited by Dr. Patton to preach at the family church. Word that he would do so spread rapidly, bringing an unusually large congregation to the timeworn meetinghouse. He regaled them with a further polished version of his Medford sermon. Grandfather William Ellery was one of his most appreciative fans. He wrote: "You cannot conceive what satisfaction it gives me to see my grandson walking in the truth with so much steadiness, and with so much eloquence and wisdom dispensing the light of the gospel. If he lives, he will be a burning and shining light." The old man's last sentence indicates graphically that while others were impressed with the "spirituality" of Channing's appearance, those closest to him were wondering if his translucent pallor didn't prophesy an early end.[66]

Meanwhile two of Boston's proudest congregations were vying for the services of this twenty-two-year-old preacher, a situation with none of the strangeness then that might attach to it now. By custom, when a pastor settled in early nineteenth-century New England, it was assumed that he would stay put, possibly for life, but certainly for some time. As the occasion arose, a church looked around for the most promising young man it could find, lured him if it could into settling, then expected him to ripen on the job. The two Boston churches that found themselves in that position in the late autumn of 1802 were prosperous, stylish Brattle Street, where aging Dr. Peter Thacher wished to find a colleague-successor, and historic, but somewhat down-at-the-heel Federal Street, where the pulpit was vacant.*

* This church, built in 1744, replaced the original barn on Long Lane, where thirty "Presbyterian strangers" had first gathered under Irish-born and Glasgow-educated Reverend John Moorhead. After some difficulty with the Presbyterian mode of church government, the male members of the congregation decided to join the company of the Puritan churches in Boston, and embraced the Congregational polity. Soon afterward (1786) they invited Jeremy Belknap, then minister in Dover, New Hampshire, to occupy their pulpit, and in 1787, to serve them as their pastor. Belknap was a man of distinctly liberal inclination and a scholar of wide repute. One of America's poineer historians, he had written a three-volume history of New Hampshire and was a founder of the Massachusetts Historical Society. Under his leadership, the "Society of the Congregation in Federal Street" became identified with every progressive movement of the decade 1787–1797. These included the institution of fire brigades, smallpox vaccination, and acceptance of the federal Constitution (the church served as the meetinghouse where in 1788 the Massachusetts Convention ratified the document). Dr. Belknap's ministry ended with his death in 1798. He was succeeded by John Snelling Popkin, who, for reasons that are obscure, resigned from his post in 1802. He accepted a less demanding pastorate in Newbury, Massachusetts, in 1804. Later he became professor of Greek at Harvard. (Jane B. Marcou, *Life of Jeremy Belknap* [New York: Harper and Brothers, 1847]; Cornelius C. Felton, ed., *A Memorial of the Rev. John Snelling Popkin, D.D.* [Cambridge, Mass.: John Bartlett, 1852]; Harriet E. Johnson, "The Early History of Arlington Street Church," *Proceedings of the Unitarian Historical Society* 5, part 2 [1937]: 15–36.)

The first enticements came from Brattle Street, followed on December 29 by an urgent invitation from the committee of Federal Street. No less a personage than Harrison Gray Otis, Boston's most public-spirited Sybarite, pressed Brattle Street's desires upon Channing. Federal Street had no such luminary, but it had something of subtler appeal to ailing William. The demands of the smaller Federal Street operation looked more manageable to him. True, with Thacher as his senior colleague, Brattle Street's requirements would probably be tractable also. But Thacher was ailing. In fact, within weeks Thacher was dead. Channing, sitting out his problem in Newport, found that Providence had made his decision for him. On January 25, 1803, he wrote from Newport to Harrison Gray Otis, politely saying no. Returning to Boston, he conferred again with the Federal Street committee, and on February 12 composed a letter of acceptance. In a revealing paragraph, he wrote: "Though young and feeble, I am encouraged to form this solemn connection from a confidence in that candor and affection I have already experienced."[67]

On June 1, 1803, at the age of twenty-three, William Ellery Channing was ordained and installed in the only pulpit he was ever to call his own.

II

Apostle to the Brahmins

SUDDENLY, the loneliness and coldness of his situation struck him. The years of theorizing about being a minister were over. He was one. He had a sacred house of his own — one of the plainest, barest, and ugliest in Boston, but it was his. The first thing he did was to panic. After all, who was he? A pale midget with a trembling voice. What powers could he possibly bring?

During the weeks prior to his installation, Channing lived in Brookline, with a wealthy parishioner, Stephen Higginson, who treated his moodiness gently, made no social demands upon him, and let him spend as many uninterrupted hours as he wished in his well-stocked library. Still, Channing felt that he was imposing upon the Higginsons' hospitality, excused himself, and found quarters with another family while waiting for his parsonage to be made ready. Though officially "settled," he asked his congregation for freedom during the summer months to make himself worthier of what was expected of him. He was still too wrapped up in his own problems to turn his attention to the world around him. Once again he was fighting feelings of weakness and corruption. The family with whom he lived found him to be an oppressive character to have about, except that he made himself as scarce as possible.[1] The thought of being sociable repelled him. He ate little, and that in an obvious hurry to get back to his brooding. It was little understood how compulsive his brooding was.

As a dog worries a bone, so Channing's mind worried any subject that absorbed him, and the subject of the moment was the origin of moral feeling. His power of concentration was so great that it actually terrified him. He confided to his journal:

"My mode of study destroys me, my health, my piety, my social feelings; and is therefore sinful.

"My long absorption in a subject enfeebles my mind, prevents its free action, casts a cloud over my thoughts, produces a painful anxiety."[2]

In truth, Channing was torn by religious doubts, and frantic to achieve certainty. His brain throbbed with the notion that without certainty, he had no business posing as a preacher. Yet, the doubts were there. He came close to throwing up ministry, but yielded to his brother Francis's urgings to give it at least a fair trial.[3] Indeed, the encounter with Francis was just the jolt he needed to get his common sense back on the track. It came to him that if God wanted angels as ministers of his word, he would have arranged it that way. Instead, the task was entrusted to mortal men, to frail earthen vessels, who as Channing described them, "need moral and religious education as truly as their hearers."[4]

A shudder of relief passed through him with the sensible realization that great spiritual conflict and a deep sense of imperfection were probably inseparable from a minister's work. Though Channing would never be wholly cured of his excessive soul-searching, he cracked his shell sufficiently, with Francis's timely help, to take a practical look at the human world he wanted so desperately to serve. And one of the plainest possibilities had to do with his own family. As Federal Street's pastor, he had a rent-free house at his disposal, and a respectable cash salary of $1200 a year. The time had clearly come for him to unite his Newport family under his roof, to provide for their support, and to set Francis free at last to marry. He dashed off a letter to his mother telling her that he had a parsonage he could not occupy, and fuel he could not burn, and that she would save the congregation much waste and worry by gathering up the children and joining him in Boston.[5] In a short time they came, ending once and for all Channing's pungent bouts with homesickness.

The arrangement couldn't possibly have been better. Channing, with an honest abhorrence of handling money, turned his salary over to his mother, and his extra fees over to his sisters. Using his mother as his banker, he drew from her the sizable sums he wished to donate to charities, and the trifling amounts he spent on himself. Moreover, it pleased him considerably to take the smallest room in the house as his study, while he shared the unheated attic with a younger brother as sleeping quarters. He wore this kind of self-denial beautifully, and enjoyed it thoroughly. This new domesticity, with more than enough to give security to his family, while he himself reveled in Spartan simplicity, brought him solemn satisfaction and peace. It occurred to him that he might relish being a minister after all, and where could the profession be more stimulatingly practiced than in early nineteenth-century Boston?

A highly self-conscious Boston, twenty-five thousand strong in 1803, was ready to make its moves in a nation that had just embraced the Louisiana Purchase and acquired a vast new frontier. With its wandering cobblestone streets and walks, its compact brick dwellings, its occasional oil street lamps, Boston resembled an insulated English market town, and Boston's burghers and their ladies sharpened the old country image by dancing the minuet after huge, belch-ridden English dinners. This society, according to Chadwick, "was as exclusive of Jeffersonian Republicans as freezing water of animal germs. A lady of the period said, 'I should as soon have expected to see a cow in a drawing-room as a Jacobin.' "[6]

Stuffy as they seemed, Bostonians, in their uniquely conservative way, were stirring. A considerable network of prominent, affluent families had emerged, with the will to invest their acquired commercial wealth in financial, transportation, and manufacturing enterprises that would change the face of New England. At one and the same time, this strong Boston breed of entrepreneurs welcomed and feared the implications of their ventures. That always unknown factor, *new people*, would inevitably be needed and attracted in considerable numbers by Boston's expanding enterprises. How were they to be disciplined to Boston's standards of appropriate behavior? To make the footing firm, Bostonians seized upon their existing, elaborate fabric of kinship ties and made from family cohesion, continuity, and stability a fortress of self-perpetuating power and prestige. Recognizing that ties of blood were not in themselves enough, the kinship elite dedicated itself to cultivating a mystique of values which circumscribed manners, drilled the young in proper goals, and defined the rules for stifling deviation.

Boston's "codfish aristocracy," in tightening consolidation, and by the strict guiding of opinion, meant not only to do well but to do good. Convinced that they were the vanguard of sound progress, Boston's patricians lived, moved, walked, and spoke as the trustees of a holy city, a light for the nation, for the entire world. Their Boston was to be a model of American citizenship, a center of culture and charity, of wisdom and stability; in short, an Athens and an Edinburgh rolled into one. Far from being otherworldly, Boston men were as genial as they were prideful and prudential. They wanted the rest of the world to know how open they were to new knowledge, new ideas, but only if the rest of the world also acknowledged how much Bostonians already knew. They felt assured, for example, that in a world governed as they would govern it — by thriving enterprise and peaceful commercial ties — war would disappear, social progress would stride on, civilization and the arts would spread, and the politics of kings would give way to the politics of merchants and philanthropists.

Many currents coursed through the Boston mind: ". . . a warm and chivalrous Tory strain, a passionate strain of rebelliousness, a strain of religious fervor, a marked and even general disposition . . . to sacrifice at other than mundane altars."[7] Personal ambition was strong, because it had to be, if wealth was to be acquired. Treasure was the handmaiden of public service. But strong also was the determination not to be taken over by money-making. One of Channing's admirers, George Hillard, told the Boston Mercantile Library Association, "The man who labors simply for the accumulation of property, and with no higher aims, surely is unworthy of a day such as ours; he has mistaken his calling."[8]

Those who said that Bostonians had divided minds put their finger on a source of tension. Especially poignant, and symbolic, was William Appleton, who confessed to his diary that even as he sat in church listening to the likes of Channing, his mind darted "from City to City, from Ship to Ship and from Speculation to Speculation."[9] Part of William Appleton thirsted for the spiritual life, but the most alive part of William Appleton was fulfilled by commerce. He felt guilty about it, but there it was. Such men as Appleton were aware that the Calvinist ethic no longer sanctified *their* devotion to enterprise and profit. No longer was earned wealth a sign of worth according to God's grace. Business success was its own exciting and absorbing reward. Channing, early in his preaching career, became painfully aware that he could not observe among his laymen any particular "fervor and happiness from the prospect and hope of heaven."[10]

There was, however, more inner tension than the surfaces revealed. Boston men placed great store on circumspection when it came to their secret thoughts. A calm countenance no matter what went on inside was part of the Puritan heritage of early persecution, and a trait extremely useful to a trading community. But tensions of principle and conscience were there, and occasionally broke through. Most Bostonians knew of the merchant in their midst who revolted against his anxieties over a missing ship. "My God," he asked himself, "can it be that I care more about the money itself than the worthwhile things I might do with it?" And he knew exactly how to nip his incipient rapacity in the bud. He added up the value of the ship and cargo and donated the amount to his favorite charity.[11]

Youthful retirement was another form of expiation. Since it was not unusual for fortunes to be made or inherited before thirty, the way was opened for some to drop out of the marketplace early and turn to a life of public service. Channing's Harvard classmate and lifelong friend, Jonathan Phillips, was one of these. Not content merely to let his money talk for him in philanthropic enterprises, Phillips served for years as Channing's unpaid lay associate in the ministry of Federal Street. Phillips was a skeptic in theology, and could find little to admire in the way most churches operated, but he saw in Channing great hope for religion's ministry to human needs. It was he who provided Emerson with the classic illustration of a Boston gentleman's habit of understatement. Speaking of his saintly friend, Dr. Channing, Phillips said, "I have known him long, I have studied his character, and I believe him capable of virtue."[12] It is indicative of how un-Bostonian Channing could be that he exuberantly described Phillips as "a remarkable man, an earnest lover of his fellow-creatures and possessed with an invincible trust in their progress."[13]

While Phillips was hardly a routine Boston phenomenon, the motives concentrated in him were liberally if more superficially spread among others. One of the hallmarks of Channing's first decade as a minister was his success as a fund raiser for charitable causes among rich and conscientious Bostonians. Slums, as we now know them, were still a thing of Boston's future, except for a squalid area on the back side of Beacon Hill. When Lafayette walked in Boston's crowded streets, he asked, "But where are your poor?" The poor were there, however, and Channing and Phillips had no trouble finding them. Channing, indeed, regularly gave away so much of his annual salary that he was virtually one of them. Francis, with some asperity, remarked that his brother William needed a financial guardian.[14] But by putting his own dollars where his preachments were, Channing opened in unprecedented fashion many of Boston's fattest purses.

The range of Boston's enterprise ethics included a John Murray Forbes, who, according to his partner, "never seemed . . . a man of acquisitiveness, but very distinctly one of constructiveness."[15] Forbes's spiritual exhilaration came from managing things skillfully and building things up. The profits were sweet, but the creative accomplishments even sweeter.

Others were attracted to the "ease of mind" — the sense of personal independence — gained from succeeding honorably in an honorable business. They believed that to do so accomplished at least as much for a man's chracter and moral qualities as prayer. The ideal merchant was a man of honor, a moralist, and ipso facto a Christian. Therefore, the heart of the commercial ethic was a man's responsibility to make something of his life, regardless of his origins. In a way it was even an advantage to rise from humble beginnings, thus avoiding the pitfalls of being born to wealthy indulgence. But those who overcame the temptations of affluence deserved full credit also. The crucial point was the fixing of *personal* responsibility.

Boston business, of course, was more than isolated individual duty. As desirable as was John Murray Forbes's aim (to pinpoint responsibility for business decisions on one man, "who has got to take all the credit or blame"), Boston-based enterprises were woven into a pattern of human relationships, in which family and friendship played formidable roles. Trust in kith and kin, especially when so much of the overseas trade rested on trust, had its distinct advantages. While it bred the hazards of nepotism, it also minimized them. In Paul Goodman's words, "The elite entrepreneur was thus not a free agent but a morally responsible person answerable to family and friends as well as to community and conscience. By deviating from expected norms, individuals not only risked censure but they also might injure the clan materially and morally."[16]

The ethic of personal responsibility was thus firmly anchored to a broader social base, a base as broad as the fair name of Boston itself. Recognition as a worthy Bostonian automatically included the virtues Van Wyck Brooks listed as "a clear, distinct mentality, a strong distaste for nonsense, steady composure, a calm and gentle demeanor, stability, good principles, intelligence, a habit of understatement, a slow and cautious way of reasoning, contempt for extravagance, vanity and affectation, kindness of heart, purity, decorum, profound affections, filial and paternal."[17] A magnificent ideal, yet, in his more impassioned moments, Channing looked at his noble fellow Bostonians and wondered if he didn't see marble busts rather than flesh and blood. As for beloved Beacon Hill, he shivered at the prospect of its becoming a mountain of ice.

The Bostonians who asserted their early nineteenth-century powers, were in dignified but determined pursuit of balance: business acumen seasoned with learning; respect for ledgers coupled with reverence for letters, arts, and sciences. It was not accidental that before the century reached its halfway mark, Boston would produce an astonishing array of intellectuals, poets, novelists, historians, scientists, preachers, educators — and reformers.

The reformers emerged more slowly than the others, yet the soil was being readied for them, albeit inadvertently, by the charitable and philanthropic interests of Boston's Brahmins. The fear that business preoccupations could turn men into mammon worshipers was assuaged by the ethic of stewardship. Amos Lawrence, reminding himself that he worked for humanity no less than for himself, soberly confided to his diary: ". . . We are to render an account of the use of those talents which are committed to us; . . . As our stewardship has been faithful or otherwise, will be the sentence pronounced upon us."[18] Lawrence was not chattering idly to himself. Over a twenty-five-year period, in which he kept secret but accurate accounts, he distributed $639,000 — a mighty sum for the times. In addition, he made a warehouse of two rooms in his home, where he accumulated relief materials for the poor.

Spurred but by no means intimidated by such sensitive chroniclers of social need as Channing, the privileged of Boston supported scores of deserving causes, from Harvard College to the poor, sick, blind, orphaned, and unemployed. Channing began early to wonder if there wasn't something wrong with a social order that spawned so many charitable needs. But he confessed this dangerous speculation only to his private journal, along with an equally perilous conjecture that perhaps charity was not enough and that the *causes* of poverty should be traced.[19]

Boston's men of enterprise were much too concerned with manicuring their souls to be tormented by secret questions about the origins of pauperism. They wanted neither research nor praise of their charity. On the contrary, a public display of their assistance to widows and orphans simply substituted for financial greed a lust for recognition. A man's philanthropic duties should be done with as little fanfare as possible, preferably with no fanfare at all.

Something of this same self-effacing penchant marked the Proper Bostonian's concern for the nation's affairs. Here again the key was responsibility rather than power. The appropriate business of the United States republic was business itself, for the lucid reason that enterprise, in its need for talent and virtue, offered to all citizens their personal chance to get ahead. Success in the marketplace, it was reasoned, bore the stamp of personal merit, not accidental advantage, and automatically involved a duty to serve the community which made such prospering possible. New England's flourishing sons felt obligated to spread in the nation New England's moral and political influence. One must be willing, in the fashion of an Adams, a Webster, a Lawrence, an Appleton, or a Silsbee, to serve even in the Congress of the United States, to endure its frequently tasteless foibles, for the sake of transmitting Boston's standards.

Boston's gentry believed that their business ethics were a standard to which the nation, in all its parts, could rally. That their actual behavior frequently fell short of these professions was a fact shunted aside in favor of riveting attention on the "values" that should govern competition, speculation, profit, and interest rates. An entrepreneur was also a fiduciary, the bearer of a sacred trust toward all who invested in an enterprise. The gravest test of overseership came on occasions of personal embarrassment. That man was most admired who without hesitation overrode his own interests rather than risk resources entrusted to him by others. John James Dixon parlayed his China trade success into the presidency of the Massachusetts Bank, which extended a $31,000 line of credit to the ill-fated Boston Brick Manufacturing Company. Dixon, out of his personal funds, reimbursed the bank to the tune of $20,000. J. M. Forbes detested slavery with sufficient passion to be one of John Brown's financial angels, but his trustee's sense of commitment to the stockholders of the Hannibal and St. Joseph Railroad, with tracks through proslavery Missouri, compelled him to keep silent publicly on the slavery issue.[20]

In time, Channing and others would raise vexing questions about a fiduciary sense more concerned with financial investments than with human lives. But it was not easy to challenge men whose mercantile ideals were to them the heart of human ideals. How, for example, could one call to account men who utterly scorned speculation as such because it undermined virtue and hard work as the reputable roads to wealth? Decent merchants were not so hell-bent to get rich that they would cultivate financial chicanery at the expense of meritorious personal effort. If they were to prosper, it would be by hard work, by prudent, elevating efforts, not by rash ventures. If this meant caution, so be it. If caution meant fair rather than exorbitant profits, so be it. It was moderation, after all, and not groveling before the golden calf that formed character. The same applied to interest rates. In the scheme of things, money for hire was intrinsically worth only so much, say six percent at most. Anything more, as John Jacob Astor was to phrase it, "narrered the mind and 'ardened the 'art."[21] To take advantage of another's need was bad business for the simple reason that it was bad human practice.

Such men as these, Boston's gentry, were the core of Channing's potential audience as he launched his ministerial career. They professed to be preserving a human climate even as they transmuted their homeland's economy. Business was not just business, it was a wide-ranging, comprehensive value-mystique, with a purpose no less than that of conserving an intensely personal and human pattern of behavior in the midst of fleet, disturbing change.

This was the prideful, self-conscious Brahmin ideal, to which William Ellery Channing was summoned to turn his attention. That he had to do so within the framework of organized religion was not without its special significance.

Men bent on cultivating a secure spiritual Eden through business enterprise quite naturally deplored the distractions of sectarian dogmatism or bigotry. Certain needs were obvious, such as confidence in the human capacity to be rational and moral. Otherwise, what sense was there in aspiring to live one's faith by performing good works? Calvinism, therefore, was a problem, but one that had to be dealt with refreshingly — by gentle winds of liberal change — rather than by demeaning polemics. Once opened, the gates of religious controversy beckoned such alien demagogues as Tom Paine, or worse, a misguided New Englander like Ethan Allen, with his scurrilous attacks on Christianity.

Far more suitable to the Brahmin mentality was the Arminian Christianity which for two generations had slowly, steadily, been making Boston its stronghold. Only Old South among Boston's nine congregational churches in 1803 remained rigidly Calvinist, and it was not irrelevant that Old South's minister, Dr. Joseph Eckley, was a Princeton man in a sea of Harvard colleagues. Arminian influence, with quiet, unspectacular persistence, had found in Boston "a middle ground between Calvinism and infidelity,"[22] and had fitted Christian theology snugly into the Age of Reason. True, there was a spectacular provincialism in this triumph. Beyond eastern Massachusetts, New England remained staunchly Calvinist; indeed, orthodoxy was most militantly alive. But in a twenty-mile radius around Boston, Arminianism was the prestigious faith, embellished by a cool-tempered, cultivated clergy and by the merchants, lawyers, and physicians who flocked to its meetinghouses. In Charlestown, a brooding champion of Calvinism, Yale-trained geographer, the Reverend Jedidiah Morse, grew increasingly resentful of the formidable "wealth, talents, and influence" being attracted to the liberal churches. Morse was not a social leveler; his interests were emphatically theological. But he sniffed incidentally a decided trend toward social class distinction within Boston's Arminian congregations.

When Conrad Wright correlated the membership lists of Boston's elite clubs and societies with church affiliations, he found a striking relationship.[23] Postrevolutionary Boston spawned more than a dozen literary, scientific, philanthropic, and social organizations for men of influence and status. Among them were the American Academy of Arts and Sciences (1780), the Humane Society (1786), the Massachusetts Historical Society (1791), and the Charitable Fire Society (1794). In virtually every instance, the organizers of these bodies were Arminian ministers, abetted by members of their own congregations.

One of the elite societies was the Wednesday Evening Club, which in 1803 (the year Channing began his ministry) had a stupendously exclusive membership of fourteen, of whom thirteen belonged to the liberal churches. King's Chapel and the First Church merited three members each; Federal Street,

Brattle Street, and the New South, two apiece; the New North, one. Old South, with its stubborn grip on orthodoxy was shut out, along with such social pariahs as Baptists, Methodists, Universalists, Catholics, and Jews.

The American Academy of Arts and Sciences had begun its career with a fair number of orthodox fellows, but by 1804 six of its seven officers listed Arminian church affiliations. When Jeremy Belknap (Channing's predecessor, once removed, at Federal Street) founded the Massachusetts Historical Society with ten charter members, at least seven of them, including Belknap, were Arminians. By 1804, when membership had expanded to fifty-five, eleven of the fifteen officers were avowed liberals. Moreover, the memberships of the Academy and the Historical Society were markedly inbred and overlapping. Wright's final example, the Anthology Society, was organized in 1805 for the official purpose of editing the *Monthly Anthology,* Boston's answer to Edinburgh's literary imperialism. A less somber but equally compelling aim was the social intercourse Boston's master intellects required: dinners of "widgeon and teal, or woodcock" — among other choice viands — enliven the society's minutes. Given Channing's digestive problems, his reluctance to be among the society's founders may well have been gastronomical. There was added reason, as we shall see, in his repugnance for separating liberal sheep from orthodox goats, or vice versa. But four of his fellow ministers, all liberals (William Emerson, J. S. Buckminster, Joseph Tuckerman, and Thomas Gray), along with the inevitable laymen from Brattle Street, King's Chapel, and Federal Street, set the group in motion; and, as it turned out, just in time to use their new magazine for a scalding review of Jedidiah Morse's literary declaration of war on the liberals: *True Reasons on which the Election of a Hollis Professor of Divinity in Harvard College Was Opposed.*

Boston's upper-crust societies and clubs thus knitted together a clique of prominent liberal ministers and laymen within the city, and to some extent from the surrounding towns as well. The ingroup feeling was further accentuated by common Harvard bonds, often involving strong personal friendships. Still, the natural tendency to favor one's own kind in pulpit exchanges and other ecclesiastical events was tempered by a gentlemanly wish for friendly relations with others, particularly with moderate Calvinists. A Presbyterian who visited the Boston Association of Ministers was anguished to discover that among the members, "some are Calvinists, some Universalists, some Arminians, some Arians, and one at least is a Socinian." He could accept this if the association met merely to "shake hands, and talk of politics and science, and laugh, and eat raisins and almonds, and apples and cake, and drink wine and tea, and then go about their business when they please." But he thought it "ludicrous" if the group had serious pretensions of dealing with "church government."[24]

Actually, the shadings among Arminians and moderate Calvinists were mild enough to make the pigeonholing of some men difficult. Channing was one of these. In the earliest years of his ministry, many were puzzled as to exactly where he stood, and he was not about to help them to decide. It was a different story, however, with out-and-out Hopkinsians. They were not concentrated in any one area, but they cultivated an unsociable aura that set them apart. William Bentley, the Salem liberal, believed that the sectlike behavior of the Hopkinsians, whom he looked down his nose at as "Farmer Metaphysicians," was motivated by class jealousy. They were on the down side of the social structure, he suggested, and were trying by their exclusiveness to climb up. Not by accident, the Hopkinsians were virtually all Yale men, who worked hard at keeping in close touch with one another. Their communications network centered in the Massachusetts Missionary Society, which was reigned over by Hopkinsians, as the Anthology Society was by Arminians, and which launched in 1803, two years earlier than the *Monthly Anthology*, a Hopkinsian journal, the *Massachusetts Missionary Magazine*.

Though a traditional Calvinist rather than a Hopkinsian, the Reverend Jedidiah Morse, D.D., of Charlestown, managed to arrange a place for himself on the board of the Massachusetts Missionary Society. According to Conrad Wright, it was Morse's way of implementing a bold scheme to realign the religious parties of Massachusetts.[25] A son of Connecticut and

Yale, Morse cherished the Connecticut pattern of fraternization among various breeds of Calvinists, coupled with ostracism for Arminians, who were mainly Episcopalian in the Nutmeg State. He bitterly resented the Massachusetts model of fraternity among liberals and traditional Calvinists, with Hopkinsians on the outside.

Far from being impressed by the Boston Brahmin wish for a noncontroversial drift toward liberal rather than orthodox religious tenets, Morse intended just the opposite. He wanted the liberals isolated, and he thrived on controversy.[26]

Morse, who was dramatically installed as minister of the Charlestown church at the very hour George Washington was taking the oath as president, was a mélange of assets and liabilities in terms of acceptance by the Boston establishment. On the debit side, he was a Yale man, an ardent advocate of orthodoxy, and an ebullient controversialist. To his credit, however, he had intellectual stature as the author of *American Geography* (which brought him membership in the American Academy and the Historical Society), came of socially impressive stock, and his position as Charlestown minister gave him self-activating rank as an overseer of Harvard College.

There was sufficient ambiguity in his status and personality to curry estrangement from his more thoroughly establishmentarian brethren, and he labored at it assiduously. His first ploy was to deliver a series of barbed lectures upholding the divinity of Christ. One of his targets was easily recognized as the revered Socinian, James Freeman of King's Chapel. Freeman overreacted by publishing a sixty-page potpourri. He called attention to several embarrassing errors in *American Geography,* charged Morse with disgraceful bigotry against Universalists, scolded him for calling Massachusetts Congregationalists degenerate, and chided him for reviling Rhode Islanders, lawyers, and Marylanders as slothful and ignorant. Summing up, Freeman accused Morse of blind hostility to anything not labeled Connecticut.[27]

Morse and Freeman were sufficiently chastened by their crossfire to lie low for some years, in addition to which the "atheistical" onslaughts of Ethan Allen caused both to concentrate on

69

the ramparts of their common Christianity. But in 1803, after preaching Channing's installation sermon, and shortly before the Harvard commencement, Professor David Tappan died (soon to be followed in death by the Hopkinsian demiurge, old Samuel Hopkins himself). Now the fat was in the fire concerning a successor to Tappan, whose genius as a Boston-variety gentleman had to be acceptable to liberals and orthodox alike.

In Boston's tightly-knit circles, gossip gushed as a year of inaction passed. There were grumblings about neglect of the student's spiritual welfare, and murmurings that funds for the Hollis professorship were being siphoned off to cover the losses of a bankrupt college lottery. The real issue, however, was theological. President Joseph Willard, a less accommodating Calvinist than Tappan, also died, throwing wide open the issue of which doctrinal outlook would dominate the influential Harvard community.* Morse, sensing a decisive moment, summoned Harvard's corporation and overseers to rebuff those who would elect "loose and erroneous" Unitarians, or other self-styled rational Christians who "deny the proper divinity of the Savior."[28]

Morse was accused in turn of intolerance utterly unbecoming one who labored in Boston's benevolent atmosphere, and the thesis was proposed that "whether the candidates for the Presidential and Theological chairs, be Calvinists, Arians, Socinians, or Latitudinarians, is not of so much importance, as whether they are learned, pious, moral men."[29]

The Harvard Corporation deliberated indecisively until February 1, 1805, when the Reverend Henry Ware, a Hingham liberal, was elected Hollis professor of divinity by a vote of four to two. Thirteen days later, when the overseers met to ratify or veto the corporation decision, Morse again took the offensive, but was silenced, as he expected to be, by a vote of thirty-three to twenty-three. Within a year, the liberals consolidated their

* Willard, had he lived, would doubtless have opposed the appointment of a liberal to the coveted chair. He is reputed to have stated that "he would sooner cut off his hand than lift it up for an Arminian professor." (Samuel Eliot Morison, *Three Centuries of Harvard* [Cambridge, Mass.: Harvard University Press, 1936], p. 188.)

advantage by electing Samuel Webber, an Arminian, to the presidency.

Morse was demolished in most eyes, though not his own. His strategy, far subtler than the liberals at first surmised, was to make certain that Ware's election was the result of an unmistakable theological confrontation. He had no intention of letting good fellowship smother the controversy. As Wright has summed up the situation: "After it was all over, the liberals would have liked nothing better than to forget the struggle. But too many bitter words had been spoken, too many pens had been dipped in acid. The Arminian movement had done its work; the Unitarian Controversy had begun."[30]

Another religious development which would cast its influence across Channing's life was the dedication on September 9, 1803, of Boston's first Roman Catholic cathedral, the Church of the Holy Cross, built but a short walk from Federal Street Church. The fact that the edifice was constructed from a Charles Bulfinch design spoke volumes, for Bulfinch was as Bostonian as Long Wharf. The further fact that financing of the cathedral came in part from Protestant purses, indicated the degree to which anti-Catholic prejudice had eased in America's Athens, in spite of a steady, albeit small, growth of an immigrant Catholic population, mostly from Ireland.

Bulfinch's participation in the Cathedral project was thoroughly in keeping with his remarkable openness of spirit. On a tour of Europe, while teaching himself to be an architect, he had been moved to tears by St. Peter's in Rome. Moreover, by filling Boston with his public buildings, homes, crescents, and churches, he quite consciously sought to give Boston's "new mind" an appropriate outward form.

Also, the American and French revolutions provided antidotes to inherited Puritan prejudices. The venerated Washington, so dear to Boston's Federalist heart, publicly denounced anti-Popery and praised Catholic patriotism. The hated French revolution, on the other hand, drove to Boston two of France's most distinguished Catholic scholars and humanitarians, Fathers Francis Anthony Matignon and Jean Louis Cheverus. Both were conscious that they had quite possibly exchanged Jacobinism for Puritan bigotry, but they set about giving the kind of example — virtue, simplicity, zeal, charitableness, cultivated sensibility — best calculated to melt lingering bias in Proper Bostonian hearts. By the time Abbé Cheverus was designated Boston's first bishop, in 1808, an unostentatious but profound mutual respect had arisen between Channing and his Catholic colleagues. The relationship was typical of an atmosphere of toleration that would last for nearly three decades, until the Connecticut blacksmith, Lyman Beecher, fulminating from his fundamentalist Boston pulpit, rekindled, with the help of others, the old flames of hate.[31]

How genuinely Bostonian was Channing as he began to mount Federal Street Church's pulpit regularly? How would he react to the theological storm Jedidiah Morse was deliberately provoking?

In the clear, distinct mentality so cherished in the Boston ethos, Channing was a true believer. He knew precisely what his business was: "My great end is the promotion of the moral and religious interests of mankind, the cause of virtue, the gospel. This is my occupation. This end may be accomplished everywhere. . . . Let me study for this. Let my exercise, relaxation, visits, prayers, all have this in view. Let me eat and sleep for this."[32]

In his journal, he scribbled an almost classic definition of "distinct conception": "We should seek to see all things in their just extent, clearly, forcibly. All thoughts . . . should be connected in their natural order . . . so as to form a complete view."[33]

As for the Boston-prized distaste for nonsense, Channing met the test well. He had no doubt that anyone who pursued nonsense pursued misery, and that the skid was an easy one from pleasure to nonsense. Still, the mind must be kept open "to every source of enjoyment, to the little pleasures which surround us." The ideal, in Channing's view, was "a succession of minute enjoyments."[34] No nonsense about that.

With respect to stability and steady composure, Channing had monumental problems, as we know. He once said that the load of anxiety he carried during his early ministry was beyond description. His nerves seemed constantly to be at the breaking point. The exertions of a sermon often brought on a fever. A particularly animated meeting or conversation invited a sleepless night. He struggled to learn how to *appear* composed, and succeeded. One day, though ill, he seemed as tranquil as a sleeping infant. When a physician looked in on him toward evening, the family was shocked to hear Channing plead for something to relieve his tension, which he said was almost beyond his bearing or power to control.[35]

The assiduously cultivated self-control, patience, and serenity became very much a part of the genuine Channing, but they were certainly not easily achieved, and their authenticity was rooted in passionate feelings at the well of his being. He went into the pulpit one Sunday as Thomas Davis, one of his dearest parishioners, lay dying. When he tried to speak to the congregation of their imminent loss, his voice failed him, he dropped his head on the desk, and burst into tears.[36] Channing was not the kind of Bostonian who made a "thing" of understating or under-expressing his profoundest feelings.

This is why, long before he embarked on his career as a social reformer, Channing spoke for the inner as well as the outer life of Boston, why he was willing to let his hunger and thirst for goodness show, why he resisted the sanctification of caution, decorum, and the calculating mind, and why he began to revolutionize Boston preaching by dipping into the natural feelings and instincts of man. Destined to be an apostle to Boston Brahmins, he would be with them, but by no means always *of* them. He would be his own man, an original force, commanded by his own visions, convictions, and eccentricities — among them a skeptical view of institutional roles and responsibilities, and an abnormally insular attitude toward politicizing the inevitable conflicts of interest in a free and fluid society.

He swiftly became the most hallowed of his clerical contemporaries, but he was vigilantly unsanctimonious in temper and spirit. His consciousness of being a vassal of Christ was overpowering, yet he was doggedly nonecclesiastical. He loved Boston dearly, fervently, with an overflowing heart, but he was not

73

a Bostonian according to many of Boston's most cherished standards. He did not, for example, share Boston's notion that *proper* and *property* were synonyms, nor its impulse to identify preeminence with the baptism of Harvard's waters. If he practiced social conformity, it was not because he believed it God-given. Actually, he found it to be something of a mockery of humanity's shaggy and exotic diversities. Respectability, family solidarity, self-consistency, decorum, moderation — all of these honored penates of the Boston hearth — he observed, yet they were not *his* household gods. Appearances aside, he was not the typical Bostonian of his day. What he did in and for Boston, he did from motives often at cross-purposes with the city's governing tastes and characteristics. He gave his genius to Boston and to mankind, but Boston's learned ignorance and pious inhumanity were his problems, not his guides. And he was such a fabulously, stunningly "good" person, so unadulteratedly whole in his acceptance of his fellow creatures, that it was years before the elitists who adored him realized that they had the spirit of an unbroken mustang in their midst.

All the while, Channing was living a personal as well as a public life. His Harvard classmate and friend, Joseph Story, began his steady judicial rise by getting himself elected in Salem to the Massachusetts legislature, in spite of his radical profession that Jefferson was neither a criminal nor an enemy of his country. Channing took substantial pleasure in Story's triumph, and legislative presence in Boston, as he did in the visits of another classmate, the Reverend Joseph Tuckerman, who dropped by frequently from his nearby Chelsea parish.

In Brookline, Channing had introduced his brother Francis to Susan Higginson. With his newfound financial freedom, Francis settled into a serious courtship, then into marriage. Nothing was farther from Channing's delighted thoughts than the possibility that his strapping, handsome brother, so unlike his puny self, would be dead within four years, and not only dead, but leaving a son, William Henry, whom Channing would raise to become his own biographer. At the moment, Channing was protesting Francis's repeated expressions of gratitude for bringing Susan

74

into his life, and for making marriage possible, by insisting that he really didn't have a sacrificial bone in his body.

Channing's celebrating mood over Francis and Susan suddenly crashed into dismay at the death of Arthur Walter, the brilliant classmate who had refused to compromise at their Harvard graduation. Walter was one of the young bloods who insisted on a no-nonsense approach to Boston's literary pretensions. If the city was to lead in American letters, it had to fashion proper vehicles. Walter, with William Smith Shaw, was among the non-clergy who helped to found the *Anthology,* and then moved to establish the Anthology Reading-Room and library, first of its species in town. Death swept Walter away before this innovation could be incorporated as "The Proprietors of the Boston Athenaeum," but his drive permeated what became Boston's only library for nearly fifty years. Characteristically, its doors were never thrown open to the general public. The Athenaeum was a debonair parent of Boston's literary birth.

Soon after Arthur Walter's death, Channing's parsonage household was sharply reminded of the student unrest that had cost Walter his degree. Brothers Edward and Walter Channing were respectively a senior and junior at Harvard where they played active roles in the slam-bang "Rotten Cabbage" student rebellion of 1807. The triggering issue is accurately contained in the title of the mutiny. Harvard's notorious buttery was still galvanizing student unrest. After the rioting, Edward and Walter trudged sheepishly to Boston, not knowing what to expect from their mother and brother. They were told that they had to fight their own battles, should do so fairly, and be willing to accept the consequences. Both boys were deprived of their degrees by the college administration, but they took their discipline gracefully and went on to brilliant careers anyway. Edward, to whom Harvard finally granted an honorary M.A. in 1819, became that same year the college's Boylston professor of rhetoric and oratory. Walter had to wait until 1867 before being granted his bachelor's degree as a member of the class of 1808, but in the meantime took an M.D. at the University of Pennsylvania, then headed for Edinburgh and London to prepare for his distinguished career as Harvard's first professor of obstetrics and medical jurisprudence and, ultimately, as dean of the Medical School.[37]

The boy wonder of the pulpit during these early years was not Channing, but Joseph Buckminster, who was called to Brattle Street Church after Channing turned down the job. Buckminster, whose life was to be brief and meteoric, had a great deal of what Channing lacked — a musical voice, wit, social grace, a Byronic appearance. He was a lustrous preacher, with a mind at least the equal of Channing's. As a budding Biblical scholar and man of letters, he was clearly Channing's superior. But he suffered from epilepsy, which in 1812 snuffed out his life.

Buckminster, unlike Channing, was not the least bit shy about staking out his anti-Calvinist position in the theological battle caused by Ware's appointment. He, Peter Thacher, William Emerson (Ralph Waldo's father), Joseph Tuckerman, Samuel Cooper Thacher, and J. S. J. Gardiner made use of the *Anthology*'s pages to sting the orthodox position. But Channing, who was on the friendliest of terms with all of them, gingerly avoided involvement. At the time it seemed inconceivable that he would land at the head of the Unitarian vanguard, and perhaps he never would have if Buckminster had lived. Not that he was clinging to orthodox doctrine; his liberal tendencies were clear enough. But he was far from certain that an angry theological blow-up was what the church needed. Ministers, he felt, had more important matters to resolve. He also believed that liberals had no monopoly on virtue. It seemed apparent to him that unless churchmen could lay down their arms and embrace one another, there was small chance nations would do so. He could look forward only with "pain to the irritations, hatreds, bitter recriminations, censoriousness, spiritual pride, and schismatical spirit"[38] should the gathering theological controversy burst into open warfare.

It is astonishing that Channing recorded not a single word of reaction or response to Hosea Ballou's historic Universalist treatise demolishing the received orthodox doctrine of atonement, which was published and widely circulated in 1805.[39] Ballou's treatise anticipated to a remarkable degree the principal lines of Channing's later writings on Calvinism, the Trinity,

76

and Jesus. Yet Channing peremptorily ignored it. His only possible excuse was that Ballou's impressive foray, coupled with a
livid counterattack from the orthodox, spelled more of what he
wanted no part of.

Channing stuck doggedly to his chosen path of exchanging
pulpits impartially with all parties, and adopted an evangelical
line in his preaching which was reconciling to Calvinists, and at
least acceptable to liberals. Then his young friend John Codman
gave him a chance to drive home his primary concern — the
basic business of the minister. Codman, after graduating from
Harvard in 1802, went to Hingham to study theology with
Henry Ware. It says something about the tenor of the times that
Ware, the Arminian who would be the object of Morse's wrath,
made no attempt at theological seduction of Codman, who was a
zealous Calvinist.

Channing, who regularly dined with the Codman family on
Saturdays, built a solid friendship with John that easily survived
their opposing positions in the later Unitarian controversy. In
1805 Codman journeyed to Scotland for further theological
study, and soon found his faith shaken, as Ware had never
attempted, by liberal Scottish divines. He wrote to Channing for
help and received back a typically personal description of the
spiritual torments he (Channing) had gone through. He urged
Codman to let his doubts and fears flow freely into channels of
self-examination; that in the end he would know where he
stood.[40]

Codman seems to have done just that, and emerged as a more
explicit Calvinist than ever before. By 1808 he was back in
Boston, where in October he was invited by the Second Church
in Dorchester to become its pastor. He wanted the job only if
the congregation understood that he was uninfected by the
Arian and Socinian "errors" that had crept into many of the
churches. He stoutly affirmed his loyalty to the Trinity, to the
assembly catechism, and to the 1680 Confession of Faith drawn
up by the elders and messengers of the Congregational churches.
Whether because of sympathy with his views, his candor, or
both, the congregation did want him. Despite being a full communion member of Brattle Street (Buckminster's church), Cod-

man asked Channing to preach the ordination sermon, and offered Buckminster the modest role of introductory prayer. Both invitations were immediately accepted. Another outspoken liberal, Thaddeus Mason Harris, was requested to extend the right hand of fellowship; and still another, Charles Lowell, was assigned the concluding prayer. Several reputable Calvinists were also added to the cast of ordaining characters, not, it may be assumed, for the sake of confusing anybody, but because party lines, though tightening, had not yet snapped completely apart. It was Channing's obvious wish that they should not, so he tailored his sermon accordingly.

Read from this vantage point, the sermon is a bewitching model of how, by projecting sufficient evangelical zeal, Calvinist feelings could be evoked while skirting Calvinist doctrines. As the Unitarian controversy heated up, liberals were accused by their orthodox detractors of fudging their real point of view. Parts of Channing's sermon were vulnerable enough to this charge to explain their conspicuous omission from nephew William Henry Channing's monumental three-volume *Memoir,* though several pages are devoted to the sermon's eloquent passages on the ministerial role. In the bulky official edition of Channing's *Works,* the sermon is totally ignored.

Using as his text Paul's exhortation to Timothy, "Be instant in season, out of season" (2 Tim. 4:2), Channing took off on what he termed "the zealous and affectionate performance of ministerial duties." To make certain that he did not lose his more rigorously traditional hearers before he got to what really concerned him, Channing summoned up a fearful portrait of the human sin and depravity confronting a pastor: "He is called to guide a wandering beast through a thorny rugged wilderness, beset with snares and beasts of prey. . . . He is sent to a world of sinners, in whose hearts lurk idolatry, sensuality, pride and every corruption. He is sent to many who are bound in fetters of iron and are perishing with the most loathsome diseases. He is indeed sent with balm for their wounds, with light and hope and consolation. But there are those, and sometimes not a few, who turn away from the proffered aid. . . . He sees immoral beings, committed to his care, advancing with rapid steps to the brink of the abyss, from which they are never to arise, and can he be unconcerned? Can he read of that fire which is never quenched, of that worm which never dies, and yet see without emotion fellow-beings, with whom he sustains the tenderest connections, hastening forward to this indescribable ruin?"[41]

This was surely the kind of hair-curling eloquence Calvinists would rejoice to hear — the dragging of Jonathan Edwards's abject sinners to the brink of the fearful abyss. Yet it is noteworthy that Channing did not try to score points for the inbred corruption of human nature. That he nicely minced around, before plunging into his central theme: ministers must be "urgent, engaged," not in serving their own "ease, or distinction, or gain," but in exploring "new means of usefulness"; not in dazzling people "with studied ornaments of rhetoric," mimicking feelings not personally possessed, but in carrying into "common walks and conversations" the deepest living realities of the Christian life.

Channing, with an eye to the gathering clouds of controversy, explicitly warned that the worthy minister would exert a steady "watchfulness over his mind, lest . . . some narrow interest, some prejudice of education, some attachment to a party, secretly insinuate itself," and incline him to a narrow, rigid view of religion. Noise and earnestness, he insisted, are very different things.

As for the art of preaching, he granted that rules were useful to teach how not to sermonize. "But when rules have done all that they can for us, they will leave us chilling preachers, unless we superadd that tenderness . . . which an engaged heart can alone breathe through our delivery." And this in turn depends upon a preacher laboring in his own life "to exhibit a uniform and interesting example of the truth he preaches."[42]

Ironically, if Codman clutched Channing's words to his bosom, it was not as Channing wished or intended. Soon after ordination, Codman exhibited as his "uniform and interesting example" a refusal to exchange with liberal ministers, and otherwise became staunchly stiff-necked about his orthodox purity.[43] Members of the Dorchester congregation assembled to discuss their pastor's behavior. Though reminded by Codman's supporters that their shepherd had plainly laid out his course before accepting the call, a bare majority of those present voted that as far as they were concerned, Codman's connection with the Dorchester flock "had become extinct." Whereupon seventy-one male and one hundred and eighty-three female members of the church and society angrily petitioned for a reversal of the society's vote. Two tense councils were held, producing confusion. Codman's detractors hired another preacher, and placed guards at the approaches to the high pulpit to keep Codman from mounting. But an undaunted Codman proceeded to preach from the lower platform. The vision of two sermons being preached simultaneously is intriguing, but it does not appear to have come off.

In the end, at still another meeting, a tie vote was broken by the moderator, giving Codman an official victory. The significance of this bizarre train of events was the degree to which sides and feelings were firming up. In spite of such meliorative efforts as Channing's, schism was more and more the spirit of the times. In 1808, the Andover Theological Seminary came into being as a stinging rebuke to the liberal take-over of Harvard three years before. A year later, the foundations of Park Street Church, conceived as a bastion of antiliberalism in the center of Boston, were laid from plans by the English architect, Peter Banner. Bulfinch, associated with the Boston "heresy," had been deliberately passed over. Buckminster noted developments in a letter to the noted English Unitarian, Thomas Belsham: "There is among us an increasing party of Calvinists and Hopkinsians who wish to promote a more *exclusive* union on the basis of the *Westminster Confession of Faith* and who will, therefore, form a schism in our Congregational connection and separate from us."[44]

Morse's well-calculated plans were unfolding. In the face of what otherwise might have been bitter hostility between them, conventional Calvinists and Hopkinsians were linking arms against the common Boston enemy. By contrast, in New York, where liberal strength was paltry, the more traditional Calvinists were livid in their opposition to Hopkinsianism, which was characterized as "at war with the philosophy of the human mind, with *common sense,* and with the word of the living God"; that it "ought to be exposed and *reprobated* in the most decided manner."[45] Old Calvinists and Hopkinsians could despise one another's views with verve, unless united by a foe fearsome to both, which was the case in Massachusetts, just as Morse foresaw.

Channing, from his Boston parsonage, wrote to his grandfather William Ellery: "My life is very tranquil. I will not mingle with the contentious of the world. Angry politicians and theologians are raging around me, but I try not to hear. . . . Certainly life is too short, its duties too numerous and weighty, to leave us much time to waste in altercation."

Politically, this was a bleak time for Boston's commercial lords of creation, who were more than ready for an altercation with the national administration. For years Jefferson had nursed the notion that the United States could skirt Europe's wars by threatening to cease trading with the outside world. In June 1807, when a British squadron in search of English naval deserters boarded and humiliated the U.S.S. *Chesapeake,* Jefferson rushed through Congress an Embargo Act, on the theory that American trade was so vital to Great Britain that she would disintegrate if it were barred. England bore the embargo surprisingly well, but the effects on New England were drastic. Jefferson's miscalculation breathed new fire into the dwindling Federalist cause. In 1807, all of New England, save Connecticut, voted overwhelmingly Federalist, making Jefferson's Republican supporters in the area furious with him. Yet in the national election of 1808, the Federalist presidential candidate, while he swept New England, was otherwise routed by the Republican Madison. In January 1809, with but a few months of his term to run, a stubborn Jefferson persuaded Congress to pass an Enforcement Act, giving federal officials carte blanche to seize cargoes suspected of being bound for foreign ports. New Englanders, now in their second winter of economic havoc, lost their endurance. With the political atmosphere charged with threats of secession, Congress gave way. On March 1, 1809, three days before his term ended, Jefferson signed a repeal of the embargo and retired to Monticello.

III

The Making of a Dove

CHANNING, as he had written to his grandfather, lived tranquilly above the political ferment, no less than he lived detached from the theological boil. He had every reason to believe that his approach was a productive one. From the first, his preaching was crowned with success. Along with Buckminster, he ushered in a new era of pulpit work. The limping Federal Street congregation became a throng that outgrew the sanctuary, until the old frame structure was taken down and replaced in 1809 by a handsome brick edifice representing Bulfinch's first and only "excursion into Gothic."*[1] Channing's nephew-biographer described the rapture with which his early preaching was viewed by Boston's pulpit connoisseurs: "The seriousness of his deportment, the depth and sweetness of his voice, the pathos with which he read the Scriptures and sacred poetry, the solemnity of his appeals, his rapt and kindling enthusiasm, his humble, trustful spirit of prayer, his subdued feeling, so expressive of personal experience, made religion a new reality; while his whole air and look of spirituality won them to listen by its mild and somewhat melancholy beauty."[2]

While much of this dramatic pulpit delivery was natural and unassuming, Channing worked long and hard at his sermons. They were painstaking creations, deliberately aimed at all who might appreciate a wide range of spiritual concerns expressed clearly, gracefully, and stirringly. As Channing quite frankly

* Salem's sarcastic Reverend William Bentley inspected the strange new edifice a few days after its dedication and said of it: "We have had Gothic theology for many generations, and the style is not yet lost." (William Bentley, *Diary* [reissued Gloucester, Mass.: Peter Smith, 1963], vol. 3, p. 482.)

confided to his journal, he strove to preach "striking, rather than melting, sermons."[3] Although he took satisfaction in the rapid growth and diversification of his congregation, he remained as honest as ever in assessing basic results. He dolefully admitted that the religious discussions of his communicants were "limited to a few topics, heartless, cold, uninteresting!"[4] His response, far from despair, was to visit constantly in the homes of his parishioners and to entice them into periodical meetings for prayer, conversation, and religious instruction. He was innovative in his approaches to these gatherings, using techniques of group interaction and "brainstorming" far in advance of his time.

Creating a precedent, he regularly gathered the children of the society about him after a service. His procedure was to come down from the pulpit, group the youngsters at the base of it, and then address a monologue to them. Though Sunday Schools were yet unknown, Channing, out of this experience, was one of the first to recognize their attractiveness. He was blessed with a scarce adult virtue in his time — a sense of respect for children and for their moral intuitions. He counted as one of the profoundest compliments he was paid during this period, a little girl's report to her mother that she "understood every word he said."[5]

While the respect of Boston audiences might be all many preachers would covet, Channing welcomed an opportunity to journey to New York, where in April 1809 he preached twice on the topic: "In God We Live and Move and Have Our Being." His impact was great enough to bring him a subsequent invitation to transfer his talents to that city, which he refused.

He was also trying his literary hand by contributing occasionally to the pages of the *Monthly Anthology*. One poem attributed to him, "Winter Night," represents one of his few dalliances with the muse:

In vain the Sun
Of Righteousness sheds bright and healing beams.
In vain does He, who died on Calvary,
Extend his hands, bleeding with wounds of love.

83

Man still is cold and wintry; still is hard,
And melts not into mercy. This vain world
Is colder than the northern skies. But FAITH
Looks o'er the icy mountains, looks beyond
The wintry clouds, and sees unfading bloom
Of paradise, sees peaceful streams of joy,
And warm effulgence of the God of love.[6]

As an essayist (a style much more natural than poetry to a sermonizer), Channing addressed himself, quite independently of Carlyle's similar concern, to "Thoughts on Dress." Dress "influences the cabinet of policy, as well as the toilet of beauty," Channing stated. Then, with tongue plainly in cheek, he acknowledged how cautiously he must proceed, since, without sober concentration on the importance of dress, "the beauties of the age would sink into lifeless indifference. . . . The amusements of shopping, that relief of tediousness would be suspended. . . . The manufacturer, the merchant, the statesman" would be deprived of a subject dear to "the prosperity of nations." How could England "fight her battles without her broadcloths?" Here was an ironic Channing, a splenetic Channing, quite at variance with the pulpiteer.

Moralists, he moaned, were helpless before the tyrannies of fashion: "They may rail and sneer; but the vain heart will still beat high for ornament. . . . Man . . . will be pleased with himself on account of the labours of the silk-worm." In a more serious mood, Channing insisted that the factual purposes of dress are "comfort and decency"; that "dress, like the countenance, is an expression of soul."[7]

In articles on "ambition" and "eloquence," he blazed a similar literary trail of eloquent irony coupled with trenchant moralizing. His Boston was growing rapidly. By 1810, its population had soared to nearly thirty-four thousand, not including an additional sixteen thousand in the suburbs. Channing's literary aspirations were growing accordingly. His spirits were also enlivened by the birth to Francis and Susan Higginson Channing of his first nephew, named William (Henry) in his honor. Yet he himself was still without wife or child.

Channing's intimate secrets of the heart during this period remain just that, in keeping with the tenor of the times. Whatever desires he may have had to bed down with his own woman were never confided to paper, nor revealed by any who knew him. Channing was in his thirties. It is inconceivable, in light of his later hearty enjoyment of matrimony, that he was unmindful of the purposes marriage might serve in his life. But such matters were simply not acknowledged by persons of his status or calling. "Victorianism" was practiced by Americans long before the fabled queen arrived on the scene.

The closest Channing came to an amorous venture before his marriage was by correspondence with Miss Eloise Payne, the daughter of a celebrated Boston educator and sister of John Howard Payne, one of America's early dramatists. Miss Payne, possibly at Channing's urgings, ventured into Newport to open a girls' school. No less an authority than Channing's brother George tells us that Miss Payne opened her "noticeable" school in 1807 or 1808, and that "until her health failed, she exerted a great influence for good in the moral and intellectual culture of girls, — not only the residents of Newport, but also of many from New York and Boston. . . . Perhaps no young lady-teacher ever enjoyed more deserved repute. . . . Her voice was delightfully sweet and winning. Her face was the index of unusual intellectual power. Her eye, lustrous and penetrating when she spoke, awakened confidence and love when she was silent. Her skill in penmanship was admirable. She attracted many, and held them spell-bound by her grace in conversation. Her religious faith yielded the fruit of holy living; so that, though her life was short, her death was deeply lamented."[8]

Channing's correspondence with Miss Payne, extending from her foray into Newport until shortly before his marriage, was about as ardent as correspondence could be in those days without becoming downright brazen. His letters were lengthy and fervent, full of preachments and moralizing, and an unmistakable tone of tenderness. Addressing her as "Dear Eloise," a most unusual burst of familiarity, he repeatedly apologized for not writing more often. He told her how his imagination played with her development as a person, how he longed for the progress of her character. He answered her questions about theologians and historians. Edward Gibbon, he said, was guilty of "the most insidious attack ever made on Christianity." He warned her to be "judicious" in the giving of her affections, but in the next breath told her that her letters gave him more pleasure than he "ought to express." He chided her ("Are *you* yet in your infancy, or do you think *me* in my dotage . . .") that she spoke so unqualifiedly of his virtues. He confessed to her what he was at great pains to conceal from virtually everyone else: that his private view of Calvinism pigeonholed it as a "dreaded system" for susceptible minds: "If it be fully believed, I think there is ground for a despondence bordering on insanity."

The closer he came to a decision about his marriage, the more nervous he grew about his relationship with Miss Payne, who sensed and complained of a change in his feelings toward her. "I could give you a great many good reasons for my long silence," he wrote. "For a long time I was fully impressed with the idea that I had answered your letter and that you were in my debt — but I now believe that I was in error — You hold the same place in my heart as ever." Having declared himself to his cousin Ruth Gibbs, Channing wrote Miss Payne that he could not tell her with "more propriety than before" that few held a higher place in his affections than she. In a "Dear John" vein, he expressed the hope that he had in Eloise "a sincere and affectionate friend, on whose attachment I may rely amidst all the vicissitudes of my life."

Two months before his wedding, Channing penned a hurried note to Miss Payne in New York, where she had established herself after closing her Newport school:

Framingham, 20 miles from Boston,
May 9, 1814

My dear Eloise —

My mother and I are taking a journey principally for health. We shall reach NY probably on Saturday, where we shall spend perhaps two days. My mother does not wish to go to a boarding house for so short a time, and will be happy to be with you, if it is perfectly convenient. I shall wish to be in your neighborhood; for to tell you a secret which you must whisper to no one, in that large city: there is

86

hardly any body I wish to see except yourself and your family. Will you then think of a house near you where I can be accommodated, and if you have not room for my mother, will you be prepared to tell us, when we drive to your door, where we can both find lodging. The prospect of seeing you again, my dear friend, gives new animation to my mind. Let me beg and if I have not lost all my authority, *charge* you to say to nobody that I am coming, for I shall want rest and cannot think of preaching. To *you* I will preach enough, and let that satisfy you —

yr affectte friend —
W E Channing

After marrying, and for the rest of his life, Channing would have many devoted female friends, admirers, and disciples. He was immensely attractive to keen-witted, strong-willed women. But he would never again, other than with his wife, have a relationship with the *tendresse* that characterized his communion with Eloise Payne.[9]

Channing lived as long as he did above the clang of theological and political strife partly because he could absorb himself in domestic concerns. The doings of his family provided both the brightest and darkest hours of his soul. For years sister Ann had known Channing's old friend Washington Allston, but the painter, so far a financial failure, had sailed off to England and Italy for seven years of study. When the prospect of possible success in America opened up for him, he returned to Boston to court and marry Ann. "We consider this a happy event," Channing wrote to his grandfather Ellery; "Your granddaughter has found . . . an excellent husband." But the ceremony, Channing reported, left him "rather solemn." Ann, he said, "is too important a member of our family to be resigned without something like sorrow."

Channing resented Allston's depressing financial struggles, remarking sourly that Bostonians "have not yet sufficient taste for the arts to give Mr. Allston the encouragement he deserves." He told his grandfather: "We have, indeed, money enough to spend on cumbrous furniture, which another generation will throw into the garret as antiquated and absurd, but we cannot afford to adorn our walls with the productions of genius."[10] Most of Allston's "commissions" consisted of painting various

87

members of the Channing clan. In despair, Allston and his bride sailed to England.

In the spring of 1810, brother Francis and sister-in-law Susan introduced Channing to their firstborn son and his firstborn nephew, William Henry. A few weeks later, Francis (who had worn himself out with overwork) suffered a violent lung hemorrhage and was rushed to Newport to recuperate. His condition deteriorated, and his family decided that he and his wife should voyage that autumn to the softer climate of Rio de Janeiro. On their nineteenth day at sea, Francis died. Not until the following spring, on a Sunday, between the morning and afternoon services, did the crushing news reach Channing.

Although he summoned up his serenest face for his mother and his congregation, Channing poured into his journal the jumbled anger and grief he felt: "A brother, — a friend — a nurse in sickness, — a counsellor. One who so often and so tenderly thought of me, — of us all, — who was guardian of our happiness. One who grew up with me. One who has engaged so many of my thoughts and feelings. The first-born, — the stay of his family. . . . Taken from the midst of us, never again to be seen and embraced on earth. . . . Taken at a distance from us. . . . His remains committed to the deep, never to be collected by us. . . . Taken in the midst of life, — a son, — a husband, — a father. . . . 'Thou shalt love the Lord thy God with *all* thy heart.' Do I understand this?"

Susan Higginson Channing was unashamedly distraught. Half wishing that she herself might die, or be drowned at sea, before completing her long, lonely trip back to Boston, she wrote to her family: "If I should never return, — and often I feel as if I never should, — tell William that I give my son to him. He must bring him up as his own, and make him as much like himself as possible."

She endured the voyage, however, and was welcomed, along with her two daughters and year-old son, into the Berry Street parsonage. Channing assumed paternal responsibility for his nieces and nephew. Susan, who never remarried, nursed her widow's grief with restless fascination. But if Channing was bothered by her, he did not let on. She had, after all, lost a most remarkable husband. As the portrait of him by Washington Allston makes evident, Francis Channing was a striking human being.

Another brace of happenings dug deeply into Channing's psyche in 1811 and 1812. He had supervised the theological studies of young Samuel Cooper Thacher, who became minister of the New South Church when Kirkland left to assume the presidency of Harvard. Thacher was an apple in Channing's eye. "Heaven," he wrote to a friend, "can hardly bestow on me a greater blessing than the friendship of Thacher." After participating in Thacher's ordination as extender of the right hand of fellowship, Channing made a journal entry which sounded the depths of his attachment: "Let me save [Thacher] if possible from my errors. Let me avoid every feeling of rivalship."[11]

The two men set to work on a mutual venture — the writing of a catechism for children on *Elements of Religion and Morality*. Early in 1813, their completed manuscript was issued by John Eliot's press with a statement on the title page that the material was "Designed for the use of the younger Children of the New South Society, and the Society in Federal Street." Channing's informal experiments in meeting with children beneath the Federal Street pulpit had crystallized, with Thacher's collaboration, into the beginnings of a Sunday School curriculum.

In their preface, the two authors stated that their "object" was "to present to the minds of children the great elementary principles of moral and religious truth, with the utmost possible simplicity of language." They believed "that the only effect of compelling a child to learn what it cannot understand would be to disgust it with its task." Mindful of the volatile theological atmosphere of the time, Channing and Thacher insisted that other churchmen who wished to use their publication should feel free to pick and choose among its varied contents; an observation, they said, that was "drawn from us by the fact that similar freedoms with other works of this kind have been, as we think, too hastily censured." To make their open-ended position unmistakably clear, the joint authors went on to say: "It has been our desire to present such views only of the doctrines of christianity

89

as all serious and practical christians may unite in. If, however, contrary to our hopes, any parents should find any sentiments in the pages not warranted by the scriptures, we most earnestly hope they will expunge it, or forbear to teach it."

Unfortunately, the contents of the catechism do not live up to the challenging tone of the preface. The language is indeed simple enough for children, but the subject matter is uniformly parochial. More than bewildering is the gulf between Channing's personally spontaneous attitude toward the learning processes of children, and the uninspired drabness of the published catechism. Channing, for example, insisted that there should be "freedom and abandon" in the cultivation of the spiritual life, that the most important beginning of all was to release children's affections toward their fellow humans.[12] But typical of the catechism is this desultory material:

III. Q. *Does God always see you?*
  A. 1. He sees me at all times all the night and all the day.
     2. He sees me when I am alone, when no other person sees me.

  Q. *How must you feel and act towards those around you?*
  A. 1. I must love and obey my parents, and be thankful to them for the tender care they take of me.
     2. I must treat with respect those, who are older than myself.

XX. Q. *But what if you are wicked?*
  A. 1. I can then never be happy. The wicked must always be miserable.

If anything, one feels a keener embarrassment for Thacher than for Channing. Federal Street's pastor was notoriously slow in acquiring the full-blown public freedom of his private liberal impulses. But Thacher, even prior to his ordination, had built a reputation as the Harry Percy of the young liberals.

Even as Channing and Thacher were laboring on their lugubrious catechism, a terrible personal blow struck them both. An attack of epilepsy killed Joseph Stevens Buckminster at the age of twenty-nine. Thacher and Buckminster were locked together in the kind of friendship the Talmud describes as "chosen" — that is, without qualification. Channing was somewhat more ambivalent. He fully recognized and respected the startling brilliance of his colleague. The death of so amiable and exciting a contemporary filled him with melancholy. Yet when he spoke to his congregation, he was strangely wooden. He said the proper things of Buckminster: "One of the brightest ornaments of his profession, and of this country, — whose vigor of mind, whose eloquence, whose piety . . . I have witnessed with increasing pleasure and increasing hope."[13] The words, however, were labored and stilted.

In a letter, he spelled out more credibly what was on his mind: "Buckminster's death gives me many painful and solicitous feelings in relation to the interests of religion in this place. People here, as you well know, are attached to religious institutions not so much by a sense of the value of religion as by their love to their minister; and I fear that their zeal will grow cold, when their ministers are removed. I wish that there were more attachment to the truth, and less to the man who delivers it. The loss of Mr. Buckminster appears to me irreparable. I know no man who unites so many gifts from nature, so many acquisitions from study, and such power of rendering religion interesting to all classes of society, especially to the improved, the polished, the fashionable."[14]

Channing *was* ambiguous — if not about Buckminster himself, then certainly about the meaning of his impact on "the improved, the polished, the fashionable." There was something "too exclusive" about Buckminster's famous conversation parties for Boston's young elite, Channing told Elizabeth Peabody years later.[15]

There were aspects of Buckminster's pulpit eloquence that troubled him. He was troubled because he sensed and feared that he himself was similarly afflicted. The best preaching, in Channing's view, "leads the audience to lose sight of the speaker in the sublimity of his themes." Otherwise, Channing bemoaned, a preacher "will be heard, admired, criticized, as an actor is, for the excitement he causes."[16] Channing feared that Buckminster and he were ripe victims for this preacher's trap.

Many years later, in 1861, John G. Palfrey, who succeeded Andrews Norton as professor of Biblical literature at Harvard, reminisced about Buckminster and Channing. "I first saw [Buckminster] in 1805," he wrote, in a vein relevant to Channing's concern, "going up to the pulpit of Federal Street Church, where the family worshipped of which I was a member. Boston was then a town of less than thirty thousand inhabitants, and much more isolated than it is now from the rest of the world. The appearance of a youthful prodigy of pulpit eloquence was the theme of conversation in all circles. I strained my eyes for the first glimpse of one so celebrated. I heard him preach occasionally from that time forward. I seemed to understand all that he said, and was captivated by it, like all around me. As I now read his sermons of the period, they do not appear to me so level to the comprehension of a child as those which I heard habitually with less interest from Dr. Channing. It must have been the exquisite charm of manner, which impressed the meaning that the language alone would have failed to convey."[17]

Channing readily accepted George Ticknor's invitation to collaborate with Thacher in arranging Buckminster's papers for publication. Channing gave a good deal of time to the enterprise, though Thacher carried the lion's share. Ticknor's recollections are instructive. "The sermons on Faith," according to Ticknor, "and the sermon on Philemon, attracted, I believe, more of [Channing's] attention than any others. In the last an omission was made at his suggestion; but it may be worth notice in reference to the opinions he afterwards entertained on the subject, that the strong phrases in the discourse that touch slavery did not excite his attention. At least I am satisfied that he made no remarks about them; and I remember the way in which he went over the whole of the sermon. What most struck me, throughout his examination of the manuscripts, was his interest in Mr. Buckminster's reputation and his care that justice should be done to it."[18]

Channing, sensing that only in part did Buckminster's written word justify the overwhelming impact of his personal magnetism, was inclined to place only the *best* of his words in posterity's hands.

By any measurement, Buckminster's meteoric life was extraordinary. He began studying Latin at the age of four, and the following year was reading chapters in the Greek Testament. By the time he was eleven, he was well prepared for college, but his father held him back for two years. At Harvard, his photographic memory and rapid reading skills were fully developed. Instead of reading across and down, he seemed to be able to gaze briefly at the center of a page and grasp and retain everything on it. His classmate Joshua Bates, later president of Middlebury College, recalled a reading experiment during their undergraduate days: "Each one in succession read aloud as rapidly as he could articulate, till one of the number, without previous notice, interposed some object between the eye of the reader and the book. It was found that Buckminster could continue to read, after the interposed object had covered the printed page, for a longer, a much longer, time than any other member of the company."[19]

Buckminster's first attack of epilepsy struck when he was an eighteen-year-old teacher at Phillips Academy at Exeter. Soon he vented his private despair in his journal: "Another fit of epilepsy. I pray God that I may be prepared not so much for death as for the loss of health, and perhaps of mental faculties. The repetition of these fits must at length reduce me to idiocy. Can I resign myself to the loss of memory, and of that knowledge I may have vainly prided myself upon?"[20]

At the unusually young age of twenty-five, Buckminster was invited to give the Phi Beta Kappa oration at Harvard. Already known as the "Chrysostom of America," his interests were at least as much literary as they were ecclesiastical. He addressed the Harvard audience on "The Dangers and Duties of Men of Letters," taking sharp issue with the likes of Federalist mandarin Fisher Ames, who dourly believed that no society with pronounced republican tendencies could possibly produce genius in the arts. Buckminster glowingly predicted the birth of a great school of American letters. Out of the young republic, he said, historians and poets would soon appear of whom posterity would stand in awe. "You, my young friends," he declared, "are destined to witness the dawn of our Augustan age, and to contribute to its glory."[21]

Buckminster was prepared to do his full part. He spent

virtually his entire small fortune buying books in Paris, when he and Thacher visited the Continent on a health tour. (Thacher was already suffering from the tuberculosis that would snuff out his life in 1818.) For the shelves of the fledgling Boston Athenaeum, Buckminster shipped home more than three thousand volumes, such was his determination to rouse Boston from its slumbers. Meanwhile, he had leaped ahead of his contemporaries in familiarizing himself with the pioneering works of German Biblical criticism and philosophy. A generation in advance of transcendentalism, he breathed aloud the venturesome notion that there was a higher poetry than "the mere language of reason." When in 1811, Samuel Dexter provided Harvard with the wherewithal for a lectureship on Biblical Criticism, Buckminster took the job. He had barely begun, when his epilepsy destroyed him.

Buckminster, both alive and dead, but especially dead, reverberated in Channing's life. Alive, he occupied so much of the limelight that Channing, and every other Boston divine for that matter, moved in his shadow. Dead, he left a vacuum which Channing was bound to fill.

Channing, though he fell far short of Buckminster's scholarly achievements, was no less concerned with spreading rational interpretations of the Bible. In 1810, he helped to found the Bible Society of Massachusetts; the following year he spoke at its anniversary convocation; the year after that he accepted the chairmanship of its executive committee. He was asked to take on the Dexter lectureship when Buckminster died, and he accepted. He bought a great many of Buckminster's books when they were auctioned, especially those on German Biblical scholarship; he dispatched orders abroad for several more. Then the taint that would always plague him asserted itself. His strength caved in under the aggressive schedule of study he set for himself, forcing him to resign.

What Channing might have amounted to as professional, though part-time, Biblical scholar is hard to say. By resigning, he cleared the way for Norton, his successor, to tower as the "Unitarian Pope" (Carlyle's phrase) over the Harvard firmament, fashioning a mere lectureship into the Dexter professorship of sacred literature, hammering out with steely logic his *Evidences of the Genuineness of the Gospels,* in which he proved to his own satisfaction, if not entirely to others, that whatever the woolly Germans might be claiming in their higher criticism, the gospels were written by the very Matthew, Mark, Luke, and John, whose names they bore. Norton, after "demolishing" Calvinism, would settle down, in Emerson's words, as "the tyrant of the Cambridge Parnassus," stoutly defending a Unitarian status quo. Channing surely would have marched to a different drumbeat, searching for the signs of Christianity's excellence in feelings no less than in logic, beyond the limits of Norton's Biblical exegesis no less than within them.

Channing must have been slightly euphoric to accept the Dexter lectureship in the first place. Given his puny health, he was already engaged in a strenuous array of activities. In addition to his preaching and pastoral duties and his responsibility for the affairs of the Bible Society, Channing in March 1812 accepted reelection to the Boston School Committee, then the following month rattled his bones on an exhausting stagecoach trip to Washington in the company of his friend Congressman Josiah Quincy. Two years earlier, Quincy had transferred his church membership from New South to Federal Street, where he worshiped until he was named president of Harvard. Channing stayed several days as a guest in Quincy's home in the capital, hoping to listen to congressional debates on the gloomy crisis with England, but the House remained in secret session throughout his visit.[22] He returned to Boston exhausted and frustrated, to learn of Buckminster's death. Even as he accepted the invitation of the Dexter fund trustees to succeed Buckminster, he was sick at heart. By a narrow margin, with Quincy in opposition, Congress had declared war on Great Britain. Voicing a sentiment which Channing strongly shared, Massachusetts Governor Strong proclaimed a public fast in mourning for a war "against the nation from which we are descended." The Federalist-dominated Massachusetts General Court issued a passionate "Address to the People," terming the war contrary to the public interest and urging that there be no volunteers from the Bay State.

The year 1812 was a time of desolation for Channing, with only a few bright hues. Walter, his brother, was awarded his M.D. The Smith School for "colored" children was established as one of the ten elementary institutions in the city, and Channing, as a School Committee member, had the privilege of casting an aye vote for the munificent sum of two hundred dollars appropriated for this "School for African Children."[23] The Howard Benevolent Society, an avant-garde relief effort for the poor, sick, and suffering of Boston, was launched, along with the picturesquely named (and still functioning) Fragment Society, to aid the worthy, destitute poor, suffering, and sick by giving them money, food, clothing, and fuel. With poverty certain to spread as a result of the war's harsh curtailment of foreign trade, Channing took grim though guilty satisfaction in Josiah Quincy's intimacy with John C. Calhoun, then a member of the Foreign Relations Committee of the House of Representatives. Calhoun tipped Quincy of the administration's intention to institute another embargo. Quincy dispatched the news to his Boston cronies Harrison Gray Otis and Thomas Handasyd Perkins, so that ships in Boston harbor, fully or partly loaded, could split and run.

On Governor Strong's appointed day of fasting and prayer, July 23, 1812, Jedidiah Morse in Charlestown proclaimed that the war was God's rebuke to the nation's sins. Channing had a different view. The war, he felt, was a purely human decision. It was unnecessary and could have been avoided. In his most measured tones, he pronounced that he was "unable to justify the war in which we have engaged."

From beginning to end, Channing's attitude toward war was consistent. War was hideous — yet he was not a pacifist. The spilling of human blood could never be anything but horrifying — still there were conceivable conditions under which war might justly be waged. Determining the distinction between a just and unjust war was not done by measuring popular sentiment. It was a task for the finest faculties of mind and conscience.

Channing's opposition to the War of 1812 was shared overwhelmingly by his fellow New Englanders, but he had not bothered to count noses. Quite possibly a majority of all Americans opposed the course adopted by the Congress and the Madison administration. Again, his position was independent of the shifting winds of public opinion, as he would repeatedly demonstrate in the years ahead. He had only one obligation: to weigh carefully every possible claim, then make up his mind.

Channing acknowledged to his congregation that the British had maliciously provoked Americans. But war, he felt, was a disproportionate response to the offenses involved. The evils inherent in such a war overshadowed the evils put forward as its justification.

For five years Napoleon had treated American shipping harshly and arbitrarily, but America had not succumbed to the temptation to make war on him. Obviously, it was not simply British provocation that fanned a war fever in the inland and western states from Vermont to Tennessee, and in the South from Virginia down. There were those in Boston who were also hell-bent to fight. A Republican paper let Governor Strong know what it thought of him, with a hot-blooded quatrain:

> *Since war is the word, let us strain every nerve*
> *To save our America, her glory increase;*
> *So, shoulder your firelock, your country preserve,*
> *For the hotter the war, boys, the quicker the peace.*[24]

Strangely, in the part of the country most acutely affected by British provocations at sea — the Atlantic coastline — there was the most formidable opposition to the war. To be sure, war might deal deadlier blows to commerce than Britain's impressment of seamen, or repeated violations of American territorial waters by the Royal Navy. Channing mentioned this in his sermon, and by doing so acknowledged that it explained some of the fury of Bostonian dissent. But he quickly explained that his dissent was different. "Loss of property," he said, "is a small evil attending this war,— its effect on our *character* cannot be calculated."[25]

There were many factors Channing might have mentioned to justify his fears for the nation's character. In the 1810–1811

97

congressional elections, a covey of new men won seats, and their bellicosity promptly earned them the term "war hawks." For the most part, they were men of Channing's age — Henry Clay and Richard Johnson from Kentucky, Felix Grundy from Tennessee, John C. Calhoun from South Carolina. They had tendencies Channing deeply distrusted. They despised the patient diplomacy of Madison and his secretary of state Monroe, and thundered that the national honor demanded a fight. They made no bones about their thirst for a war with Great Britain, which if successful, would justify gobbling up Canada, legitimize the slaughter of stubborn Indians on the frontier, and swing open vast new forest lands for expansionist settlement. This was hardly the spirit of benevolence Channing cherished for America.

Channing inexplicably mentioned none of this in his sermon. Instead he resorted to a theme, dear to his heart to be sure, which was bound to rouse universal applause from his listeners. He asked them to consider with whom America automatically allied itself as it waged war against England. The answer was obvious: Napoleon. Two years earlier, on the occasion of another public fast day, Channing had starkly expressed himself on Bonaparte's depredations. Napoleon's nation, he exclaimed, "lusts for war, and her leader seeks world domination. Religion, virtue, and liberty wither under her power, and she breathes an air polluted with infidelity, impiety and atheism."[26] Had Channing been an Englishman, he would have counted Britain's military resistance to the Corsican a just cause.

Now with his nation at war with the Mother Country, he was doubly desolate: "When I view my country taking part with the oppressor against that nation which has alone arrested his proud career of victory,— which is now spreading her shield over desolated Portugal and Spain,— which is the chief hope of the civilized world,— I blush,— I mourn. . . . Let our government know that we deem alliance with France the worst of evils, threatening at once our morals, our liberty, and our religion."[27]

Within a month, Channing again climbed his pulpit steps to speak out on the war, this time in response to President Madison's proclamation of a day of "Humiliation and Prayer, appointed in consequence of the declaration of war against Great

Britain." Channing, hoping to address posterity as well as his congregation, prepared his discourse with razor-like precision. When a free society is split asunder, as America was over "Madison's War," what is the relationship between the citizen and his government? What crucial principles must be identified, understood, and firmly grasped? With prophetic wizardry, Channing outlined a case that he could have delivered as relevantly during America's torment over Vietnam.[28]

Regarding war itself, Channing declared it to be "in all circumstances, at all times . . . a tremendous scourge." Nevertheless, there are conditions in which war "may be the last and only method of repelling lawless ambition, and of defending invaded liberty and essential rights." Even then, "we should deeply lament the necessity of shedding human blood." When the screw turns, and a just war becomes unavoidable, the community of which we are a part "claims and deserves our prayers, our cheerful services, the sacrifice of wealth, and even of life." Could he view the nation's war with Great Britain in that light, "what different feelings" would he express. Instead he was compelled to believe that the ministry was "precipitated into a war which . . . cannot be justified, and . . . which promises not a benefit . . . to this country or to the world."

What should a citizen do when he finds himself in this solemn situation? It was Channing's conviction that citizens should not go charging off into ill-considered civil disobedience, not at least until they had rigorously reviewed for themselves the role properly constituted government, whatever its faults and follies, plays as "a divine institution, essential to the improvement of our nature, the spring of industry and enterprise, the shield of property and life, the refuge of the weak and oppressed."

He emphasized that he was not calling for mute submission. The citizen, he said, has rights as well as duties: "The Government is instituted for one and a single end, — the benefit of the governed, the protection, peace, and welfare of society: and when it is perverted to other objects, to purposes of avarice, ambition, or party-spirit, we are authorized and even bound to make such opposition as is suited to restore it to its proper end, to render it as pure as the imperfection of our nature and state will admit."

Indeed, Channing went on, when a government "wantonly disregards the ends of social union; when it threatens the subversion of national liberty and happiness," the citizen acquires the right, "not only of remonstrating, but of employing force for its destruction." Channing hastily added that such action "cannot be exercised with too much deliberation." Let us remember, he pleaded, "that the best government will partake the imperfections of all human institutions, and that if the ends of the social compact are in any tolerable degree accomplished," it would be madness to destroy a blessing possessed for a blessing only imagined.

"The last dreadful resort," Channing continued, "is never justifiable until the injured members of the community are brought to despair of other relief, and are so far united in views and purposes as to be authorized in the hope of success." The uncharacteristically expedient tone of Channing's last phrase took on added meaning with his next sentence: "Civil commotion should be viewed as the worst of national evils, *with the single exception of slavery"* (italics mine). This sentence must have sent a tremor through a congregation unaccustomed to hearing their pastor's view of slavery. But in the two parts of the single sentence, Channing summarized the paradox he would wrestle with for years — how to end slavery and avoid civil war at one and the same time.

Acknowledging that the United States had come into being through civil war, Channing pled for recognition of the unique character of it: "The government which we shook off was not seated in the midst of us. Our struggle was that of nation with nation, rather than of fellow-citizens with one another. Our manners and habits tended to give a considerateness and a stability to the public mind which can hardly be expected in a future struggle." It was almost as if Channing had closed his eyes and conjured up a vision of the uninhibited slaughter which would ensue should Americans take up arms against one another. At any rate, it was a vision that would haunt him for the rest of his life.

As if seeking to shake a specter from his mind, Channing invoked the Constitution, "the great design of which is to prevent the necessity of appealing to force." In a despotism, he said, there is no way to influence public affairs "but by convulsing the state." Under the Constitution, governments and public policies may be changed "without the horrors" of a violent revolution. The Constitution's two most critical features, he continued, are the voting right and the right of freely discussing public issues: "Resign either of these, and no way of escape from oppression will be left you but civil commotion."

Refining his point further, Channing contended that the right of election quickly loses its meaning unless freedom of opinion, of speech, and of the press, "the very soul of republican institutions," is stubbornly protected and fully exercised. "Nothing awakens and improves men so much as free communication of thoughts and feelings," he rhapsodized. If the right of free discussion is abandoned, if convictions are awed and suppressed by threats, if a government succeeds "in silencing every voice but that which approves them; if nothing reaches the people but what would lend support to men in power,— farewell to liberty. The form of a free government may remain, but the life, the soul, the substance is fled."

Channing had earlier applied this reasoning to the Federalist-sponsored Alien and Sedition Acts. Now he had cause to apply it again. Because his hearers knew the details, he kept his remarks pungently brief:

"We have lived to hear the strange doctrine that to expose the measures of rulers is treason; and we have lived to see this doctrine carried into practice. We have seen a savage populace excited and let loose on men whose crime consisted in bearing testimony against the present war; and let loose not merely to waste their property, but to tear them from the refuge which the magistrate had afforded, and to shed their blood. In this, and in other events, there have been symptoms of a purpose to terrify into silence those who disapprove the calamitous war under which we suffer; to deprive us of the only method which is left of obtaining a wiser and better government. The cry has been that war is declared, and all opposition should therefore be hushed. A sentiment more unworthy of a free country can hardly be propagated. If this doctrine be admitted, rulers have only to declare war, and they are screened at once from scrutiny. . . . The press, which is to expose inferior abuses, must not utter one rebuke, one indignant complaint, although our best interests and most valuable rights are put to hazard by an unnecessary war. . . . Our peace and our interests require that a different sentiment should prevail. We should teach our present and all future rulers that there is no measure for which they must render so solemn an account to their constituents as for the declaration of war; that no measure will be so freely, so fully discussed; and that no administration can succeed in persuading this people to exhaust their treasure and blood in supporting war, unless it be palpably necessary and just."[29]

Superimposing Channing's doctrine of dissent on America's Vietnam experience reveals that he laid the foundation of an enduring national concern. Channing, one can assume, would not have been confused. He was neither time-bound, nor tradition-bound in his devotion to meaningful dissent.

Only a few weeks before Channing spoke, Boston had been alerted by the city government to the possibility of mob action against opponents of the war. There were, as noted, elements in the city no less hawkish and chauvinistic than those in Baltimore — the "savage populace" Channing referred to — who had carried out the so-called Baltimore Massacre. This frightening event, neglected in most accounts of American history, is chronicled, fortunately, in the sixth volume of Henry Adams's *History of the United States*. Its significance was not lost on Channing, and he was to use it in the future on issues not nearly so agreeable to the merchant-gentry of his congregation.

On June 22, 1812, shortly after the United States launched hostilities against Great Britain, a gang of patriotic commandos occupied the printing office of the *Federal Republican* in Baltimore and smashed it to smithereens. The editors, Jacob Wagner and Alexander C. Hanson, had certainly done little to endear themselves to hawkish fellow citizens. Their assault on war-minded congressmen, and on Madison himself, was as slanderous as any in the press of the time, which was considerable. It is fair to say that they were extremists. But until war was actually declared there was no physical retaliation.

After the raid, the newspaper's editors managed to resume publication in nearby Georgetown. Some of their Baltimore friends saw to it that the sheet was circulated, but also spread a rumor that the new printing facilities had been set up at an address in Baltimore, which they openly specified. A group of about twenty antiwar Federalists, commanded by Generals J. M. Lingan and Henry Lee, the celebrated Revolutionary War hero and former governor of Maryland, occupied and barricaded the house named by the *Federal Republican*'s backers, anticipating an attack. An alcohol-fortified waterfront mob, led by a mysterious French agent provocateur, obliged. As the assailing force stormed the door, Lee's garrison opened fire. A terrible bloodbath was averted when Baltimore's mayor rode up with a troop of cavalry, and convinced the besieged Federalists to accept sanctuary in the city jail. That night the mob broke into the jail. In the melee, several of Lee's associates managed to flee, but eight, less fortunate, were beaten to a pulp, and then tortured through the night on the jailhouse steps, to see if they were dead.

At noon the next day, the mob finally permitted city authorities to assume charge of the carnage. Lingan was dead, and Lee, among others, was cruelly crippled.

As Channing could plainly see, the damage done by this incident to the war hawks' cause was immense, perhaps irreparable, but he was not content to leave it at that. In the same spirit in which he would later hold some of the abolitionists accountable, Channing exhorted antiwar editors not to abuse their freedom, for this, he said, "may be as fatal to our country as its relinquishment." The truth must be told, he continued, but let it "be told for a good end; not to irritate but to convince; not to inflame the bad passions, but to sway the judgment." He mourned "that so much is continually published among us for no other apparent end than to gratify the malevolence of one party by wounding the other. The consequence is, that . . . fellow-citizens burn with mutual hatred, and some are evidently ripe for outrage and violence." While this must never

103

be used as an excuse for suppressing free discussion, Channing declared, "every man should feel the duty of speaking and writing with deliberation." In summary, Channing invoked the duty "to hold fast and to assert with firmness those truths and principles on which the welfare of your country seems to depend; but to do this with calmness, with a love of peace, without illwill and revenge."

Channing's critics repeatedly point to such passages as evidence of his wishful romanticizing. Surely he did not believe that his fellow countrymen were angelic enough to follow his advice! In truth, he did not. He fully expected his counsel to be more honored in the breach than the observance. Also, he expected it on occasion to be denounced. Channing was clearheaded enough about the deformities of man's present state. What the ministry of religion meant to him was thè chance to teach and demonstrate, in all circumstances and conditions, that humanity is not locked into its imperfections; that all occasions, even the worst, are potential gateways to emancipation. Far from being facile purism, his addresses on the "Duties of the Citizen in Times of Trial or Danger" reveal an acute sense of the need to keep idealism relevantly related to actual social conditions and consequences. As Max Weber would note some seventy years later, a signal element of Channing's genius as a moral force was the degree to which he consistently tried to avoid permitting "a gulf to emerge in men's feelings between the presumed requirements of Christianity and that which is brought about by the social system . . . in terms of consequences and preconditions."[30]

Channing was human enough and imperfect enough to have a fling that did disregard the hard realities of the external world. When news of Napoleon's overthrow reached Boston in June 1814, a group of fifteen of the most Brahminish of Boston's Brahmins gathered at the home of Lieutenant Governor William Phillips to prepare "a solemn religious festival" to celebrate Bonaparte's humiliation. Channing, the only clergyman in the lot, was elected to preach the sermon.[31] True enough, New Englanders, even the Republican segment, had endured two emotionally frustrating war years. Some kind of emotional binge was badly needed, and the downfall of the Corsican tyrant was a wildly exciting event to Boston's men of substance, Channing included.

Every square foot of King's Chapel was filled with the perspiring influential of Boston when Channing took his place in the high pulpit. The warm June day, thoughts of his forthcoming marriage (only a month away), the long years of bitter brooding about Napoleon, the packed sanctuary — all these produced an adrenal response in Channing. He quickly moved to a resounding peroration: "The oppressor is fallen and the world is free!" That most respectable of congregations burst into wild applause. Channing was stunned, we are told. Summoning his calmest ministerial manner, he reminded the suddenly hushed assembly that they were in the presence of God.[32]

The world was *not* free, as normally he would have been the first to recognize and point out. But this was not the normal Channing. He was carried away, and let himself be carried away. God had cast down the predator! Henceforth, Christianity and peace would rule! Only once did he revert to his usual style of suggesting how thorny and demanding was the pathway to the kingdom of heaven, when he said, "I am not forgetful of the solemn uncertainty of futurity." For the most part, that June day, he *was* forgetful.

Who could wonder? Two years of the hated war had been for most New Englanders a sponge of gall. But the economic consequences were far less harsh than anticipated; in fact, they were surprisingly benevolent. While some shipowners and merchants suffered considerably, spreading their misery to their various classes of employees and dependents, others prospered. The British blockade was not levied against the New England coast until May 1814. Meanwhile, many of Boston's traders, scornful of their own government's laws (after all, it was not *their* war), did a thriving business with the enemy in the Maritime Provinces and Quebec. In addition, legitimate overseas commerce funneled through New England seaports, and was then sent by wagons and sleds to inland states. Unexpectedly, the war turned New England's economy toward manufacturing; as if by magic, there were suddenly almost half a million spindles whirring in the region.

Despite these windfalls, New England's Federalists mulishly insisted that the war was ruining them. In a fashion repeated by prospering businessmen who intoned their abomination of Franklin Roosevelt and his wild-eyed radical advisors, Boston's unreconstructed Federalists seemed to believe, and constantly to publish, horrors in the making. Wrapping themselves in piety, the Federalist majority in the Massachusetts General Court rejected a resolution of gratitude to a naval hero as "not becoming a moral and religious people."

Once Napoleon had been disposed of, it seemed conceivable that the Boston establishment might undertake an agonizing reassessment of position. However legitimate their strictures against the war hawks' lust for Canada, it had not happened, and now the United States stood nearly naked before the overpowering sea and land might of Great Britain.

The events of the summer of 1814 brought that reassessment. From Washington came word that the national government could no longer provide a military shield for Massachusetts. The Royal Navy, encouraged by the refusal of Federalist governors in New England to place their state militias under war department orders, raided various parts of the coast virtually at will. In September, a British invasion of Boston loomed as a distinct possibility, yet many of Boston's burghers were emotionally unable to shake off their sulk.

Channing was not one of them. On September 18, 1814, now married, Channing reassumed his natural role of relating religious principles to conditions and consequences.[33] The purpose of religion, he told his anxious congregation, is to offer "instructions suited to every condition, whether of individuals or communities." The country's reverses in the war, depressing and unnerving as they were, compel each individual "to ask himself what are his duties, what the times demand from him, in what manner he may contribute to the public safety."

Channing proceeded to outline five principles with which citizens who had conscientiously opposed the United States declaration of war could now apply their religious convictions to the existing situation. First, he said, every individual must search out, confess, and renounce the flaws in his own character,

106

Channing's mother

Channing as a student

Samuel Hopkins

Channing's summer house at Oakland, R.I.

The Old Federal Street Meetinghouse in which Chan-ning was ordained

Channing in middle age
(After a portrait
painted in 1839 by Gambardella
that Channing considered his best likeness)

*Bishop Jean Louis Lefebvre de Cheverus
(Portrait by Gilbert Stuart.
Courtesy of the Museum of Fine Arts, Boston.
Bequest of Mrs. Charlotte Gore Greenough Hervoches de Quilliou)*

Charles Follen

Joseph S. Buckminster
(After a portrait by Gilbert Stuart)

which contributed to the nation's moral bankruptcy. Coming over to Jedidiah Morse's earlier point of view, Channing declared that the war's dismal course had indeed been a sign of God's judgment on a spiritually floundering people. God, he said, is "a moral governor, the friend of the righteous, the punisher of the wicked. . . . A virtuous people, fighting in defense of their altars and firesides, may look to God with confidence." Look inward, he warned, and let the soul-searching be more than a superficial confession: "We owe to ourselves and our country deep sorrow for our sins."

Having advised general penitence, Channing moved to his second point, "instant and fervent" prayer. "Let us pray to God," he continued, "that he will not forsake us in this dark and menacing day . . . that he will be our shield in battle, and will send us deliverance." How could Channing now invoke God's aid in a war he had condemned only two years earlier as palpably malicious? Channing gave his audience credit for grasping the cause of his turnabout: "It will not be imagined from these remarks, that by importunity of prayer God can be bent to favor an unjust cause. But when our cause is just; when, instead of waging offensive war, we gather round our city and shores for defence, we may be assured that sincere prayer, united with a sincere purpose of obedience, will not be lost."

For his third principle, Channing resorted to patriotism, which he claimed was enjoined, under certain circumstances, by Christianity's "disinterested and benevolent" spirit. The circumstances he had in mind were double-edged: when one's community is genuinely threatened by hostile forces, it must be defended; but even then, patriotism must be purged of "every mixture of injustice toward foreign states." The question, he said, was no longer one of carrying "invasion, slaughter, and desolation into an unoffending province, not whether we will give our strength and wealth to the prosecution of unprincipled plans of conquest, but whether we will defend our firesides and altars, whether we will repel from our shores a hostile army."

Channing felt that the answer was plain: "However unjustifiable may have been the measures by which we have been reduced to this mournful extremity, our right to our soil and our possessions remains unimpaired; the right of defence can never be wrested from us; and never whilst God gives means of resistance, ought we to resign our country to the clemency of a foe."

Channing's fourth point was the need to distinguish between irrational and rational fears. The imagination, he said, is prone to enlarge panic until it "spreads like lightning from breast to breast." Before a blow is struck, "a people are subdued by their fears." On the other hand, the key to real fortitude, courage, and resolution, is to take full account of the rational dangers, which Channing described as formidable. He referred to the relatively small but powerful British task force threatening the New England seacoast as "a veteran army, trained to war, accustomed to success, fresh from conquest, and led by experienced commanders." This, he said, "is not to be despised." He pled that Bostonians fortify their minds "by reflecting on the justice of our cause, that we are standing on our own shores, and defending invaded rights." In such circumstances, he declared, the best way to demonstrate a love of peace is to show that it "has not originated in timidity." For the benefit of those shaken by the thought of being killed, Channing reminded them that "Death awaits us all, and happy he who meets it in the discharge of duty . . . happy is the martyr to the cause of his country, who, in obedience to God, opposes his breast to the sword of her invaders, and repays with life the protection she has afforded."

A more conventional distillation of the patriotic doctrine of self-defense, with theological underpinnings, is impossible to conceive, yet Channing stoutly avoided jingoism on the one hand and pious sentimentality on the other. While holding his audience morally accountable, surrendering nothing to their more primitive urges, he nevertheless kept in close touch with their instincts and aspirations. This talent was the nub of his constantly intensifying appeal to a following that included the lowliest and mightiest of his fellow citizens.

Channing's fifth and concluding point illustrated his ability not only to be tuned in to his people's passions, but to be sensitive in a principled way. Reminding them that their religion required benevolence "even towards our personal and national foes," he warned against poisoning patriotism with malignancy. "The brave are generous," he declared, particularly "when our foe is an illustrious nation, which for ages has defended and nurtured the interests of religion, science, and humanity." True, this paragon nation was sending her forces against American communities, "but let us not forget that our own government first sent slaughter and conflagration into her unoffending provinces." If English armies must now be met by Bostonians in battle (God in his mercy forbid! Channing prayed), "let us fight not like beasts of prey to glut revenge, but to maintain our rights, to obtain an honorable peace."

The invasion of Boston never came off; Channing's high-minded counsel was not tested; the war droned on in its indecisive and generally inglorious manner. Channing meanwhile had his hands full with some of his friends. The Federalist establishment of Massachusetts, smarting from the invasion scare, summoned a New England Convention in Hartford to mull over various embitterments and to consider revisions of the Constitution. The reference to constitutional change was actually a compromise between Federalist moderates and extremists. The moderates had no stomach for secession. They did hope, however, to win concessions for their region from the national government, and reasoned that the Hartford meetings would be a safety valve to let off some of the mounting steam for disunion. Channing, whose devotion to the union never flagged no matter how much fear and trembling there was among the New England gentry over a westward shift of power along an expanding United States frontier, favored the moderate cause. The more violent wing of the Federalist leadership, numbering some of Channing's intimates, was too soured to care about the union.

Convinced that the British invasion of New Orleans would succeed and that Aaron Burr's secession scheme for the Louisiana Purchase would materialize, they hankered for a new Constitution, with ironclad protection for New England's interests, and confined to the original thirteen states. If they could win acceptance for this impossible dream, fine; otherwise they were for making a separate peace and going it alone. Channing breathed a sigh of relief when moderates gained control of the secret sessions in Hartford and succeeded in issuing an unhysterical report. The convention statement piled condemnation on the Madison administration and the war, but stated that attempts to change the Constitution "upon every abuse of power" were irresponsible. Secession was ruled out as being both inexpedient and unnecessary. The roots of New England's distresses were neither deep nor permanent, the report went on, having resulted from a combination of bad administration, and a wrongheaded partisanship in the European war. A proposal was made that New England assume responsibility for its own defense and sequester federal taxes for that purpose. Several constitutional amendments were halfheartedly suggested. The thunder about making a separate peace was silenced.

If Channing nursed a notion that high principle had prevailed, he was wrong. The safety valve worked, but it did so because cool Federalists, like George Cabot and Harrison Gray Otis were haunted by the growing strength of the Republican party in New England. The Federalists controlled all five states by the slimmest of margins. If the extremists among them had prevailed at Hartford, there might well have been civil war in New England. At the very least, Federalism would have signed its political death warrant by exposing itself to the stigma of being unpatriotic. Moderation turned out *not* to be its own reward. The Madison administration suddenly found itself riding a wave of good news, first from New Orleans, where a new hero, Andrew Jackson, broke onto the surface of American political life, then from Ghent where a peace treaty was signed, in which there was neither gain nor glory for America or Britain. New England's Federalist decision makers were made the political scapegoats for the government's own inept handling of the war. A brand of disloyalty, from which it never recuperated, was fastened on the Federalist party. The doctrine of states' rights, however, not only escaped disgrace, but within a few years was being stoutly championed by states like Virginia, which had damned the Hartford Convention as traitorous.[34]

Channing's Federalism was more than skin-deep, but he never succumbed to excesses of party loyalty. After the King's Chapel celebration of Napoleon's defeat, he was harshly attacked by a Boston pamphleteer using the pseudonym Messala, who charged him with converting the pulpit "into a theatre for political lectures." According to Messala, Channing, by consenting "to become the instrument of a party," by lending himself to "the bitterness of faction," and by meddling "in the fury of party collision," should be considered and treated "as a common political brawler."[35]

Channing understood how someone as emotionally pro-France as Messala obviously was, had to be offended by his pulpit performance at King's Chapel. He had his own regrets about that. But he knew that the charge of cloaking Federalist partisanship in his pulpit robe was unfounded. As much as he admired the contributions of Federalism to American life, he was well aware of its supporters' frailties. Many years later, in his *Christian Examiner* essay on "The Union,"[36] he reviewed the thoughts that occupied him during these war years. The country, he felt, would always owe a tremendous debt to the Federal party for organizing the government, for carrying the nation safely and honorably through the most tempestuous days of the French Revolution, for averting war with Great Britain during the shaky early years of the nation's existence.

He fully acknowledged, however, that the party "in some respects failed of its duty to the cause of the Union and of freedom." The reason for this, Channing wrote, was not the "treachery" of which it was falsely and tragically charged after the Hartford Convention, but "despondence." This was "the rock on which Federalism split." Here Channing spoke from personal knowledge. "Too many of its leading men" distrusted democratic institutions and "the moral ability" of the people to sustain them. "By not confiding in the community, they lost its confidence. By the depressed tone with which they spoke of liberty, their attachment to it became suspect. The taint of anti-republican tendencies was fastened upon them by their opponents, and this reproach no party could survive." To illustrate, Channing singled out George Cabot, the dean of the Federalists of his time. He represented the Boston ideal of independent judgment and integrity in its purest form, Channing said. Yet he lacked "a just faith in man's capacity of freedom, at least in that degree of it which our institutions suppose." Cabot, in Channing's self-revealing view, "had too much the wisdom of experience. He wanted what may be called the wisdom of hope."

Then, in one of his most eloquent paragraphs, Channing explained why he could never be a partisan Federalist, or a skeptical conservative of any kind: "We apprehend that it is possible to make experience too much our guide. . . . There are seasons in human affairs, of inward and outward revolution, when new depths seem to be broken up in the soul, when new wants are unfolded in multitudes, and a new and undefined good is thirsted for. These are periods when the principles of experience need to be modified, when hope and trust and instinct claim a share with prudence in the guidance of affairs, when, in truth, *to dare* is the highest wisdom."

Channing was already a seasoned and celebrated Proper Bostonian in his mid-thirties when news of the Treaty of Ghent reached Boston, but far from following the Cabot path of darkening even this blessing with Federalist foreboding, he went radiantly into his pulpit to "Thank God!" that now, with "a spirit of mutual forbearance among our citizens," the country could resume its stride.

Channing's "wisdom of hope" was attuned to the times. Most Americans, including most New Englanders, burst out of the gloomy cocoon of war in high spirits. If the fighting on the whole had been a costly fiasco, it had also produced intriguing, unanticipated results. New England, as mentioned, was rapidly transforming itself from a maritime to a manufacturing region. West Florida had slipped, almost unnoticed, within the nation's boundaries. There was a subtle but pronounced renewal of national pride and purpose, produced by apparent release at last from the interminable bloodletting of Europe, which seemed ready for its own era of peace. Americans, their Capitol in ruins, plagued by sectional rivalries, the national credit in peril, sensed that they were free as never before to get down to the work of settling the west and making money.

For Channing, neither settling the west nor making money claimed high priority, though he was not opposed to either as long as correct principles were observed. What goaded him was a dream he had long nursed — a peace movement that would free man forever from the scourge of war. He observed with wonder and fascination the festivities in Boston following the arrival of news from Ghent. Church bells all over the city, including those of Federal Street, rang out. An oratorio in celebration of peace was sung at King's Chapel, with uniformed British officers in attendance. A parade and fireworks followed. A peace ball was staged at the Concert Hall, where British officers were again present, this time as "favorite partners of the young ladies."[37] If bitter foes, on such short notice, could join in the revelry of peace, surely there must be some way to assure that peace would be man's lot.

Encouragement came from Channing's octogenarian Grandfather Ellery, who, while diffident about quick success, was heart and soul behind Channing's dream: "Peace and liberty are the great objects of my delight. . . . However gradual may be the growth of Christian knowledge and moral reformation yet, unless it be begun, unless the seeds be planted, there can be no tree of knowledge, and, of course, no fruit. The attempt . . . to produce peace on earth and good-will towards men is humane, Christian, and sublime; and if persevered in, will, I don't doubt, in due time be successful."[38] William Ellery, like his grandson, was piqued by the "applauding" of martial virtues, and responded to a noticeable rise, in Europe no less than in the United States, of antiwar sentiments. A widespread weariness with military slaughter spawned by a quarter century of international conflict gave popular impetus to a peace movement.

Keyed up, Channing invited a group of peace supporters to meet with him in his study — the breeding pen without equal of high-minded causes. There on December 28, 1815, twenty-two crusaders for the abolition of war ratified a constitution establishing the Peace Society of Massachusetts. Channing was heartened to learn that a similar group had banded together in New York City at the urging of David Low Dodge.

Some months earlier, Channing had received a letter from William Pitt Scargill, an English peace enthusiast, enclosing a copy of Scargill's pamphlet on *The Impolicy of War* and exhorting Channing to bend his best efforts against war.[39] But the man who stimulated him most was the saintly Rev. Dr. Noah Worcester, whose Arian views on the Trinity had cost him his pulpit in Thornton, New Hampshire, but who then turned a major portion of his gentle, persistent energies to the cause of peace. Their lives were already intertwined in the erupting theological controversy of the period, and the peace issue brought them closer. At the 1815 annual meeting of the Massachusetts Convention of Congregational Ministers, Dr. Worcester successfully introduced a resolution for the appointment of a five-man committee to draft plans for correcting "the public mind on the subject of war." Channing and Worcester, along with President John T. Kirkland of Harvard, Dr. Osgood of Medford, and Mr. Foster of Brighton were appointed.[40] The meeting in Channing's study followed, thrusting him, even in this most pacific effort, into a controversy.

As one of the senior counselors of the Peace Society, he had to bring his moderating skills to bear on a split between those who were total pacifists, and those, like himself, who drew a distinction between the just and unjust use of force. If the Peace Society was to amount to anything, he reasoned, its ranks must include all friends of peace whatever their differing views on the legitimacy of defensive war; otherwise the base of influence would be narrowed to the few who believed in absolute nonresistance. When the Convention of Congregational Ministers assembled in the spring of 1816, Channing delivered the first of his addresses on war.[41] He spent the first ten minutes or so detailing the *"miseries and crimes"* of war. In deliberately shocking language he pictured a battlefield: "Here are heaps of slain, weltering in their own blood, their bodies mangled . . ." He then followed the track of a victorious, pursuing army: ". . . You see the roads strewed with the dead; you see scattered flocks, and harvests trampled underfoot, the smoking ruins of cottages, and the miserable inhabitants flying in want and despair; and even yet, the horrors of a single battle are not exhausted."

Channing next discussed the causes of war, each one a moral issue in his opinion: the passion for excitement, hazard, tumult;

the lust for triumph and power; the myth that the field of battle is a field of glory; false patriotism; childhood conditioning that war is part of the fixed laws of human nature.

If the causes have moral origins, then the cures must be moral also, Channing went on. To eliminate the seeds of war, more seeds of harmonious human relationship and association must be sown. For this reason Channing felt compelled to suggest "an important caution": "Let not the cause of peace be injured by the assertion of extreme and indefensible principles. I particularly refer to the principle that war is absolutely, and in all possible cases, unlawful, and prohibited by Christianity. This doctrine is considered by a great majority of the judicious and enlightened, as endangering the best interests of society; and it ought not therefore to be connected with our efforts for the diffusion of peace, unless it appear to us a clear and indubitable truth."

With the passing years, Channing's horror of war constantly deepened, and with each successive address on the subject, his language grew stronger and more colorful. But if he was one of the first to expound the idea of conscientious objection to particular wars, he could never bring himself to join the ranks of absolute pacifists. In his 1838 lecture on war, delivered as a memorial to Noah Worcester, he set forth a doctrine of selective conscientious objection.[42] No Christian, he said, has a right to take part in a war simply because his government asks or requires it. If it is a war which his conscience repudiates, "let him deliberately refuse. If martial law seize on him, let him submit. If hurried to prison, let him submit. It brought thence to be shot, let him submit. There must be martyrs to peace as truly as to other principles of our religion."

Still, when Channing was driving at Newport with his young protégé Frederick Farley, the two men fell into discussion of a recent pacifist tract by Samuel J. May. Channing, clenching and waving his small, delicate fist, said: "Brother Farley, sometimes we *must* fight."[43]

To the congregational ministers, Channing traced with considerable care why he felt that way. National subjugation, he said, is a greater evil than a war of defense. A community, it seemed to him, possessed "the indisputable right to resort to such a war, when all other means have failed for the security of its existence or freedom." He asked the clergymen to imagine that they were asked to restore peace to "a contentious neighborhood." Wouldn't they feel foolish, he queried, insisting that whatever the threat or provocation, all acts of self-defense would be treated as crimes. Equally useless, he declared, is an effort to apply this principle to the pacification of the world.

As for the Scriptural injunction, "Resist not evil," favorite of the absolute nonresisters, Channing coolly commented that the "Scriptures are given to us as reasonable beings." Unless circumstantial exceptions can be made to "resist not evil," civil government is "prostrated"; citizens could not even employ the aid of the laws to enforce their rights. One of the primary purposes of organized society, said Channing, is precisely "to *resist* evil men." With these words Channing synthesized two of his current involvements — the leadership thrust upon him, willy-nilly, of the liberal theological cause, and the prominence he welcomed in education for peace.

Channing explained his abnormal welcoming of the spotlight on the peace issue in the opening paragraphs of his address to his ministerial colleagues. "After the slumber of ages," he said, "Christians seem to be awakening to a sense of the pacific character of their religion . . . I was unwilling that this subject should be approached and dismissed as an ordinary affair. I feared that in the pressure of business, we might be satisfied with the expression of customary disapprobation; and that, having in this way relieved our consciences, we should relapse into our former indifference, and continue to hear the howlings of this dreadful storm of human passions with as much unconcern as before."

Toward the end of his remarks, Channing lectured his brother ministers on the specific contributions they might make to world peace. They could admit the painful truth, for example, that "under no religion have intolerance and persecution raged more fiercely than under the gospel of the meek and forbearing Savior." Christians, he continued, "have made the earth to reek with blood and to resound with denunciation." Little wonder,

Channing noted, that "while the spirit of war has been cherished in the very bosom of the church, it has continued to ravage among the nations." The twin causes here pleaded with mounting animation. "Were the true spirit of Christianity," Channing declared, "to be inculcated with but half the zeal which has been wasted on doubtful and disputed doctrines, a sympathy, a cooperation might in a very short time be produced among Christians of every nation, most propitious to the pacification of the world."

Activities and events swirled through Channing's life during the second decade of the nineteenth century. He became increasingly caught up in Harvard's affairs,[44] first as an elected member of the college corporation, then as a member of various committees dealing with commencement exercises, chapel worship, mathematics texts, theological instruction, and aid to divinity students. In addition to his sermons, he was doing more and more writing for the journals. There was the mixture to which he had grown accustomed of bitter and sweet intimate experiences. In 1815, he had to swallow the desolate news from England that sister Ann had died. Once again he turned to his private journal to lash out against an intolerable grief. There had been so many! But the same year brought a compensating satisfaction. His brother Walter was made first professor of obstetrics and medical jurisprudence at the Harvard Medical School. Meanwhile Channing was composing memorials to Congress on peace, carrying on an alarmingly profuse correspondence, busying himself with contributing generously to an array of pioneering social service ventures, preaching at various ordinations and installations. For a man with a debilitated constitution, it was a remarkable performance.

The most indelible event, of course, was his marriage, after so many years of bachelorhood, to his first cousin, heiress Ruth Gibbs of Newport.

The two had grown up together; Ruth, two years older than Channing, exercising, if his memory be trusted, a continuous spell over his affections. Years after, he told Elizabeth Peabody how Ruth's "beautiful locks" had fascinated him. She was truly "a dancing shape, an image gay," he confided.[45] Why had he delayed putting the question so long? According to Miss Peabody's recollection, Channing had explained that "the minister of Christian morality must have clean hands, and the fact that my wife was so rich in this world's goods deterred me for years from endeavoring to win her from her luxurious home, to share privations and burdens which duty compelled me to bear."[46]

There are difficulties with this rationalization. As the ministry went, Channing was well paid and well housed. True, he gave his money away with almost reckless abandon, but he didn't have to. In addition, he never offered a satisfactory explanation for changing his mind and marrying Ruth after all. Those closest to the couple believed, justifiably or not, that Channing became increasingly distressed as Ruth turned down one suitor after another, realizing that he was the one she wanted, and that unless he took the initiative she would end up an old maid.[47]

That Channing was not necessarily a sophisticate in such matters was attested to by his sister, who observed: ". . . With all his admiration of the gentler sex, he lived to the age of thirty-four . . . ignorant of the warmest affections of the heart."[48] But after two years of marriage, he was preaching on the subject as if he were curator of the institution. His parishioners were given the benefit of his opinion that of all God's female creatures, America's women were the most blessed.

"The culture which is bestowed on the female mind, and which distinguishes modern times from the most refined periods of antiquity, — the respect which is accorded to woman, and which Christianity has done so much to inspire,— the reverence which prevails for the marriage vow, and the indignation which falls on conjugal infidelity,— the habit by which we are marked, of looking to our homes for the greatest part of our happiness, and the mixture of freedom and delicacy with which our general intercourse is conducted,— all contribute to elevate among us the female character, to render woman the associate of man's most refined pleasures and pursuits, and to confer on the conjugal connection a tenderness and dignity which have rarely distinguished it."[49]

Channing believed this (or he wouldn't have said it). He was describing how things genuinely were, and remained, in his own marriage, and, quite possibly, among the majority of other upper-class Bostonians.

But two sharp-eyed and sharp-tongued Englishwomen, Harriet Martineau, whom Channing enjoyed immensely, and Mrs. Frances Trollope, anything but Channing's type, saw things quite differently as they went about America taking voluminous notes for their subsequent, best-selling revelations.[50] Miss Martineau was irritated. "If a test of civilization be sought," she wrote, "none can be so sure as the condition of that half of society over which the other half has power, — from the exercise of the right of the strongest. Tried by this test, the American civilization appears to be of a lower order than might have been expected from some other symptoms of its social state. The Americans have, in the treatment of women, fallen below, not only their own democratic principles, but the practice of some parts of the Old World."

Mrs. Trollope was considerably testier: "In America, with the exception of dancing, which is almost wholly confined to the unmarried of both sexes, all the enjoyments of the men are found in the absence of the women. They dine, they play cards, they have musical meetings, they have suppers, all in large parties, but all without women. Were it not that such is the custom, it is impossible but that they would have ingenuity enough to find some expedient for sparing the wives and daughters of the opulent the sordid offices of household drudgery which they almost all perform in their families."

Channing, who could take satisfaction in marriage singularly companionable, and remarkably free from the slights, cruelties, and pains Miss Martineau and Mrs. Trollope spied out in the land, told his congregation of the care to be taken in getting married in the first place. This "most solemn engagement of life," he said, must never be "an act of rashness and unreflecting passion. . . . Let the heart take counsel of the understanding. Let the future as well as the present be brought into the account. Let not the eye or the imagination be trusted." So far, Channing might have been discussing the purchase of a parcel of land. But then . . . "Let the young man or young woman in-

128

quire, Is this a friend with whom I would wish to spend, not only my youth, but my age, not only my health, but my sickness, on whom I can lean in my griefs, to whom I can confide my trials."

Channing's further views were of a kind to delight Miss Martineau or Mrs. Trollope — and Mrs. Channing, from all indications. He said that there should be "an habitual flow of minute and kind attentions" between husband and wife; they should "cultivate each other's society, include each other in all their plans, share the same pleasures. . . . There should be few solitary joys."

Channing was what he was for reasons largely his own. But over and over again the influence of his Grandfather Ellery traces itself through his life style. An anecdote of the old gentleman's early married life was frequently on Channing's lips. For some years after marrying Ann Remington of Cambridge, Grandfather Ellery, like most other husbands, spent his evenings drinking and gossiping at a Newport pub. His wife, like most other wives, stayed home, where she passed some of her evening hours scribbling an account of the day's events on the margins and blank leaves of her almanac. Once, she recorded, as the day's most precious event, that her husband had spent the evening with her and the children! William Ellery happened to peek. He said nothing at the time, just put on his coat and walked to the public house where his cronies were hard at their drinking. He announced that he had come to take a parting cup with them; that from now on he would seek his evening pleasures at home. Edward T. Channing, who wrote his grandfather's authorized biography, gave this tale its appropriate denouement: "Some disbelieved, others scoffed; — could this be true of a man of his gayety and spirit? But their surprise and boisterous ridicule he was prepared for, and, true to his purpose and word, he left them, and was ever after a thoroughly domestic man. And such was the effect of his resolution upon them, that, in no time, the party was broken up, and succeeded by pleasant meetings in each other's families."[51]

Channing, who had obviously thought it all out with great care before leaping, was from the first day of his marriage "a thoroughly domestic man." With that remarkable moral consistency which was his hallmark, he practiced in marriage precisely what he preached.

Ruth Gibbs Channing moved with ease into the center of her illustrious husband's life. She herself had lustre aplenty. Her father, George Gibbs II, had been Rhode Island's foremost tycoon. At his death in 1803, he left a fortune estimated at £700,000, a huge sum for those days, divided so that his widow (Channing's father's sister) and each of his seven surviving children enjoyed independent wealth. Gibbs, who in 1792 had formed a partnership with his brother-in-law Walter Channing, had wide-ranging interests, including mills, rum distilleries, a remarkable amount of choice real estate (Newport, Boston, New York, Philadelphia), and about seventy-five sailing vessels. Channing's brother George, who served his business apprenticeship with Gibbs and Channing, claimed, from his knowledge of the company's books, that Mr. Gibbs was at one time "more extensively engaged in mercantile pursuits than any other man in New England." In 1868, when his *Early Recollections of Newport* was published, George Channing estimated that "very many of the richest men in New York, Boston, Philadelphia, and Baltimore, to-day, are the descendants of men whose wealth had its rise and growth from their connection, as agents," with Gibbs's enterprises.[52]

The Gibbs family practiced their Episcopal religion at Old Trinity Church in Newport, where George Gibbs had been a staunch supporter and vestryman; thus on July 21, 1814, when Channing and Ruth Gibbs were married in her mother's Boston mansion, the officiating clergyman was the Rev. Dr. Gardner, Episcopalian rector of Boston's Trinity church. After the required festivities, the couple left to honeymoon at one of the most attractive of the Gibbs estates, Oakland, some six miles from Newport, where the Channings would spend virtually every summer of their remaining years.

The Oakland house, on eighty breathtaking acres, was purchased by George Gibbs in 1796, and furnished by him with the choicest objects his ships could bring from Europe and Asia. Ruth's younger sister, Sarah (always called Aunt Sarah because she never married), was Oakland's permanent mistress until her death at the age of ninety-one, at which time the estate was sold to August Belmont, who in turn sold it to the Vanderbilts, whose use of the property gave it a considerably flashier tone than the atmosphere cultivated by Sarah Gibbs and the Channings. Sarah's personality was enshrined on the acres when she built and endowed a chapel, St. Mary's, in memory of her parents. Washington Allston embellished the interior by designing a carved mural monument, stretching from floor to ceiling. Channing composed the chapel's memorial inscription.[53]

On their return to Boston in September, the Channings moved into the Berry Street parsonage, but Ruth's mother, whose home on Mt. Vernon Street was not only one of the city's most fashionable, but spacious enough for two families to live in with reasonable privacy, strongly urged William and Ruth to join her. As a long, hard winter eased, it was done. Ruth was thirty-six when she married, and already annoyed by an arthritic condition that would worsen. Two years later, she gave birth to her first child, a daughter, who died within twenty-four hours. Francis Channing's widow, Susan, wrote a note to her mother describing the tragedy's toll: "Ruth's sufferings have been dreadful . . . William is miserably, I have never seen him look worse, and he says that he never felt so good for nothing. He has preached only one half day for five weeks; last Sunday he could only get through the communion service and christen a child — but for his great anxiety and suffering about Ruth he would probably have been well, but it has been impossible for him to gain strength. He means to try riding on horse back, and if that does not answer he will go on a journey if his wife should get well enough to permit him to leave her."[54]

As far as is known, Channing did not become an equestrian. Any journeying more distant than Newport was put off until 1819, when he would invade New York City and Baltimore as the reluctant but aroused champion of the Unitarian cause. New England's long-simmering theological feud had finally erupted into open hostilities.

IV

Among the Pharisees

THE LAST THING CHANNING WANTED was an unmendable rip in the hallowed churchly inheritance of the Puritan fathers. Yet as long as there were those who considered categorical theological definitions to be essential to the soul's salvation, Channing's outlook made schism inevitable. It was the *categorical* element he resisted. Every Christian, as far as he was concerned, had unalienable access to whatever doctrinal beliefs created a viable personal mixture of reason, revelation, righteousness of life, and charity of heart. Nobody, according to Channing, believed what was false because it was false, but because it seemed to be true.[1] Everyone, therefore, had an obligation to learn how what appeared false to him could seem true to somebody else. In that spirit, there could be healthy inquiry, even controversy, without spleen, and without wreckage.

Channing struggled manfully to introduce a wholly new tone of religious controversy. He would be gratified to see that the passage of a century and a half has greatly increased the resonance of that tone. But for the New England of 1815, his hopes were towering. Moreover, how could people who truly, deeply *believe* in the soul's life-and-death need for correct doctrine be sweetly reasonable? That was the reef on which Channing's sweet reasonableness foundered. He blinked and found himself leading one theological phalanx against another.

As Chadwick cheerily pointed out in his 1903 biography of Channing, anyone who tries "to write a history of the Unitarian Controversy in its various expressions during the fifteen to twenty years that corresponded with its liveliest ebullition" would have little space left in his volume for anything else.[2] But if Channing's contributions are to make sense, they must be set in a proper frame. How could this low-pitched, introspective semi-invalid let himself be catapulted to polemical leadership in a controversy he considered wasteful and unnecessary, convinced, as he was, that there were worthier issues on which to spend his cramped energies?

There are at least three answers. First, while Channing could serenely absorb denunciation of his own doctrinal views, he could not suffer in silence assaults on his integrity as a minister of religion. Second, he could not ignore what he considered to be serious misrepresentations of the liberal position. Third, he could not stand idly by in the face of an effort to lock the gates of Christian fellowship.

Sighted through orthodox spectacles, the scene was very different. By the time the provocations that piqued Channing had occurred, Jedidiah Morse and his fellow Calvinists felt that they had already been pushed beyond endurance. What was at stake, as far as they were concerned, was not personal sensibility, but Christianity itself. Moses Stuart, the able and peaceable Calvinist scholar at Andover Theological School, went to the heart of the matter in a letter to Edward Everett, dated December 25, 1813. "Mr. Channing," he wrote, "is undoubtedly a man of sense; but so long as it stands written, 'He that believeth not shall be damned,' so long I must believe that *unbelief* is always criminal in the sight of God."[3]

That Channing was a good man ("a man of sense"), Stuart did not doubt, but God's sovereign sway required that penalty must surely be visited on the sin of unbelief. The orthodox standard of belief for Congregational churches was familiar enough. First and most decisively, there was the absolute sovereignty of God. Next came the means by which the omnipotent God reveals himself and his methods of dealing with men. He reveals himself in three persons through Holy Scripture, which is the final authority for human faith and action. By this authority men are elected to salvation or condemned to perdition by a divine decree promulgated before the creation of the world. Those chosen for salvation can neither refuse the gift of grace

133

nor act in such a way as to cause it to be withdrawn. Jesus Christ, an equal member of the Godhead, and both God and man, had obtained the salvation of the Elect by accepting the just punishment due to all men because of the essential depravity of their nature since Adam's fall.[4]

To be sure, Hopkinsians, following Edwards's lead, insisted on tinkering. They doubted that there was a *physical* transfer of Adam's guilt and of Christ's righteousness, yet total depravity was precisely that — total and innate in a *moral* sense. Vicarious atonement remained vicarious, but could no longer be explained as a cold exchange of victims. God's moral government, the Hopkinsians said, demanded penalty for sin, but not necessarily from the sinners. Because Christ bore the punishment, universal forgiveness was morally possible for God. Election and reprobation remained election and reprobation, but the Hopkinsians shifted them from before to after Christ's atonement. Thus God's mercy and justice were impregnated with the experience of atonement as the decisions of election and reprobation were made.

One can see why conventional Calvinists were shaken by these innovations; still, the fundamentals of the creed were unscathed. But with the various breeds of liberals, this was not the case. They did not accept all of the fundamentals. Far from it. And these heretics, quietly, gradually (insidiously, from the orthodox point of view), had been creeping along. Now and then, some radical in advance of his brethren would openly utter a horrifying thought, and a clearheaded orthodox believer would strike back.

But in general, the doubters seemed to know what they doubted far better than they knew what to put in the place of what they doubted, so they curbed their tongues. Their thinking was obviously at odds with that of the fathers, but what did Holy Scripture say? That became the great issue. Were the Calvinist doctrines really there in sacred writ? As William Channing Gannett described it: "Many a Massachusetts minister, in the quiet of his study, bent over the holy book with his ten fingers between the leaves, drawing up lists of texts on this side and on that, trying to focus the rays of Bible light into one clear word."[5] What was truly at issue was the nature of man and his ability to contribute to his own salvation, but few were ready to blurt that out. Instead, the liberals and the evangelicals eyed one another with increasing suspicion over which way the Bible's doctrinal winds blew. Both proclaimed their devotion to Biblical guidance, but liberals contended that human explanations of scripture, as in the creeds and confessions, were superfluous. Let the Bible express its mysteries, if such they were, in its own words.

The most freewheeling of the early liberals had been Jonathan Mayhew of Boston's West Church. With rare candor Mayhew ticked off his heresies. While other doubters prudently pecked at creedalism, he denounced it; where they practiced private theological judgment unobtrusively, he declared its practice to be a public duty; where they nursed quiet reservations about the Calvinist decrees, he openly denied them. As early as 1755 he expressed in print — albeit fine print — his disbelief in the Trinity. He knew that he was not alone. Charles Chauncy at First Church in Boston, and Ebenezer Gay in Hingham were as unorthodox, only more circumspect. They and others adopted a laconic strategy. The questionable aspects of creedal orthodoxy were simply not mentioned from the pulpit. Their place was taken by Biblical phrases of contrary implication. It became increasingly fashionable for sermons to stress broad toleration. Candidates for preaching licenses were pointedly not questioned about their orthodoxy. There was a lively circulation of the works of such English Unitarians as Thomas Emlyn, Samuel Clarke, and John Taylor. The evangelicals were at first bemused by the dissimulation, but they were not duped. Only the initiative of Jedidiah Morse was awaited to transform bemusement into attack.

The first Boston church openly to admit to Unitarianism was King's Chapel — not Congregational, after all, but Episcopalian, and therefore alien to the Puritan heritage. With no responsibility to the established church of Massachusetts, and with its ties to the Church of England torn by the revolution, King's Chapel in 1782 invited an avowed Unitarian and Socinian, James Freeman, to become its reader; later, its minister. He was of the Mayhew mold; that is, he was not content simply to slip Bible phrases into the place usually reserved for Trinitarian doxologies, or quietly to drop Athanasianism from his sermons. Freeman had the Prayer Book to read from, and its Trinitarian passages, among others, made him gag. The people of King's Chapel, because they shared at least some of his theological nausea, urged him to purge their liturgical manual.

Freeman, a mild soul, was reluctant to push his luck too far. For someone with whom to discuss his dilemmas, he turned to the London Unitarian Theophilus Lindsey, a recent experimenter in liturgical reform. To Lindsey, Freeman wrote of his shyness about blue-penciling the Prayer Book as drastically as Lindsey had. He described how appreciatively his people responded to his restraint, and added that Priestley's and Lindsey's books were attracting wide interest, especially among the increasing numbers of ministers and laymen who were hesitantly abandoning Trinitarian orthodoxy. He said that while there was only one other minister, William Bentley of Salem, who preached of a human Jesus, there were constantly more churches in which the worship was flavored by Unitarianism. In Freeman's words: "There are . . . others, more cautious, who content themselves with leading their hearers, by a course of rational but prudent sermons, gradually and insensibly to embrace it. Though the latter mode is not what I entirely approve, yet it produces good effects."[6]

The evangelicals were not deceived. It was the very gradualism and insensibility of the process, to them stealth, that stoked their fury.

The year 1800 was a depressing one for the orthodox. A liberal, James Kendall, was settled as minister of the original Mayflower church in Plymouth, where only five years earlier a militantly Calvinistic confession had been adopted. In such a short span, Plymouth Calvinists had become a minority, and had been forced to withdraw and to form a new church. The Boston heresy was spreading contagiously beyond the confines of Boston. From Worcester County eastward, according to orthodox calculations, three out of every five Congregational churches had slipped into the clutches of clergymen tainted with unbelief. Moreover, in evangelical eyes, the refined plundering of God's elect Congregational communities by respectable men of the cloth was weakening the barricades against worse infidels: the workbench and farm-chore freethinkers who spouted Tom Paine and Voltaire between squirts of tobacco juice; and those higher bred, of Thomas Jefferson's ilk, who undermined piety with their downgrading of received institutions of faith.

Admittedly, village infidels and Jeffersonian anticlerics, lumped altogether, were a fraction of a fraction of the total populace. But what about Baptists who, here and there, threw over the traces and babbled against the sacred decrees of election and reprobation? They could out-evangelize the evangelical Calvinists, yet heresy was festering in their ranks. And the Universalists! With their tireless itinerant preaching, and closeness to common, isolated country folk, they were transforming vicarious atonement into a mockery called universal salvation. Then, there were the self-designated "Christians," come-outers from the Methodists of the South, the Presbyterians of the middle states, and the Baptists of New England, whose two positive fundamentals were the Bible and individual freedom to interpret it. Their devil was sectarianism. Unlike the Boston liberals, they were earthy and full of evangelistic zeal.

No one could forge a united front among these restless bodies. They were deeply suspicious of one another. But when their separate efforts were added up — liberals, freethinkers, Universalists, radical Baptists, "Christians" — it was evident that a sizable revolt against Puritan theology was under way. Liberals and Calvinists predominated because they had powerful institutional bases from which to operate, but they were by no means alone in the struggle to reshape the American religious mind.

The liberal victory in Harvard College ushered in a decade of intensive pen and printing press skirmishing, first through the orthodox *Panoplist* and the liberal *Anthology*. By 1812, liberals decided that a more audacious voice was needed. The *General Repository* was launched, with young Andrews Norton as editor (Mr. Norton, he preferred to be called, rather than Professor, Reverend, or Doctor). Norton's first article, printed under a masthead motto of *Nec temere, nec timide,* was boldly entitled

"Defence of Liberal Christianity." Although Norton's long career as a defender of liberalism's own orthodoxy was introduced with this initial radical blast, the magazine itself was not a sensational success. Within a year, Channing and some of his friends decided that rather than congratulate themselves on the quality of the *General Repository,* they would reach for a greater quantity of support. Noah Worcester was persuaded by Channing to become editor of the newly born *Christian Disciple,* a position he held from 1813 to 1823.

The peace-loving tendencies of Worcester and Channing were in evidence in the pages of the *Christian Disciple,* which specialized, issue after issue, in the celebration of practical religion, Christian character, and open-mindedness.

Meanwhile, heterodoxy had found other outlets. A hymn book compiled by William Emerson and Joseph Buckminster daringly included Pope's "Universal Prayer." A Boston publisher reprinted a revised rendering of the New Testament, embellished with Unitarian footnotes by its English editors. The volume's lively reception prompted one shocked orthodox divine to describe it as "the amended Bible which the Iscariot bands of professed Christianity are laboring to thrust into the hands of the simple, — straining into the cup of salvation the venom of Socinian blasphemy."[7]

Early in the game, Calvinist spokesmen intermittently charged the liberals with evasion — hiding their Unitarianism behind mincing words. But not until Morse found a devastating way to use the accusation did it become a major object of contention. Occasionally, a liberal would torment the Calvinists in similar fashion, as Thacher did in a scathing *Anthology* article on the Andover Theological School creed, a papering over of differences between old Calvinists and Hopkinsians. Thacher, who was impatient for full-scale theological combat, ridiculed the Andover covenant as "the first instance on record of a creed being originally formed with a designed ambiguity of meaning, with the express intention of permitting men of different opinions to sign it."[8]

When Channing had written to Worcester to persuade him to become editor of the *Disciple,* he had stressed that contention was the last thing he and his friends, including Thacher, wished to indulge in. It was utterly foreign to Channing to dissimulate. Yet who can wonder that Morse was looking for a chance to draw blood. There was something maddening about the way liberals hacked at Calvinism with one hand, and held up a flag of innocent benevolence with the other. When Morse's opportunity came, he made the most of it.

Morse's portrait in William Buell Sprague's *Annals of the American Pulpit* pictures him as an Ichabod Crane of the Puritan pantheon: spare bent frame, long thin neck, pinched sour face. Yet, grim general of the orthodox forces that he was, Morse was personally a man of warmth and sensitivity. When he warned Lucy Osgood, daughter of Channing's old friend Dr. Osgood of Medford, that Worcester's *Bible News* was a short cut to the everlasting bonfire, he did so with a pleasantness Lucy never forgot. One of his many kindnesses was the rescue from debt of the father of the Universalist firebrand, Thomas Whittemore.

Morse was installed as minister in Charlestown in 1789 at a salary of eleven dollars per week, plus house and firewood. He promptly asked for a reduction to ten dollars per week because his people had not recovered from the burning of their homes by British troops after the Battle of Bunker Hill.

Morse's installation sermon, strangely enough, was preached by Channing's liberal predecessor at Federal Street, Jeremy Belknap, who used the text, "Neither as lording it over God's heritage, but as examples to the flock." Chadwick aptly commented: "No man of his time so lorded it over God's heritage as Dr. Morse."[9] Yet Morse was not personally vindictive, nor were his cohorts Jeremiah Evarts, Moses Stuart, Leonard Woods, and Samuel Worcester (Noah's brother). They were gentlemen of the same stripe as Channing, Norton, Buckminster, Tuckerman, and S. C. Thacher. Morse genuinely believed that he was called upon, most urgently, to defend "the faith once delivered to the saints." And he paid dearly when his Charlestown parishioners, enchanted in the end with Unitarianism, grew weary of Morse and gave him his walking papers. But before his dismissal,

Morse achieved his goal: he smoked the Unitarians, even (perhaps especially) Channing, into the open.

The manna that fell into Morse's hands originated in England. Thomas Belsham, a disciple of Priestley, had fumed almost as much as Morse over the prim refusal of Boston liberals to show their hand. Their denial of the Unitarian label was one thing, but their silence on Calvinist dogmas was another. English liberals, under Priestley's sway, had quite self-consciously appropriated the Unitarian name for their Socinian* concept of Jesus, while most Boston liberals were Arians: portrayers of Christ as a being somewhere midway between God and man. Channing was particularly anxious to clear himself of any guilt by association with Priestley, but the rush to take sides illustrates how much suppressed feeling seethed in liberal circles. Channing and Thacher, with evident relief, admitted the concealment and absolved it. Others confessed it and chided themselves for indulging.

The orthodox experienced their own sense of release. For a decade, they had restlessly probed for hard dialogue, only to find themselves smothered in soft talk of practical religion and toleration. The motives of the liberals can be described in many ways — a mature sense of priorities, Christian benevolence, discretion, stalling, cowardice, duplicity. All of these were certainly operative — if not in each individual liberal, then in various mixtures within the liberal group as a whole. Channing's

---

* According to the Racovian Catechism (1605), which reflected the veiws of Faustus Socinus and his followers in Poland and Transylvania, God had made Christ a perfect man, and had endowed him with special authority as prophet, priest, and king. By the end of the eighteenth century, Socinianism in a modified form had generally supplanted Arianism among English Unitarians. The Socinian Christology in England was best articulated in the writings of Joseph Priestley. Arianism has a much older and more complex history, but the term was loosely applied to the view that Christ, though inferior to God, was more than man, and that he had a spiritual existence which predated his humanity. Arian views predominated among New England proto-Unitarians. Notable exceptions were James Freeman, minister of King's Chapel, and William Bentley of Salem's East Church, both of whom had been influenced by Socinian views. For a fuller discussion of Socinian and Arian doctrines at this time, see Earl Morse Wilbur, *A History of Unitarianism* (Cambridge, Mass.: Harvard University Press 1945), vol. 1, pp. 409–419, and Conrad Wright, *The Beginnings of Unitarianism in America* (Boston: Starr King Press, 1955), pp. 200–222.

conscious motive, and quite likely his instinctive one as well, was a profound wish to avoid controversy over issues that had little relevance to *real* religion as he understood it. He and many of his riper associates could foresee that open doctrinal dispute was a Pandora's box. Once released, the demons of controversy would tear the dear old church of the Puritan forefathers apart. They didn't want that. Yet, some of the younger men, like Thacher, who sensed that it was inevitable, were probably more in touch.

For years, there had been the curious situation in which liberals, presumably intoxicated by reason, were seen clutching the letter of holy writ, and crying out that *they* were the Bible men, while the orthodox, presumably in possession of complete revelation, sought opportunities to "interpret" Scripture. Those alleged to be the freer thinkers wrapped themselves in nebulous thought and obscure words, while those alleged to have closed minds defended the proposition that in religion there was a duty to think clearly and to speak distinctly.

From the Calvinist point of view, the liberal challenge was double-faced. Exposure was essential. Morse had a burst of inspiration as to how it might be done.

In 1812, Belsham had issued his *Memoirs of the Life of the Reverend Theophilus Lindsey*. One of its chapters dealt with American Unitarianism, with lengthy citations of Freeman's old letters to Lindsey, plus more recent examples of correspondence from American liberals. The policy of cultivating liberalism gradually and quietly was frankly discussed.

Morse decided, in the spring of 1815, that by handling the matter adroitly, he could do serious damage to the liberal ego. There was nothing particularly lurid in Belsham's chapter, but when Morse prefaced its thirty-eight pages by ten of his own in a pamphlet reprint, he succeeded in suggesting a close identification between the Boston liberals and the English Unitarians.

Morse rushed his brainchild through the press, and arranged for Jeremiah Evarts to write a review of it for the June issue of *Panoplist*. Meanwhile, he fired off presentation copies to key figures, one of them old John Adams, living in stately retirement in Quincy. If Morse expected a scream of outrage from the ex-

President, he was disappointed. Across the top of his letter to Morse, Adams wrote, "This letter must not be printed." After telling Morse that he had leafed through the pamphlet, Adams sniffed that he found nothing unfamiliar in it. As for Morse's statement that for thirty years Unitarianism had been infecting the churches of New England, Adams said that he could testify from personal knowledge that Unitarianism had been around for at least twice that long, and happily so. Adams gruffly asked Morse if he really expected to teach him "anything new in favour of Athanasianism" by sending the pamphlet. "You may depend upon it," Adams wrote, "your exertions will promote the church philosophick [Adams meant agnosticism and atheism] more than the church Athanasian or presbyterian." Adams concluded with the pronunciamento: "This and the coming age will not be ruled by Inquisitions . . ."[10]

If all of the liberals turned out to be as imperturbable as Adams, Morse's booby trap would be a dud. But he had counted on there being few Adamses.

The pamphlet was a rousing success, exhausting five printings within a month. The orthodox rejoiced in this apparent confirmation that the liberals were Pecksniffian Unitarians in disguise. The liberals screamed that they were being falsely accused of deceit and hypocrisy.

Evarts, meanwhile, constructed his *Panoplist* review with the hard-hitting skill he was famous for. A layman and onetime New Haven lawyer, Evarts had accepted the editorship of the *Panoplist* in 1810, at Morse's urging, and quickly distinguished himself by his forcible style and analytical powers.[11] With evident relish Evarts shaped his arguments to intensify the hostilities Morse's pamphlet had already let loose. Three points were clear, Evarts wrote: first, the liberal party held Belsham's Unitarian beliefs; second, they publicly concealed these beliefs while stealthily spreading them among the people; and third, there were definitely two parties, liberal and orthodox, and the sham of coexistence within the standing order of Congregational churches should be ended. For confirmation, he reproduced a letter to Belsham from William Wells, Jr., a Boston bookseller, reporting how rapidly, with its quiet strategy, the liberal faith was spreading.[12]

Boston Congregationalism was rocked. The liberals had to respond or lose face completely. They were furious. Even Channing, with his monumental distaste for controversy, was at last indignant. Sadly indignant, to be sure, but indignant nonetheless. Words he had written a month earlier for the *Christian Disciple* were unexpectedly prophetic. He had said then that men of liberal mind were all too often "defective in fervor." Those given to reflection and free inquiry easily slid "into a moderation of feeling bordering upon coldness," and "indifference about opinions."[13]

The time had come for liberals to demonstrate that they had feelings. Channing, ready to assume leadership that all agreed was naturally his, conferred with Thacher, who was prepared to sound off if Channing didn't. Instead of addressing the *Panoplist* directly (Evarts, as was the custom, had run his review anonymously), Channing prepared his defense in the form of an open letter, dated June 20, 1815, to Thacher, " . . . on the Aspersions contained in a Late Number of The Panoplist, on the Ministers of Boston and the Vicinity."[14]

Channing first dealt with the charge that he and his fellow liberals were Unitarians in the Belsham sense. While it was certainly no crime "to think with Belsham," Channing wrote, the plain fact was that the great majority of his colleagues shrank from some of Belsham's views "with as much aversion as from some of the gloomy doctrines of Calvin." As for the word "Unitarianism," Channing said that he accepted it as expressing "the character of a considerable part of the ministers of this town and its vicinity, and the Commonwealth." While there were a few in the liberal ranks who agreed with Belsham on the humanness of Jesus, and some who hadn't made up their minds, Channing continued, most, like himself, were convinced that Christ "is more than man." Channing complained bitterly that the *Panoplist*'s reviewer had lumped together several of Belsham's views having nothing to do with the issue at hand — his materialistic philosophy, his necessitarianism in morals, his sympathies with the French Revolution — and then piled all of these sins onto the heads of the liberals. Channing labeled this "as criminal an instance of unfairness as is to be found in the records of theological controversy."

To illustrate how theological controversy should be conducted, Channing declared that nothing he had said should be construed as "casting the least reproach on those amongst us, who believe in the simple humanity of Jesus Christ." He differed with them, yes, but had no disposition whatever "to deny them the name and privileges of Christians."

The second section of Channing's rebuttal dealt with the deep wound of "hypocritical concealment." With great pains, he clarified the motives of the liberals. In the first place, he said, his colleagues could not have conspired to hide their agreement with Belsham and the English Unitarians, since most of them held contrary views to begin with. As for their scrapping of the Trinity, that was anything but a secret, even though Morse and Evarts seemed to indicate that it was somehow the heart of the liberal plot. Channing recounted how he had scrupulously avoided giving anyone the impression that he accepted the Trinity. "My worship and sentiments have been Unitarian, in the proper sense of the word," he exclaimed.

Admittedly, he and his colleagues seldom or never introduced the Trinitarian controversy into their pulpits, Channing went on. "We preach precisely as if no such doctrine as the Trinity had ever been known." Why? Not to give a false impression, but because the exclusion of controversy was best for all concerned. "We all of us think it best to preach the truth, or what we esteem to be the truth, and to say very little about error, unless it be error of a strictly *practical* nature," Channing said.

As striking proof, Channing called attention to the way he and his friends dealt with Calvinism. Trinitarianism, he said, was a minor error compared to the awesome extravagance of the Calvinist teaching "that God brings us into life wholly depraved and wholly helpless, that he leaves multitudes without that aid which is indispensably necessary to their repentance, and then plunges them into everlasting burnings and unspeakable torture for not repenting."

Surely, Channing said, no one would contend that the liberals had anything to fear from exposing such tragic nonsense as this to their people. "On the contrary, we could hardly select a more popular topic. . . . We could . . . render the name of Calvinist as much a word of reproach in our societies, as that of Unitarian is in some parts of the country. But we esteem it a solemn duty to disarm, instead of exciting, the bad passions of our people."

Turning to the third point of the Evarts attack, Channing asked, "Why is it that our brethren are thus instigated to cut us off, as far as they have power, from the body and church of Christ?" No one, he wrote, accuses us of turning our backs on Jesus Christ; no one claims that we "neglect to study his works"; no one charges that "our lives are wanting in the spirit and virtues of his gospel." Why, then, were the orthodox being rallied to separate themselves from the liberals? Simply, Channing answered, because the liberals, after the most sober investigation, "cannot find in the Scriptures, and cannot adopt as instructions of our Master, certain doctrines which have divided the Church for ages, which have perplexed the best and wisest men, and which are very differently conceived even by those who profess to receive them." Channing was as specific as possible: "It is, in particular, because we cannot adopt the language of our brethren in relation to a doctrine which we cannot understand, and which is expressed in words not only unauthorized by the Scripture, but, as we believe, in words employed without meaning (unless they mean that there are three Gods) by those who insist upon them. This is our crime, that we cannot think and speak with our brethren on subjects the most difficult and perplexing on which the human mind was ever engaged. For this we are pursued with the cry of heresy, and are to have no rest until virtually excommunicated by our brethren."

There it was, all out in the open finally, and since controversy was now destined to flourish, Channing took the offensive. The Trinity, as far as he was concerned, was the woolliest possible subject for debate, but the Trinitarians had chosen it, so let them squirm a little. Were they monotheists or tritheists? Let the question be discussed, but not, he prayed, with "hatreds, bitter recriminations, censoriousness, spiritual pride and schismatic spirit." Above all, let everyone repudiate the ultimate temptation to say, "Stand off, we are holier than you."

Having been goaded, Channing let his passion flow and demonstrated how effectively his rational temper could control it. Although it was the last encomium he wished, he was a superbly civilized controversialist, a tough but gracious opponent. He had faithfully mirrored and crystallized a new and more open American approach to faith, and had done it in a manner calculated to reassure those who were still hesitant about their own emancipation, while exuding reconciliation toward the most obstinate defenders of orthodoxy. He was saying to Boston, and through Boston to the country: Look, this is the way it is. In this great, diverse, free-breathing land, we are going to live with multiple theological persuasions. Either we let these ambiguities tear us apart, or we use them in our separate ways to undergird a transcending unity of compliance with the ethical principles of Jesus. If some of us are to be persecuted and reviled for approaching American religious life in this fashion, so be it. But I for one, believe that what I am saying makes sense — emotional sense, as well as rational sense.

Channing was certainly not the first to offer this kind of spiritual nourishment to America, but no one before or since has done it with a more exquisite right to say: Don't just mark my words; observe how I actually behave.

As Channing suspected, he made no converts among the orthodox leadership. Morse had gauged the pent-up frustrations of his allies well. One of them, Dr. Samuel Worcester, Noah's brother, had already paid his pound of flesh in two ways. Liberalism had seduced his brothers, and he had been turned out of his Fitchburg pulpit for his loyalty to the old faith. Still, Channing was jarred that this respected, scholarly fellow minister should strike so hard, not once but three times. But Channing, having committed himself, honored his commitments. He answered the first and second of Worcester's attacks. Worcester's third letter wandered into such a bog of technical Trinitarian discussion that Channing did not reply. He willingly conceded that Worcester could examine the head of a pin far more learnedly than he, but did it matter?[15]

Through and beneath everything Worcester said ran the insistent theme: Unitarians must be driven from the church as betrayers of sound doctrine. As Channing put it, this was "infinitely the most important part" of Dr. Worcester's letters; everything else was "comparatively trifling." Still Channing was willing to discuss, up to a point, Worcester's doctrinal issues. He pointed out that while Worcester doggedly proclaimed the necessity of Trinitarian doctrine, he neglected to point out what its great significance was. With a show of weary patience, Channing tried an oversimplification of his own. Wasn't it true, he asked Worcester, that the orthodox and the liberals were separated by adverbs alone? "According to Trinitarians," Channing wrote, "Jesus who suffered and died on the cross, is a derived being, *personally* united with a self-existent God. According to the Unitarians, he is a derived being, *intimately* united with the self-existent God. . . . Ought distinctions so subtle and perplexing to separate those who love the same Divine character and respect the same Divine will?"

If Channing thought he had given Worcester a way off the hook, he was wrong. Worcester rushed his second blast through the press, while Channing was still catching his wind. It was a replay of the first letter, only more insistent. Once more Channing took up his pen, and once more covered the now familiar terrain: "What are the questions which divide us? First, whether the One God be three distinct substances, or three persons, or three *'somewhats'* called *persons,* as Dr. Worcester says, for want of 'a better word'; and secondly, whether one of these three substances, or improperly called persons, formed a personal union with a human soul, so that the Infinite Mind, and a human mind, each possessing its own distinct consciousness, became a *complex person."* With a touch of exasperation, Channing declared: "The difference between Unitarians and Trinitarians lies more in sounds than in ideas."

When an undismayed Worcester fired off his third round, Channing turned his attention elsewhere. By this time Worcester was making distinctions of whether the word "persons" as in the Trinity had a biological or a spiritual significance and it was obvious that he had wandered into a trap of his own setting. He was as incapable as Channing was of using the word "person" as a spiritual designation isolated from biological and psychological implications.

What neither Channing nor Worcester grasped was that both were fighting what was essentially a sham battle. Their real contention was over the place of man in the great cosmic drama. For Calvinists like Worcester, there was magnificent emotional satisfaction in the classical orthodox portrayal of that place — the chilling tumble from innocence of Adam and Eve, the resulting wrath of God's condemnation, blessed ransom by the Son of God, and a new birth. Rooted in the souls of men like Samuel Worcester was the awesome Calvinist portrayal of the human condition. It was not simply a matter of word meanings, as Channing insisted. Channing felt that the Calvinists were being semantically capricious because he could not conceive of the human situation as they did — literally anarchic, where everything hurts because it should hurt. The issues were not verbal as Channing claimed, but existential. Liberals did not experience existence as Calvinists did; therefore they did not need the shuddering Calvinist conception of reality. For Morse and the others, virtue was cruel, rectitude was cruel, God's justice was cruel (crueler than injustice), because there was no escape from it, given man's nature. But since neither Channing nor his adversaries were able to bring all of this into the open, they fought for the most part an ersatz contest.

The mid-twentieth-century theatre of cruelty is a far more candid portrayal of Calvinism — in a secular style — than was the early nineteenth-century Calvinist portrayal of itself. And the modern liberal seems no more able to respond directly than did the prototype Unitarians of New England. He does not feel unbearable pain. Pain is there, but it is bearable. And so it was with Channing. The pain of the human condition was seldom out of his thoughts, but even less seldom did he doubt the underlying benevolence of the cosmic scheme. The Calvinists who confronted him saw unbearable pain as the true condition of a human world sunk in sin. It was not divine benevolence such a world required; it was God's terribly just taming of a collectively guilty human race.

Worcester published his third salvo, but then, like Channing, broke off the contest. For the next few years, the crucial confrontations would take place within individual churches, with the conservatives demanding either reaffirmation of old doctrinal covenants or adoption of new creeds as tests of church membership, and with the liberals resisting both. Morse, who felt that the jugular strike was at the ministerial level, called for consociations of clergymen in the Connecticut style, from which liberals would be excluded unless approved by ecclesiastical courts.

Channing, who had sadly concluded that the doctrinal differences were probably irreconcilable and was willing to live with the situation, assailed Morse's effort. In a piece laboriously titled "The System of Exclusion and Denunciation in Religion Considered,"[16] he argued that the health of the religious enterprise could only be strengthened by welcoming men of good character, whatever their doctrinal opinions. Appealing to history, he asked to be shown how the spirit of bell, book, and candle had ever benefited the church. "Could the thunder and lightnings of excommunications have corrected the atmosphere of the church, not one pestilential vapor would have loaded it for ages. The air of Paradise would not have been more pure, more refreshing." In an unusually caustic mood, Channing chided the orthodox for appointing themselves to sit in judgment on their liberal brethren as if they were "exempted from the common frailty of our nature." The conservatives, Channing said, shield themselves behind the notion that the apostles condemned heresy. He baited them to demonstrate that they were the true successors of the apostles, and promised to obey them "cheerfully" if they could. Then, in one of his finest descriptions of man's multiform perceptions of reality, Channing wrote: "Men differ in opinions as much as in features. No two minds are perfectly accordant. The shades of belief are infinitely diversified. Amidst this immense variety of sentiment, every man is right in his own eyes. Every man discovers errors in the creed of his brother. Every man is prone to magnify the importance of his own peculiarities, and to discover danger in the peculiarities of others. This is human nature."

How should we proceed? Channing wanted to know. By subverting free inquiry? By suppressing human nature? Why encourage people to study Scripture, if at the same time we warn them that they will be driven from the church unless they find there what the self-appointed watchdogs of doctrine expect them to find? In conclusion, Channing spelled out the melancholy results of an exclusive and denunciatory policy — more dismal and horrifying pages in Christian history — and called instead for the triumph of a free, candid, and charitable temper.

And yet, Channing was a remarkably parsimonious contributor to the Unitarian controversy: an open letter to Thacher, two replies to Worcester, and the piece denouncing denunciation and exclusion — all in the months of 1815. Four years would pass before he marched to the front of theological combat again, this time to preach the most widely read and discussed sermon of his career. However, because Channing, with his special place in the scheme of things, had been willing to be the leading edge of the Unitarian thrust, other liberals took the offensive. John Lowell, for example, who had inherited Fisher Ames's place as factotum of Proper Bostonianism, went to press with a pamphlet aggressively asking on its title page, "Are You a Christian or a Calvinist?" The question was provoked by another that was making the rounds: "Are you of the Boston or the Christian religion?"

As far as Lowell could see, the great theological Armageddon was no more than a mean attempt by Yale and Connecticut to vent spleen on Harvard and Massachusetts. The significance of Lowell's toplofty pamphlet was not in its logic but in its hue. The tone established by Channing deteriorated quickly, which was reason enough for him to turn his attention elsewhere, hoping for the best.

The best, as far as Channing was concerned, was certainly not doctrinal controversy. Sharp as he proved himself to be in a clash, he detested every moment stolen from his life as parish minister, citizen activist, and private person, especially when those moments forced him into the role of public luminary. Writing to his widowed sister-in-law Susan, he confessed to feeling "almost an insuperable reluctance" about preaching and making parish calls when "people have taken it into their heads that they are to see or hear something like a prodigy." In his heart, Channing said, he carried "a conviction which contradicts this opinion of the world and renders their applause painful, mortifying." As for fame and general notice, he was convinced that they were not his "right," and he prayed that they would never be his "wish and end."[17]

The powerful strain of introspection in Channing's makeup protected him from being seduced by his growing public image, but it also intensified the response of others to him, especially idealistic young men just entering the ministry, and idealistic young ladies excited by a theological controversy.

In great demand as an ordination sermonizer, Channing, shortly before writing his "Letter to Samuel Thacher," traveled to Salem to preach at the installation of John Emory Abbot as minister of North Church. Tucked unobtrusively into the congregation was an eleven-year-old girl who already considered Channing to be the most phenomenal human being alive. Her name was Elizabeth Palmer Peabody, the eldest of a local dentist's three daughters. Elizabeth's "excited state of sensibility"[18] had been generated two years earlier when her mother brought her to hear Channing speak from the same pulpit. With photographic detail, she remembered seeing "a small man, with rapid, nervous motion, dressed in a traveller's greatcoat, go into the pulpit, and, without sitting down (for he was a little belated), take up the hymn book, turn its leaves quickly, and enter the desk; then slowly lifting up his large, remarkable eyes, with the expression of *seeing something,* begin to read the devotional hymn."[19] Channing's expression gripped young Elizabeth because of an eerie sensation that he was actually "communing with God, face to face."[20] It meant to her that "any man now, like a prophet of old," could talk with God "as friend with friend."[21]

Dr. Peabody's precociously observant child also noted how "pale and ill" Channing appeared. Surely, she thought, he will soon die. When he came two years later to preach for the ill-fated young Abbot,* the fact that he had survived added to her

* John Emory Abbot (1793–1819) was born at Exeter, New Hampshire, the son of the principal of Exeter Academy. Educated at Bowdoin College, he

infatuation. That Sunday she heard her hero elaborate on what he understood it to mean to preach Christ.[22] It was not, he said, "to make fiery partisans, and to swell the numbers of a sect; not to overwhelm the mind with fear, or to heat it with feverish rapture; not to form men . . . to a superficial goodness, which will secure the admiration of mankind." All of this, Channing vowed, falls "infinitely short of the great end of the Christian ministry." The true purpose of that ministry, he went on, is to help men to become "perfect in heart and in life, in solitude and in society, in the great and in the common concerns of life."[23]

Anticipating the laureate sermon he would preach in Baltimore four years later, Channing treated Abbot's Salem flock to a sample of his controversial conception of reason's relationship to revelation. Christian preaching, he declared, must be done "in a *rational* manner. . . . By this I mean that a Christian minister should beware of offering interpretations of Scripture which are repugnant to any clear discoveries of reason or dictates of conscience. This admonition is founded upon the very obvious principle, that a revelation from God must be adapted to the rational and moral nature which He has conferred on man; that God can never contradict in his word what He has himself written *on the human heart*." (Italics mine.)

This was an important passage in the delineation of Channing's thought. The heart is involved in reason no less than the brain; or, to put it another way, the whole man is involved in reason.

He concluded his remarks to the Salem congregation by underlining the point: "Some preachers, from observing the pernicious effects of violent and exclusive appeals to the passions, have fallen into an opposite error, which has rendered the labors of their lives almost wholly unfruitful. They have ad-

---

pursued his theological education at Harvard and under Channing's direction. He was ordained the minister of North Church, Salem, on April 20, 1815, when Channing delivered the ordination sermon. He was widely admired for his saintliness and eloquence. He died of tuberculosis at the age of twenty-six after returning from Havana, where he had unsuccessfully sought relief from his affliction. (See Henry Ware, Jr., "Sketch of the Life and Character of the Late Rev. John E. Abbot," *Christian Disciple*, n.s. 2 [January–February, 1820]: 32–46.)

dressed men as mere creatures of intellect; they have forgotten that affection is as essential to our nature as thought, that action requires motive, that the union of reason and sensibility is the health of the soul."

That Channing tried to practice this kind of intensity on the sidewalks as well as in the pulpit was symbolized in an item of chitchat making the Boston rounds at the time. When Mr. Channing asks how you are, the story went, and you reply that you are well, his next remark, "I am very glad," is spoken as if it were of real importance to him.[24]

In the "Era of Good Feelings," as contemporaries labeled it, following the second war with England, the old struggle between Federalists and Republicans waned. Relations with Great Britain sweetened. Partial disarmament provided a foundation for lasting peace with Canada. Channing bitterly regretted that disappearing national political discords had to be replaced by a theological cacophany, and he did his best for the next few years to live above it. Of considerable help may have been the news that his black parishioner and friend, Prince Saunders, had arrived in London in 1815, where he became "quite a lion, and surpassed the other passengers [Edward Everett, George Ticknor, et al.] in temporary importance."[25]

The following year, probably at the suggestion of Bishop Cheverus, who wished to provide workingmen of modest means with the incentive to save, Channing was one of three Boston clergymen and forty laymen who organized the Provident Institution for Savings, the first public savings bank to be incorporated in the United States. Earlier that year, he had published in the *Christian Examiner* some of his exploratory thoughts on the causes and cures of poverty, and had then done what he could to keep the wolf from the door of Cambridge's fledgling clergymen by helping to found and to fund the Society for the Promotion of Theological Education at Harvard.

By the following year, Channing was enthusiastically proposing construction of a vestry hall alongside the Federal Street meetinghouse to be used "for *catechizing* and instructing the children of the Society," and as a "very much needed" singing school ("Though our singing is . . . improved, we all of us feel that it might be rendered a more interesting part of public worship").* Channing also suggested that the new building might permanently house the day nursery for underprivileged youngsters already being conducted in temporary quarters by some of the young women of Federal Street and New South. In addition, he envisioned expanded adult classes and discussion groups in the new facility, along with a circulating library, of which he himself would be the librarian.[26] His plan was accepted, and within little more than a year, the building was completed.

James Monroe, the newly elected President, brought his road show of national reconciliation to Boston on July 2, for a five-day stand. Though he had won the election handsomely, there had been no Massachusetts electoral votes in his total. But Federalist hearts melted as Monroe made his way to Faneuil Hall for the annual Independence Day oration. By invitation of the selectmen, the orator was Channing's brother Edward, who praised the lack of partisanship in Monroe's administration and extolled Boston's prospects for intellectual development.

Monroe was sufficiently impressed by one Channing to want to hear another. On Sunday, July 6, after a glittering Saturday night party at Harrison Gray Otis's, Monroe sat in the Federal Street pew of Colonel T. H. Perkins and listened to Channing preach on patriotism and general benevolence.[27]

By the time Monroe left Boston, he was the lion of Federalist land. The *Boston Columbian Sentinel* sent him on his way by coining the "Era of Good Feelings" phrase.[28]

Early in September, the Rev. Lyman Beecher, the muscleman of orthodoxy, preached in Boston for the first time and launched a bitter assault on Unitarianism from the pulpit of Park Street Church. Channing's only response was to write to the Rev. Mr. Nichols of Portland, Maine, urging "occasional meetings among ministers who are scattered over the country and who agree in wishing to promote a serious as well as catholick Xy, for the

* The Federal Street Church had rented an organ which was — for those days — of unusual size and power. In 1811 a contract was made with William Goodrich for a new organ. This cost $1700 and was not completed and installed until 1822, the hired organ being used in the meantime.

purpose of mutual encouragement and counsel."[29] This was Channing's first indication that the widening theological gulf required a knitting together of raveled liberal forces.

And raveled they were by the death in Moulins, France, of Channing's beloved Samuel Thacher. Channing's personal grief was sharpened by the morbid excitement in orthodox circles over the fact that of the nine Congregational churches in Boston, six had lost their liberal ministers by death in quick succession: Buckminster in 1812, John Eliot in 1813, John Lovejoy Abbot in 1814, Samuel Cary in 1815, John Lathrop in 1816, and Samuel Thacher in 1818.[30] No reputable Calvinist came right out and said it, but a nonverbal communication was in the air that Jehovah was dealing with his foes in his own way. It was the kind of thing that made the hair at the back of Channing's neck tingle.

Still shying away from belligerency, Channing waited until his heart was bursting with happiness at the birth of his daughter Mary (October 8, 1818), before taking another swipe at Calvinist pretensions. The occasion was Mary's baptism, which he used to propose a new interpretation of the ancient rite.[31]

Why baptize a child, he asked, before the child can understand or want it? Some, he said, answer this question by claiming that baptism "communicates to the infant divine grace, that it is a regenerating ordinance, that when the water touches the body, God's spirit touches the mind, and that a new nature is thereby implanted." For Channing, this was slippery theology. He preferred to think of the rite as pointing its primary meaning toward parents, reminding them of the "great ends for which a human life is given." Let the solemnity of baptism inspire parents "to treat the infant with *reverence*," he declared. Let it help them to welcome a child "as the heir of unknown worlds, to see in its early intelligence the dawning of a light which is never to be quenched."

Mild as these words were in their criticism of the traditional view of baptism, they signaled a fire in Channing that would soon find an outlet in Baltimore. It was an outlet he badly needed, because he seethed with frustration not only at the madness of theological controversy, but because the nation, in its euphoria of "good feelings," had just perpetrated an outrage against the Seminole Indians of East Florida. General Andrew Jackson, with the sanction of Congress, had cruelly decimated a segment of the Seminole tribe for offering sanctuary to escaped slaves. Another and stronger reason for Jackson's move was the sheer desire to rob the Seminoles of their land. A piously pliant Congress approved, justifying Jackson's excessive brutality under "the laws of war."

Channing, feeling hopelessly outflanked, wrote to Noah Worcester that he could see no gain in further railing against the government. He proposed instead that their peace society should use the tragedy to "bring home to men's minds" the necessity of abolishing once and for all war's "horrible laws." If the rules of war excuse such outrages, he asked, "can war too soon be abolished? Is it not time to exert ourselves to prevent the recurrence of this infernal state of things?" He appealed to Worcester to run a series of articles taking this tack.[32]

The year 1819 was blown into being by winds of economic panic, caused by commodity inflation, wild speculation in western lands, overextended investments in manufacturing, mismanagement of the second U.S. Bank, collapse of foreign markets, and the constriction of credit. Channing's attention to the human consequences was diverted, however, by a train of events that led him to Baltimore, and to the preaching of the best-remembered sermon of his career.

In 1816, a group of prominent Baltimore citizens had appealed to leaders of the liberal faith in Boston to help them to establish a Unitarian church. The call was answered by Dr. James Freeman of King's Chapel. On October 12, a discreet advertisement appeared in the Baltimore press announcing that "Divine service will be performed by the Reverend Dr. Freeman of Boston, to-morrow, at the Hall belonging to Mr. Gibney, in South Charles Street, to commence at 11 o'clock, a.m. and at 3 p.m."[33]

On October 13, Freeman preached the first avowedly Unitarian sermons ever heard in Baltimore. His congregation was "large and respectable," much to the chagrin of the city's ortho-

156

dox majority. Youngsters were encouraged to throw stones through the windows of Gibney's Hall. Ministers threatened excommunication of any of their flock who were brazen enough to attend. But Freeman was so well received that he stayed on for two more Sundays of missionary preaching. A hard-core group of those who had heard him continued to hold weekly meetings in homes, where future plans were laid. By February 1817, the band felt fortified enough to found a church. Rejecting for prudential reasons the name of "First Unitarian Congregation," they christened themselves "the First Independent Church of Baltimore."

In deference to their racism, the founders vested the new society's affairs in nine trustees to be elected by "white members." An initial fund of $17,350 was subscribed for a building, and a French artist, Maximilien Godefroy, was commissioned to design an edifice to cost $20,000. Godefroy designed the striking structure which the congregation still occupies, but at a cost, together with land, of about $100,000. (It took the congregation sixty years to crawl out from under its debt.) By 1818, the society was on the hunt for a minister, and fastened, understandably enough, on Jared Sparks, a protégé of the celebrated Mr. Channing.

There was nothing in Sparks's Connecticut boyhood to foreshadow his later fame as preacher, editor, scholar, and "patriarch" of the field of American history. Born among the poorest of the poor, he learned carpentry in order to support himself, and tramped more than three hundred zigzag miles in northern New York in search of a teaching job. Somehow he talked himself into Exeter Academy as a student, where he wrote an autobiographical essay on the topic, "Intense application to study not detrimental to health." At the age of twenty-two, he clawed his way into Harvard, but was soon compelled by financial circumstances to take a tutoring job with the Mark Pringle family at Havre de Grace, Maryland. His Harvard friends, most of whom believed that civilized society extended no further from Boston than Dedham, were shocked that Sparks could think of going so far away. But the decision to do so was the most crucial of his life. His living quarters were in the local post-road tavern, a stopover for the stage traffic to and from Washington. In the space of a year, Sparks met many of the nation's great, among them Channing and Josiah Quincy, who stopped at the inn during their trip to Washington in 1812. Channing was drawn to Sparks, and Sparks was deeply impressed by Channing's account of his own earlier experiences as a tutor in the South. Back in Boston, their relationship grew, with Sparks a frequent guest at the parsonage. Channing urged the young man to enter the ministry, seeing in him the kind of personality needed by the liberal Christian groups that were beginning to sprout in the hinterlands. After stints as a Harvard tutor and as editor of the *North American Review*, Sparks heeded Channing's advice and became a minister. In August 1818, Sparks received an invitation to appear in Baltimore as a candidate for the new Unitarian pulpit. After seven sabbaths of preaching, he accepted the job, and promptly invited Channing to preach at his ordination, set for Wednesday, May 5, 1819.

A considerable amount of stage-managing, under Sparks's personal direction, went into the planning of the ordination. By mutual consent among Boston's leading liberal clergy, the time had come for their cause to make a national impact. Baltimore, a vital outpost far removed from Boston, was just the place to bring it off. No less than seven of the most potent Unitarian spokesmen in New England were lined up by Sparks to participate in the Baltimore event. Channing was appointed to make the hard-hitting, comprehensive statement of the Unitarian position. The legion of brethren backing him would make certain that his remarks received the widest possible public notice.

Channing, whose frail body rebelled against long overland journeys, bundled his wife and her sister into a stage for New York, where they took a rest stop of a few days, while Channing preached to a small group of New Yorkers who had expressed interest in forming a liberal church. Meeting with the group in a private drawing room, he spoke extemporaneously, trying out some of the material he had been carefully weaving together for Baltimore.

The three arrived in Baltimore in ample time for Channing to regain his strength and to finish his manuscript. There they were joined by Sparks, Henry Ware, Sr., John Palfrey of Brattle Square, Edes of Providence, Eliphalet Porter of Roxbury, Parker of Portsmouth, and Ichabod Nichols of Portland.[34]

Palfrey gave a dinner for Sparks on the evening before the ceremony, and final plans were made for the publication of Channing's sermon. The first printing, it was decided, would be two thousand copies, an unusually large pressrun for the time. It proved to be hopelessly inadequate.

The acoustics in Monsieur Godefroy's handsome Unitarian structure, a daring example of modern design, were abominable. One of Baltimore's divines told his congregation: "There has been a new Church erected in our city for the dissemination of pernicious doctrines, but by the grace of God, nobody can hear what the minister has to say."[35] Actually only those sitting in the first three rows were able to hear Channing as he preached. The others had to wait to read the sermon in the edition printed almost immediately in Baltimore by Benjamin Edes. Because he was unable to check advance proofs, Channing always referred to the first edition as "unauthorized." The numerous editions which followed were designated as "authorized."

Whether or not he could be heard, Channing did not short-change the Baltimore congregation in effort. His sermon contained some fourteen thousand words, and at his rate of delivery consumed an hour and a half. Chadwick, who was given the original manuscript by Channing's granddaughter, Grace Ellery Channing-Stetson, said of it: "There could not be a greater contrast than between the smooth and limpid flow of the printed page and the brokenness and mending of the manuscript, the writing unconscionably bad, the erasures and interlineations numberless. It is hard to conceive how Channing could preach with that even stream which was habitual with him from such a manuscript."[36]

Using the simplest possible title, "Unitarian Christianity," and the simplest possible text, "Prove all things; hold fast that which is good" (1 Thessalonians 5:21), Channing moved through four main points: first, an outline of the principles Unitarians used in interpreting Scripture and the results they achieved; second, a laying bare of the unreasonableness of the

Trinitarian dogma; third, a refutation of a dual personality for Christ, coupled with a ringing affirmation of his unified nature; and fourth, an exposition of the moral nature of God.

Obviously, these points spark little modern passion, yet there can be no better proof of their edge and pertinence in Channing's time than the feverish controversy they provoked. Presses worked overtime to fill demands for Channing's text, and for the attacks made upon it. Not until Webster, in 1830, published his famous reply to Hayne, was there a piece of literature in America with a larger circulation than the Baltimore sermon. Channing accomplished precisely what he and his colleagues intended. If the orthodox insisted upon drawing a rigid line between themselves and the liberals, then all would know where the liberals stood, and why.

The tendency of later generations has been to remark on the absence from the sermon of Channing's central theme — the dignity of human nature, the greatness of the human soul. This is myopic. Far from neglecting his "sublime idea" of human potentiality, Channing permeated his theological points with it.[37]

When speaking of the Unitarian method of dealing with the Bible, Channing pled that man cannot be trussed in a straightjacket of mechanical textualism. He possesses the gift of reason, and he must use it. The Bible, he said, "treats of subjects on which we receive ideas from other sources besides itself,— such subjects as the nature, passions, relations, and duties of man." Forecasting the mind-set of transcendentalism, he declared that of course man had to "restrain and modify" the language of Scripture by the truths "which observation and experience furnish."

In the same vein, Channing objected strongly "to the contemptuous manner in which our human reason is often spoken of by our adversaries." That the use of reason in religion had its perils, he readily granted. "But we ask any honest man to look back on the history of the church," he said, "and say whether the renunciation of it be not still more dangerous." God, according to Channing (in a phrasing remarkably similar to Einstein's), does not "sport with the understanding of his creatures." God has given us rational faculties, he went on. We may let them sleep, "but we do so at our own peril."

When protesting against the "irrational and unscriptural" (in that order) doctrines of the Trinity and the twofold nature of Christ, he again appealed to the inherent right of human beings to the dignity of making sense of what they are expected to believe.

Regarding the moral perfection of God, Channing repeated his theme that if the Calvinist conception of the Deity was correct, then God had a lower moral nature than man, since by the plainest principles of human morality, any child brought into the world with "a natural constitution of the mind, unfailingly disposing it to evil, and to evil alone," would be absolved from guilt; "that to give existence under this condition would argue unspeakable cruelty; and that to punish the sin of this unhappily constituted child with endless ruin would be a wrong unparalleled by the most merciless despotism."

Repeatedly, Channing tied his distaste for Calvinism to the potential greatness of the human spirit. By exhibiting its harsh and tyrannical God, Calvinism, Channing claimed, "tends strongly to pervert the moral faculty, to form a gloomy, forbidding and servile religion, and to lead men to substitute censoriousness, bitterness and persecution for a tender and impartial charity."

As for himself and his colleagues, Channing said, they believed that the brightest image of God they could bear was that of love and liberality, especially toward those who differ in religious opinion: "We think that in nothing have Christians so widely departed from their religion as in this particular. We read with astonishment and horror the history of the church; and sometimes, when we look back on the fires of persecution, and on the zeal of Christians in building up walls of separation, and in giving up one another to perdition, we feel as if we were reading the records of an infernal rather than a heavenly kingdom. An enemy to every religion, if asked to describe a Christian, would, with some show of reason, depict him as an idolater of his own distinguishing opinions, covered with badges of party, shutting his eyes on the virtues and his ears on the arguments of his opponents, arrogating all excellence to his own sect and all saving power to his own creed, sheltering under the name of pious zeal the love of domination, the conceit of infallibility, and the spirit of intolerance, and trampling on men's rights under the pretense of saving their souls."

The Baltimore sermon was an effort of greater subtlety than is usually acknowledged. There was not a single premise in the Calvinist system that Channing did not isolate, examine, discard, and replace. Dogmatic scripturalism was supplanted by a Bible accountable to human reason and experience; the Trinity was superseded by a unified, integral Creator-Father; a schizoid divine-human Christ became a stable, homogeneous, suffering, and conquering teacher and master; a God capable of perpetrating the "horrors" of total depravity and predestination was replaced by a paternal Deity whose moral perfection was both understandable and imitable in human terms; the ancient Anselmic notion that man, by sinning against an infinite being, was poisoned by an infinite guilt, was supplanted by the situational argument that a man's guilt must be measured by his nature and power of choice. The supreme object of religious practice, therefore, was not to avoid punishment, but to cultivate and communicate virtue.

And as for virtue — here Channing came to the root of things: "We believe that all virtue has its foundation in the moral nature of man, that is, in conscience, or his sense of duty, and in the power of forming his temper and life according to conscience. We believe that these moral faculties are the grounds of responsibility, and the highest distinction of human nature, and that no act is praiseworthy, any farther than it springs from their exertion."

With this reaffirmation of his "sublime idea," Channing automatically cast aside the last of the great Calvinist theses — that God was the irresistible executor of all moral actions and man merely a static recipient. In Channing's view, loving God and following Christ involved an active human striving toward God's moral perfection, and a conscious, animated paralleling of Christ's style of life.

Channing and those associated with him were committed heart

and soul to the organized Christian enterprise. They saw the church as a fundamental element of what civilization in general, and American society in particular, could and should become. They genuinely believed that the great human drama of potentiality was undergirded in a cosmic sense by the infinite justice, goodness, and holiness of the Supreme Being, and that the church's central task was to make this understandable to man's mind and motivational in his heart.

The liberals were also aware that *except* in the vicinity for Boston, the church was a dwindling practical influence in the lives of those Americans, increasing in number, whose deepest moral convictions revolved around creative human power, creative human dignity, and creative human reason. Throughout the rest of the country, the only formal alternatives available to such men and women were the Calvinist bodies, the Roman Catholic church, or the shouting sects — each of them elated with a belief in its own exclusive orthodoxy, none of them receptive to inquiry and thinking for oneself. Understandably, the freer-thinking American was either turning quietly away from the church, or becoming positively hostile, not only to the church but to Christianity The orthodox called them "infidels," lumping the Unitarians with them, and completely missed the point.

Far from being infidels, Channing and his fellow Unitarians wanted to provide a relevant, rational Christian option. By enshrining reason, experience, and conscience at the heart of Christian life, by declaring that revelation and salvation must be measured by human character rather than by dogmatic pronouncement, they genuinely sought the renewed Christian loyalties and energies of a disenchanted but productive and inventive segment of the American people.

This was what Channing's Baltimore sermon was all about, and the tumult it caused suggests that it struck home. According to Jared Sparks, whose ministerial career was launched by it, "We have had nothing calculated to do so much good as this sermon. It is written in a clear, persuasive style, but a popular manner. It embraces the whole subject in a small compass — it can be understood by all. It is important to circulate it as widely as possible."[38]

The Baltimore effort had cost Channing a good deal. His sparse physical strength drained dry, he spent the next day in seclusion, seeing only a few close friends. On Friday he was ready to tackle some of his accumulated correspondence, and sent his wife and sister-in-law off to Washington to see the sights. He was mentally bowed down as well. In spite of the apparent clarity of his Baltimore pronouncement, he experienced, and believed that all men shared, a shattering duality — the consequence of some deep, aboriginal blight in his nature; the daily warfare waged among the parts of his being, out of which stemmed the pride and contempt, the sin and savagery, that Calvinists in their bizarre way tried to bring under control.

He knew that only a fool — and many such would rejoice over his sermon — could gaze around and smile with unblemished optimism. Yet he could not, and he would not, lose sight of the wonder and frequency with which kindness, the soul-anchored *goodness* of man, broke forth. No one had received a fuller measure of that goodness than he, in the form of a continual succession of redemptive instants and happenings. In them, the meaning and glory of man were revealed. This had been his position as he stood behind the Baltimore pulpit. He would sustain it, by more special pleading when necessary, but above all in the human causes for which he would spend himself.

By Saturday he was ready to contemplate the long, jolting return trip to New York and Boston. He asked Sparks to excuse him from the round-the-clock liberal preaching scheduled at the Baltimore church, then set out for New York, where he paused long enough to address an overflow crowd in the hall of the medical college.

Back in Boston, Channing did his best to indicate that his interest lay elsewhere than in further theological controversy. As the financial depression of 1819 deepened, Boston's expanding population (nearly forty-three thousand) erupted with more and more of the visible poor. Bishop Cheverus wrote in alarm that "the state of commerce is such that in our port there is not one vessel for England."[39] With discussion of the causes and remedies of poverty in the air, Channing expressed his own views.[40]

He was profoundly distressed, he said, by the tendency among the well-to-do to excuse themselves from welfare efforts on the grounds that "poverty grows from charity," and that the only way to check the poor was to make their condition "intolerable." He was appalled, he said, at how many were adopting a philosophy of "the less we give, the better." The only comfort he could take from the situation was that it at least brought the subject of poverty into the open, where it could be openly discussed.

He readily acknowledged that almsgiving was sometimes harmful in its effect. Charity, he said, "partakes of the imperfection of all human things. . . . Every virtue produces occasional evil." But the notion that the best way to prevent poverty was "to take from men all expectation of relief if they became poor" was monstrous. In the first place, it could be implemented, he said, only by driving "all human feeling from our breasts," and turning "our hearts to stone." In addition, he continued, it would not work: "Men are not to be kept from poverty by being taught that poverty is a helpless state, any more than they are to be kept from crimes by multiplication of capital punishments." Indeed, Channing said, if no other relief from poverty is available, the poor will find "the temptations to escape it by fraud and violence . . . irresistible."

Channing was not prepared to put forward sweeping *programs* of economic, social, and political change, aimed at the redistribution of wealth and the structural abolition of poverty. He was absorbed with the moral meaning of the questions *then and there* staring his privileged fellow Bostonians in the face.

What about charity? Should they give it, or withhold it? Channing gave them this advice: "The occasional abuses of charity are not to discourage us in exercising this virtue. . . . Does anyone ask, 'Why shall I pity and help the poor man?' I answer, because he is A MAN; because poverty does not blot out his humanity; because he has your nature, your sensibilities, your wants, your fears; because the winter wind pierces him, and hunger gnaws him, and disease racks and weakens him, as truly as they do you. . . . To some this may seem declamation. There are some who seldom think of or value *man as man*. . . . Poverty separates a fellow-being from them, and severs the

165

golden chain of humanity. But this is a gross and vulgar way of thinking, and religion and reason cry out against it."

It was completely unrealistic of Channing to dream that having spoken his piece in Baltimore, he would be relieved of further controversial involvement. Conservatives in the north were as aghast over his text as were their orthodox Baltimore brethren. Calvinist pens went furiously to work to belabor and demolish this latest blast of godlessness, and, as usual, one pamphlet provoked another in a seemingly endless chain. When Unitarianism was repeatedly attacked as "a half-way house to infidelity," Channing felt obliged to answer in an article published later in 1819 in the *Christian Disciple*. The following year, in the same periodical, he made public his "Moral Argument Against Calvinism," which, while vigilantly avoiding personal references to his attackers, was a body blow against the conservative cause. It was here that Channing wrote his celebrated line: "It is an important truth, which we apprehend has not been sufficiently developed, that the ultimate reliance of a human being is and must be on his own mind."[41]

There was really not much more he could say to expose the root of his rejection of Calvinism. After tracing all of the other reasons for doing so — the doctrinal reasons, the Biblical reasons — in the end it came down to a personal commitment grounded in divine immanence and rational ethics; Christian only because that was the symbolism Channing knew and loved. How much plainer could he be? So, for the next six years — until December 7, 1826, when he preached on "Unitarian Christianity Most Favorable to Piety" at the dedication of the Second Unitarian Church of New York, he remained aloof from polemical penmanship.

However, there were others only too eager to scratch their opinions onto sheets of paper. Moses Stuart addressed Channing directly in one hundred and eighty pages of alternating grief and wrath, ending with a question that seemed to be torn from his depths: "When shall we bring a united offering to our common Lord, if men like you, who stand in eminent and responsible stations, treat those whom they profess to own as *Christian brethren,* in such a manner, and strive to degrade and render them contemptible."[42]

Channing could scarcely believe what he read and could not bring himself to reply. But since Stuart had defended Trinitarianism on scholarly and textual grounds, Andrews Norton volunteered to respond on an equally scholarly basis. That brought the brighest academic ornament of orthodoxy, Dr. Leonard Woods of Andover Theological Seminary, into the wordy contest. With the publication of Woods's pamphlet, Unitarianism wheeled up one of its most formidable guns: Henry Ware of Harvard. And so it went.

For three years "the Woods'n Ware" controversy raged, emotionally inflamed by developments in Dedham. The traditional, if confusing, ecclesiastical practice in New England Congregationalism was to have a church within a church. The covenant-signing communicants, or "members" proper, composed an inner body (more consecrated, more zealous), on whom courtesy bestowed the privilege of leading in church affairs. Right belief, which meant acceptable orthodoxy, was normally one of the requirements for admission to membership in the inner circle. Ringing the inner circle was the rest of the parish — the Congregationalist townspeople, some of whom occupied pews on Sunday morning, and all of whom, under the old Massachusetts Constitution, were subject to taxation for the support of the ministry, just as they were taxed for the support of the common school and the constable. The system was known as "the standing order."

In Dedham's First Church, in 1818, the pulpit became vacant just as the theological controversy reached a boil. The sentiment in the parish was strongly liberal, while that in the inner circle church was predominantly conservative. Two thirds of the parish voted for a liberal clergyman, Alvan Lamson of Cambridge, but the members of the church later voted eighteen to fourteen *against* Lamson.[43] When the stalemate seemed unresolvable, the dissenting majority within the church withdrew to form a new church, declaring that they considered themselves to

167

be the legitimate possessors of the church's real estate, endowments, communion silver, and other property.

Although Channing had served as a member of Lamson's ordaining council, he did his best to ignore the tempest once it headed toward nasty litigation. The church minority, which sided with the parish majority, reorganized, elected new deacons, and then sued for recovery of the church's property. The case was widely recognized as a bellwether, and was bitterly fought all the way to the Unitarian-dominated Massachusetts Supreme Court. In 1820, the court ruled that "where a majority of the members of a Congregational Church separate from a majority of the Parish, the members who remain, though a minority, constitute the Church in such Parish, and retain the rights and property belonging thereto."[44]

Everywhere the orthodox screamed foul, as well they might. Isaac Parker, the judge who wrote the decision, was a staunch Unitarian. It was clear to church conservatives that they were about to be "plundered," in community after community, of properties they considered to be rightly theirs. As the tide ran, there was no choice for convinced evangelicals, in the steadily mounting number of towns where liberal parish majorities were insisting upon liberal ministers, but to withdraw to form their own theologically pure churches.[45] A careful, though probably incomplete, report prepared in 1836 by a committee of the Massachusetts General Association lists eighty-one "exiled churches," which by withdrawing from their parishes surrendered parish and church funds valued at some $366,000 and meeting-houses valued at $243,000 more.[46]

In some instances — Channing's Federal Street in 1819 being one — entire congregations became Unitarian without splintering. (Boston's churches, incidentally, were not subject to the "parish" and "church" distinction, nor were Boston's citizens taxed for ministerial support.) But there were many towns throughout the Commonwealth where both parish and church remained peaceably faithful to orthodoxy.

All in all, about one quarter of the Congregational churches in Massachusetts were Unitarian by the time the tempest of division had run its course. Of the twenty-five original churches in the eastern part of the state, twenty enlisted in the Unitarian cause; in Boston only Old South maintained the faith of the founding fathers. Along the Massachusetts seaboard, the Unitarian gale swept up the ablest clergymen, the leaders in the professions and public service, in education and in the arts — in fact, the bulk of the Brahmins. Characteristically, George Ticknor, fresh from his European triumphs, joined Channing's church, and remained for all of his life a devoted member, even when his revered pastor's unanticipated radicalism went too far.

Thus whether he wished it or not, Channing had become the prime embodiment of a religious movement. The Unitarian controversy echoed far beyond the confines of Boston, and wherever its sounds were heard, the name Channing leapt to mind. From Philadelphia south to Baltimore and Charleston, then west to Kentucky, Ohio, and Illinois, and finally back along the eastern seaboard from New York to Portland, the religious ferment centered around Channing. But no men were ever less temperamentally suited for piecing together a forceful, disciplined movement than Channing and the other senior leaders of the Unitarian cause. At the very moment when they might have struck hard to mobilize and organize amorphous liberal religious sentiments erupting across the countryside, they were firming their determination not to become a "sect." Their motives were honorable enough. What they had seen of sects seemed mostly odious. Yet, it should also have been apparent to them, and wasn't, that the logical evolution of their reformist zeal was toward an independent and effective liberal church on a national scale.

A few younger men, with missionary ambitions, were emerging. One of the most resourceful of them, Ezra Stiles Gannett, became in 1824 Channing's longtime associate and eventual successor in the pastorate of the Federal Street Church. Personifying organizational statesmanship, Gannett was the moving spirit behind the birth in 1825 of the American Unitarian Association. But it was a discouraging business. Regretfully describing the unfulfilled potential of early Unitarianism, historian Joseph Henry Allen lamented that if there had been ten like Gannett, they would have spread Unitarianism "like a prairie fire from border to border of our country."[47]

Quite aside from the questionable realism of Allen's appraisal, the early format of the American Unitarian Association was designed to defuse the zeal of others like Gannett. In spite of his great administrative skill, Gannett was unable to overcome the foot-dragging of those like Channing, particularly in the Boston area, who deeply distrusted the setting up of strong denominational machinery. They were not about to put authority into the hands of an association, and to make certain, they saw to it that the association remained pinchpenny poor. Channing wished the Association no harm, but quickly refused the offered presidency.

Membership was set up on an individual rather than institutional basis, but even this tepid approach to organizational unity failed to mollify most Boston Unitarians. The association's first public roster listed only sixty-five Bostonians in a total membership of eight hundred and ninety-one, and less than half of the Boston churches offered financial help.

The conclusion is inescapable that with a charismatic prophet in Channing, an organizational genius in Gannett, and a ripe field for harvest, Unitarianism could have become a formidable institutional movement. That it did not must be attributed to what can be called either a quirk or an ornament in Channing's makeup, which was widely shared by the older Boston Unitarian elite. The Unitarians in Channing's circle had profound confidence in the written word as a means of spreading liberal faith, but they had no such confidence in denominational organization. Being a small, even struggling, religious *body* was not the kind of thing that nagged at their elevated minds. What mattered was quality. If prodigious efforts were to be put forth, let them be expended by men thinking and writing, and not by men running on treadmills of institutional machinery.

So Unitarianism did not become an expanding, multiplying, proliferating organizational church, but Unitarian writers and writings, with Channing as the acknowedged fountainhead, did exercise amazingly widespread influence not only on the nineteenth-century mind of America, but in Europe as well.

The cost in institutional terms, however, was incalculable.

While it can be argued on several counts that Unitarianism could never have captured America's popular religious imagination, it seems more likely that Gannett's proselytizing instinct was correct. At any rate, it was the Channing instinct that prevailed.

TWO

"Maturing Gracefully and Radically"

V

I Have No Fear
of Revolutions

THE LORD WAS BUSILY GIVING AND TAKING AWAY as Channing entered the second decade of the nineteenth century. Grandfather Ellery's death had to be expected — he was ninety-two — but it was still a shock. The proud old man was self-possessed in his final moments. On his last day, he got up and dressed himself, but a weak spell sent him back to bed. His doctor found his pulse almost gone, and administered wine. William Ellery seemed to revive. "Your pulse beats very well," the physician told him. "Charmingly," the patient replied. In a few hours, but not before saying that he knew he was done for, William Ellery died.[1] The Channings consoled themselves with the two sons, William Francis and George, who, in quick succession, entered their household.

Channing was riding a professional crest. The recently organized Unitarian Society in New York urged him to become its minister and to lead a crusade for enlightened religion. In declining, he pleaded public, domestic, and private considerations, but one of the strongest reasons, certainly, was the obligation he felt to the Federal Street congregation, which had briskly followed him into Unitarianism, increased his salary, appropriated funds for the assistant he requested, and filled the pews whenever he preached.

The new parish activities building on Berry Street, adjoining the church, gave him a center in which to grind some of his special axes. He used it in May 1820, as an assembly point for the liberal ministers of Massachusetts, where the still-existing Berry Street Conference was organized to hear annually "an

175

address from one of our number, . . . reports as to the state of our churches, and . . . the best methods of advancing religion."[2] Channing delivered the founding address, restating his Baltimore portrayal of the role of reason in relation to revelation.

A few weeks later, the Harvard Corporation, in recognition of his standing in the community and service to the college, voted to award him an honorary doctorate. On August 30, he became the Rev. William Ellery Channing, D.D.[3]

The 1820's were to be years of expansion and deepening of his social concerns, but the process began inauspiciously. A public issue came to a head which galvanized the cautious and conservative side of his nature. For some time there had been popular agitation in the Commonwealth for a constitutional convention, but the Federalists had intuitively fended it off. Meanwhile, the separation of Maine (until then a part of Massachusetts) began to look more and more desirable to Federalist politicians. Maine was showing signs of republican restlessness and discontent, and who among the better classes of Massachusetts needed that trouble? Far better to have their own snug little Federalist enclave. In order to allow Maine separate statehood, the ruling elders of Massachusetts decided to risk a constitutional convention. As it turned out, it was too late even in Massachusetts to reverse the decline of Federalism.

In August, when communities went about the business of electing delegates, 410 of Boston's Protestant voters wrote in the name of Bishop Cheverus — a puzzling phenomenon since two of the city's most esteemed Unitarian clergymen, Charles Lowell and Channing, received only eight and three votes respectively. Because 855 votes were required for accreditation, the convention was deprived of the bishop's participation.[4]

Many of Channing's parishioners, friends, and colleagues were elected, however — among them John Adams, Daniel Webster, Governor Levi Lincoln, Justices Joseph Story, Lemuel Shaw, and Isaac Parker, and the Rev. Joseph Tuckerman.

The conservatives at the convention concentrated on repelling the democratic spirit of the time by advocating reverence for the existing 1780 constitution. This included provisions for public support of Harvard, a religious test oath for office holders, and the religious establishment.[5]

No issues were more hotly contested on the floor of the convention than those affecting church and state relations. Day after day advocates of Jeffersonian separation clashed with defenders of establishment. Baptists, Methodists, and Universalists argued against the standing order, while most Unitarian and Trinitarian Congregationalists subordinated their bitter differences to their common privileges. There were defections, but no great number.

The floor leader of the status-quo forces was Channing's old friend Joseph Tuckerman, who was only willing to divest the constitution of its inoperative requirement of church attendance, and to add unincorporated religious societies and Catholics to the sects and denominations a citizen might specify as recipients of his religious taxes. When a delegate from Pittsfield, with considerable backing, introduced an amendment substituting *voluntary* support of religious instruction for state support, Tuckerman mounted a counterattack. Sounding the unassailable theme that free government "must be founded in religion; or in other words, in the virtues that are derived from religion,"[6] Tuckerman graciously conceded that some governments in the past had exploited religion to their own advantage. He mentioned Constantine as an example that came quickly to mind. But he could see no such possibilities in Massachusetts in 1820, where Christianity in "a pure state" was much enjoyed, and where freedom of conscience could be assured without exposing religion, morality, and the state to "the awful consequences" of separation.

On the test oath for officeholders, Tuckerman deferred at first to the leonine leadership of Channing's distinguished parishioner, Daniel Webster, who argued that the people had a right to demand an oath as provided in the 1780 constitution. Tuckerman backed him up by introducing one proposal after another for retention of a religious test. The essence was always the same: "I, ———, do declare that I believe in the Christian Religion."[7]

In December, with the convention's debate in full flow, Channing took to his pulpit to throw his prestige behind Tuckerman,

Webster, and company. In a sermon entitled "Religion a Social Principle,"[8] he painted a glowing picture of the central role of religion in society. Religion is not just a private relationship between man and his God, he said; it is a pervasive social principle. No one brings his religion into the world with him; society makes it available to him after he gets there. "Therefore Society ought, through its great organ and representative, which is government, as well as by other methods, to pay homage to God, and express its obligation." It was the proper function of a state constitution to safeguard public morals, he said, by granting elected officials the "power of providing religious instruction." Because religion is indispensable to a free society, it merits "any grateful offering from the state which upholds it."

Within days, the reigning Universalist spokesman, Hosea Ballou, rushed to the printer with a pamphlet of "strictures" on Channing's sermon.[9] Beginning in a soft and conciliatory vein, Ballou congratulated Channing on his eloquent description of the social meaning of religion. Then, with his accustomed thoroughness, Ballou dissected tissue by tissue Channing's defense of religious establishment and state support. Using history as his reference, he culled countless illustrations of how governmental meddling in religious matters had invariably corrupted Christianity. Channing, by his mistaken logic, was encouraging religious oppression, he said. If government officials are empowered to support religions they consider "social and salutary," what is to keep them from also determining, by law, which religious expressions are to be considered "subversive"? Surely, Dr. Channing would not want that! It should be quite obvious to Channing and to everyone else, Ballou continued, that men have never been made inwardly religious by law. "The internal principles of religion cannot be controlled by legislation, and therefore stand in no need of its aid."

Channing's infuriating practice of treating Ballou as if he did not exist leaves us with no indication of his personal reaction to the "strictures." We do know that in later years, he was anxious not to publicize his earlier defense of establishment. When "Religion a Social Principle" appeared in an 1830 edition of his collected works, the title was changed to "Importance of Religion to Society." All references to state support of religion were deleted. Only that part of the sermon that Ballou had praised was retained. Indeed, when in May 1830 Channing preached the annual election sermon, he had come around to Ballou's view: "Am I now asked how government is to promote energy and elevation of moral principle? I answer, not by making the various virtues matters of legislation, not by preaching morals, *not by establishing religion* [italics mine]; for these are not its appropriate functions. It is to serve the cause of spiritual freedom, not by teaching or persuasion, but by action; that is, by rigidly conforming itself, in all its measures, to the moral or Christian law; by the most public and solemn manifestations of reverence for right, for justice, for the general weal, for the principles of virtue."[10]

By 1833, when Massachusetts finally dismantled its church establishment and abolished tax-supported religious instruction, Channing was ready. But in 1820, he, along with Tuckerman, bemoaned the constitutional amendment, approved by the voters, which abolished the test oath for public office, and rejoiced that no basic change in the standing order was submitted to the voters at all.

Something fundamental was going to have to happen to Channing to shake his lingering esteem for the politically moribund, old-line, Federalist-Congregationalist (now largely Unitarian) aristocracy. Perversely enough, what paved the way was the wretched state of his health.

Except for the quiet, refreshing summer weeks spent at Oakland, the Gibbs's place outside of Newport, Channing's life was a perpetual jumble of conflicting demands. His protégés — John Pierpont and Orville Dewey, among others — thirsted for his attention. His dear friend, the distinguished young Boston attorney John Gallison, an activist member of Channing's beloved Peace Society, died at the age of thirty-two, and Channing was asked by the *Christian Disciple* to write the appropriate memoir.[11] A new liberal weekly, the *Christian Register,* with David Read as editor, was launched on April 20, 1821, bearing Channing's blessing and promise of literary contributions. From across the Charles River came Harvard's invitation to deliver the Dudleian Lecture;[12] it was virtually a summons. Channing obliged, and made a piercing impression on a senior named Ralph Waldo Emerson, the lean, laconic son of his old friend William Emerson. The Dudleian Lecture format was a topical straightjacket, restricted by probate to discourses on "The Evidences of Revealed Religion." Channing presented himself to the Harvard body as an eloquent supernaturalist (as was young Emerson at the time), giving little indication, except in his lofty enthusiasm, that he had recently "discovered" Wordsworth, whom he considered a magnificent antidote to Unitarian failures of "imagination and poetical enthusiasm,"[13] and the revolutionary German philosophers, Kant, Schelling, and Fichte.

From Baltimore, Jared Sparks bombarded him with correspondence. Late in 1820 he sought Channing's approval and counsel concerning a periodical he planned to introduce in Baltimore. Channing not only gave encouragement, but frankly expressed the hope that Sparks's publication would prove to be livelier than the *Christian Disciple*. "We want a more various and entertaining work than we now have, and I wish that it may appear in a different part of the country," Channing wrote.[14]

A heartened Sparks brought out the first issue of his *Unitarian Miscellany and Christian Monitor* in January 1821. He thought he was following Channing's advice in making the magazine controversial, hard-hitting, and militantly liberal, but soon learned that Channing had retreated again into his shell of caution. After five months of publication, Sparks received a deflating letter from his mentor: "We think you identify yourself too much with the English Unitarians, men whose peculiar circumstances have given them more of a sectarian spirit, than we wish to cultivate."[15]

Sparks, who would soon be elected chaplain of the House of Representatives (a development attributed by jolted evangelicals to "shrewd Massachusetts politicking"),[16] was not easily put off. In a letter introducing the Rev. Mr. Little, a recent preacher to Washington Unitarians, he urged Channing's co-operation with Little in soliciting funds for a church building in the Capital. Mr. Little was one of the English Unitarians.

Under the various pressures, Channing's weak health led him

to morbid speculation. In a letter to his widowed sister-in-law Susan, offering additional financial help for his nephew William's schooling, he plaintively told her that his generosity was "not altogether disinterested." He lived, he said, "in the expectation of not living long, and should I be taken, there are services which Wm. can then render me more effectively perhaps than anyone else. I should esteem his friendship for my son a great blessing."[17] By the summer of 1821, his sluggishness drove him to the mountains of New Hampshire and Vermont in preference to the familiar haunts of Newport, hoping that by lifting up his eyes unto the hills, he could snap himself back to something more nearly resembling life.

It seemed to work. Channing jotted down his pleasure at establishing a newfound friendship with the White Mountains, "more intimate than I have formed with any part of nature." His mind enlarged and swelled, he said, "with these majestic forms, which claim kindred with the skies."[18] Yet, when he was back in his Oakland retreat in September, he felt let down. His exhilaration among northern New England's hills and streams eroded remarkably fast, striking him as a gloomy specimen "of the life I have led for many years. One day undoes the work of many weeks." A stubborn cold caught somewhere along the way left him "without one additional particle of strength."[19]

He lingered in Rhode Island through September and October in a state of physical dejection, unable to return to his pulpit, his mind toying with various ideas. Aroused by his discovery of Wordsworth, he wrote that he now smiled when he heard poetry shrugged off as "light" reading: "The true poet has far-reaching thoughts, a perception of the harmonious and exquisite relations of the universe, an eye that pierces the depths and mysteries of soul, placing him amidst the most gifted and exalted intelligences."[20]

Then, in November, an event occurred in Boston that goaded him, however reluctantly, to march up the steps of his Federal Street pulpit. The Rev. John Newland Moffitt, a Methodist revivalist, created a sensation with his baptism by total immersion of some fifty converts, mostly women, in the Charles River, near what is now the site of the Massachusetts General Hospital. The following Sunday, Channing, wrapped in his pulpit robe for the first time in many months, declared that there were far more effective ways of dealing with sin and evil than by reaching for startling effects.[21] In a conversation after the sermon with young Josiah Quincy, he paid tribute to the fabled eloquence of George Whitefield, the great evangelist of prerevolutionary days, and ridiculed the notion that Moffitt was comparable.

Once back in harness, Channing manfully applied himself to what *he* considered to be more effective ways of dealing with sin and evil. In the face of an orthodox revival that was beginning to cut into Unitarian ranks, he persuaded luminary George Ticknor to take over a class of boys in the Sunday School. On a frosty February night in 1822, Channing played host at his house to a group of men who organized themselves into the Wednesday Evening Association, whose purposes were to extend the knowledge and practical influence of "true religion," to promote plans for the reform and improvement of society, and "to produce a unity of purpose and effort among Unitarian Christians."[22] For years the group pried into Boston's pockets of poverty and deprivation, nursemaiding innumerable reform ventures, but Channing, having served as its awakener, found himself growing weaker and sicker with each passing winter day. The effort of a Sunday sermon forced him to rest and be carefully tended for several days. He was of little use any longer to Jonathan Phillips, with whom he normally divided the visiting of the poor and other pastoral work.[23]

Convinced that he had become a burden both to his congregation and family, he began to cast about for ways to break out of his imprisoning ailments. At one point he seemed to think that if he could return to where it all began — to Richmond, Virginia, where his health first broke down — he might be able to reweave the old threads and start anew. President Kirkland of Harvard wrote him a letter of introduction to one William Wickham, Esq., of Richmond, whose sons were "devoting themselves to appropriate pursuits" in Cambridge.[24]

It was never used, because Channing, with sober second thought, yielded to the urging of family and friends that he take a year's leave to travel abroad. The members of Federal Street

Church officially granted him a sabbatical, expressed an "earnest wish . . . to do all in their power to conduce to the restoration of his health," and authorized the standing committee to raise "the sum of one thousand dollars to defray the additional expense of the year."[25] The additional expense was for the preaching services of Orville Dewey, the Channing protégé, whom Channing had recruited to fill his pulpit.

Having made a decision, Channing found his spirits lifting. He became quite keyed-up at the prospect — as he told his congregation on the Sunday preceding his sailing date — of "traversing countries which have kindled my imagination almost from infancy, whose literature has been the food of my mind, and where nature and society present aspects hardly to be conceived amidst the freshness of our own institutions."[26] But even in his high state of excitement, Channing could not escape his New England conscience. He insisted to his congregation that the throbbing of his imagination at the prospect of seeing Europe's sights was no more than a by-product of his *real* reason for going — the duty to restore himself to personal improvement and public usefulness.[27]

The next evening, he sat down at his writing desk and wrote two unusually manic letters. In the first, to his sister-in-law Susan, he enclosed one hundred and fifty dollars to be used for her children. He told her that "one mitigation" of the hell he had endured in recent months was learning "what a place I hold in your heart." But even such an outpouring could not down his nagging sense of duty. "I cannot escape some bitter feelings," he wrote, "when I think how much more good I might have done to my friends than I have done. But I hope to return, renovated in health."[28] The second letter was to "My Dear Mother." For her he enclosed a hundred dollars, which he begged her to spend on building up her health! What he had in mind, he did not say. Promising to remember her in his daily prayers, he assured her that he was setting off on his adventure with "a cheerful, confiding mind."[29] The tone was that of a man exceedingly febrile about fleeing an environment that incessantly reminded him of his limitations.

On Thursday, May 30, 1822, William and Ruth Channing said

good-bye to their three children and sailed for England. Clutched under Channing's arm were a notebook, a volume by John Playfair, and Brande's *Manual of Chemistry*.[30]

Substantial and remarkable things happened to Channing during his wanderings in England and on the Continent. Though he was miserly about recording his experiences, there was no mistaking their transforming effect upon him, and they had little to do with his physical health. He met people such as he had never before known — Wordsworth and Coleridge, for example — and discovered that they were acquainted with his work and anxious to impress him with their own brilliance. Coleridge was so thrown off stride by the Channing "presence" that he compensated by babbling interminably, then had the gall to write later to Washington Allston that he found Channing to be the truest of conversationalists — one who "has the love of wisdom and the wisdom of love."[31] The underlying rancor Coleridge felt at being upstaged by a provincial American clergyman apparently continued to assail him. Some years later, when Channing's essay on Napoleon was being widely read in England, Coleridge told an interviewer that Channing had cribbed its basic points from him during the preacher's visit. Though Channing felt obliged to set the record straight, he did so with his customary benevolence. He could explain the gaffe, he said, only by supposing that the interviewer had misunderstood Coleridge. "I have quite a distinct recollection of my only interview with Mr. Coleridge," he went on, "and cannot remember that Bonaparte was even once named." Channing also mentioned that his own recollections were confirmed "by a friend who was present." The "friend" was his wife.[32]

With Wordsworth, who was unawed, there was real give and take in their picturesque meeting. The two took a long walk together, and then a sunset buggy ride through Rydal Mount, chattering "so eagerly as often to interrupt one another."[33] Wordsworth recited poetry by the yard. Channing in turn carved a sharp image on Wordsworth's memory. Twenty years later the poet could still solemnly repeat Channing's conversational statement that "one great evidence of the divine origin of Christianity was, that it contained nothing which rendered it unadaptable to a progressive state of society, that it put no checks upon the activity of the human mind, and did not compel it to tread always blindly in a beaten path."[34]

Traipsing through France and Switzerland, Channing realized that he was enjoying himself in spite of his aching bones and sour stomach. The assertive, soaring quality of the Alps greatly intensified the feelings he had first experienced in the Green and White Mountains. If it was the soul's duty to elevate itself, there was real help to be found in nature's powerful handiwork. He toyed with the idea of staying longer in Switzerland, but prudently rejected it when he visualized what a Swiss winter might be like.

November of 1822 found the Channings in rain-drenched Florence, and it was a chill rain, but the old city's art treasures outstripped their advance billing. It dumbfounded Channing that the masterpieces were largely ignored by a population that apparently preferred the trite holy images of the Virgin within the churches.

Whether in Florence, Naples, or Rome, the riddle of Catholicism intrigued and puzzled him. He took special pains to be present at holy day ceremonies, and came away shaking his head at what he felt to be an absence of the "pulsation of moral life."[35] One tableau of "moral inanity," which he couldn't get out of his mind — and it bothered him deeply, he said, because of his love for Bishop Cheverus — occurred as he watched a company of priests, some with "fine-looking, intellectual heads," performing a ritual before an image of Mary. As Channing described it, "They all took hold of hands, making a circle, and were expressing symbolically a very sublime idea, when the whole effect was destroyed for me by seeing one of them most intently engaged in contriving, in the midst of the solemnities, to get a pinch of snuff!"[36]

Channing, who was capable of warming to the mysticism in Catholic worship, was too tightly locked into his background to cope with such flagrant violations of decorum. He was massively deficient in knowledge of the subtleties of Catholic dogma, and was prejudiced against the "superstitions" which he automatically associated with it. Yet his intuitions permitted him to appreciate the rich emotional life of the Catholic church, so different from his own Unitarianism. He acknowledged his admiration for the "wonderful flexibleness" of Catholicism, its "most skillful adaptation of itself to the different tastes, passions, wants of men." While insisting upon its unity, "it has a singular variety of forms and aspects . . . it has a gorgeous ritual," he noted. A visitor in Rome could see "by the side of the purple, lackeyed cardinal the begging friar; when, under the arches of St. Peter, he sees a coarsely dressed monk holding forth to a ragged crowd; or when, beneath a Franciscan church, adorned with the most precious works of art, he meets a charnel-house, where the bones of the dead brethren are built into walls, between which the living walk to read their mortality,— he is amazed, if he gives himself time for reflection, at the infinite variety of machinery which Catholicism has brought to bear on the human mind; at the sagacity with which it has adapted itself to the various tastes and propensities of human nature."[37]

His prejudice reasserted itself, however, when he tried to assess the meaning of what he persisted in calling *worship* of the Virgin. "The great idea of this Catholic deity [sic] is purity, chastity," he wrote, "and yet . . . the country where she is worshipped is disfigured by licentiousness beyond all countries of the civilized world."[38]

The personalities, sights, sounds, and smells of Europe set his mind to racing over social, political, and moral questions. His experience with affluence and poverty in the United States had not prepared him for the numbing extremes he found in Europe's great cities. What was he, as a traveler, to make of the deformities of human nature spread so insistently before him? He had no doubt what he was called upon to do. "He who travels without learning to love his race more would do far better to stay home," Channing wrote. "It is a poor business to rake into the corruptions of human nature, unless one believes in its capacity for restoration, and approaches its defilements only to cleanse them."[39]

So Channing began to mobilize and organize on paper precisely what the pressure points of enlightened social policy should be: education that opens the "faculties and affections" of every person whatever his rank or condition; economic arrangements that put human improvement first, property and profits second; an end to the "ruinous" notion that respectability and high social status are identical; replacement of civil society's abounding "restraints" with a new, great aim of "development"; reentry into society's mainstream of the poor; recognition that government, with its array of institutions, laws, and resources, exists primarily to promote respect and progress for *all* of its citizens, but especially, because of their degraded condition, for "the poor, weak, helpless, suffering."[40]

To flesh out his Elysian prospectus, Channing called for an intellectual elite — "a body of enlightened, studious men," who do not form a "party" or faction, but "consider their light as a good given to be diffused, and as a means to maintain an improving intercourse among all orders."

Next Channing turned to the rich, of whom, he assumed, there would always be a passel. But instead of "herding together, and linking themselves to one another by common pleasures, privileges, refinements," let them "regard property as a trust for the good of those who are in want."

Then lumping the learned and the loaded together, he stretched out their special guidelines: "Let there be no literary *class*, no *class* of the rich. The learned, when forming a distinct class become jealous, exacting, domineering, and seek to maintain their sway, even at the expense of truth. Scholars already begin to find the benefit of quitting their pedantic cells and mingling with general society; but still they associate too much with the rich and refined, — still they seek honor and power. Their high office, of being lights to society, is overlooked. How the rich injure themselves by a clannish spirit, corrupting one another by rivalry in show and expense!"

These meditations forecasted a more elastic and emancipated interpreter of human matters. Boston was in for a trauma when this travel-weary but travel-stimulated preacher came home. First, however, the Channings were to experience a trauma of their own — a ghastly one.

While still in Florence, Channing became absorbed with long-

ing thoughts of his children. To ease himself he wrote a voluminous letter home, full of free associations about the care and
culture of the young. His own children, he prayed, would become "simple and unaffected in character and manners, and
sincere, frank and undisguised in language and conduct."[41]
Recognizing that such lofty objectives came not by the waving
of magic wands, he began to sketch out a philosophy of child
nurture. As so often happened with him, thought piled upon
thought until his pen scratched out something of a classic.[42]

Children could learn to love long before they learn the meaning of the word, he wrote, if their parents truly love *them*. He
was certain that "the bad feelings of infancy, which we charge
upon nature, are very often to be traced to the impatience, and
want of self-government, and abuse of power, in older people."
It was also his strong conviction that "an amiable, generous
temper, uniformly expressed by those around them, will prove
equally contagious."

But Channing never described just one surface of a subject.
Turning this one sideways, he warned of an "injudicious fond-
ness" that could twist a child toward selfishness. "To prevent
this," he said, "[children] must see, that, whilst they are loved
tenderly, they are not loved blindly and without judgment; and
they must see, too, that others are loved as well as themselves.
. . . They should never imagine for a moment that their own
happiness is more important than that of older persons, or their
rights, interests, and feelings more sacred; but they should early
learn the essential equality of human beings and the respect due
to human nature in every condition."

But there was still more to be said. Too much must not be
expected of a child at first. Children begin as self-centered
creatures, "by necessity, and innocently." They start life with
an exclusive consciousness of their own pleasures and pains.
Only gradually do they comprehend that "others feel as keenly
as themselves." They need help to learn how "to place themselves in others' situations," and this help is best given by the
"unaffected delight" of example.

On December 17, the Channings reached Rome, where they
found a package of letters waiting for them, with frightful news.

Their youngest child, George, was dead. So too was Walter Channing's wife, Barbara Higginson Perkins, who had left behind a five-year-old, Channing's namesake nephew. Channing turned his soul inside out.

"I am afflicted indeed," he wrote in a letter home. "God has visited me with the heaviest loss I can experience, save one. My sweet, lovely boy! Is he indeed gone? and am I no more to see that smile which to me and to his mother was like a beam from heaven? He was a most gentle creature. I can remember his occasional cries of distress, but never one of passion. My health did not allow me to carry and play with him, as I had been in the habit of doing with my other infants; but when I was amusing myself with Mary and William, he would creep to me and climb into my lap, and win from me, by his benignant smile, the notice which I was giving to them. The accounts we had received of him before this last sad news were most encouraging, and we were anticipating the happy moment when we should take him to our arms and press him to our hearts. . . . And he is gone! and when we return, if that blessing is in store for us, we shall look for him in vain! O, the void in a parent's heart, when a child is taken . . ."[43]

Then came the inevitable Channing upbeat. As much as he suffered, he would not succumb to "dejection." Death, he was sure, "is not that wide gulf between us and the departed which we are apt to imagine. . . . Francis, Ann, my child, and our beloved Barbara, are gone from us, but are not lost to us."

For Channing, the plausible way to comfort his shattered wife and to keep himself from utter dejection was to put down his awful homesickness, devote himself to the restoration of his health, and practice in the months ahead what he described as the traveler's art — uniting "minute observation with large comparisons." As the new year began, he wrote his mother that while the symptoms of his old ailments persisted, and probably always would, he now felt that "a life of moderate effort in my profession, together with regular exercise, will not only preserve, but gradually augment my strength; and this hope gives me a cheerfulness and gratitude very necessary in my present circumstances."[44] On his forty-third birthday, he was again in Florence on the first leg of the journey *home* — a word he underlined in his letters — and in a mood to count blessings. His life, he thought, "though no exception to the common lot, though checkered with good and evil, has, on the whole, been singularly favored."[45]

Two weeks later, the Channings were at Fontainebleau, soaking in a guide's accounts of his old nemesis Napoleon. There was a brief stop in Paris, while he drew breath for the channel crossing, then on to England where his Anglophilia was nourished, and his ego massaged by a round of contacts with leading Unitarians, literary figures, and lords and ladies. One of the first drawing rooms opened to the Channings was that of aging Mrs. Anna Letitia Barbauld, the poet and critic, whom Charles Lamb cursed as a blight "of all that is Human in man and child." Channing's impression was a polar opposite. "I never saw a person of her age who had preserved so much of youth; on whom time had laid so gentle a hand," he wrote. "Her countenance had nothing of the rigidity and hard lines of advanced life, but responded to the mind like a young woman's."[46]

There was an unexpected bonus in the visit. Mrs. Barbauld's celebrated niece happened to be there. Lucy Aikin had placed herself in the front rank of historical writers with her *Memoirs of the Court of Queen Elizabeth,* published five years earlier. As the Channings arrived in England, London booksellers were doing a brisk business in her latest, *Memoirs of the Court of King James I.* Sympathetic waves vibrated immediately between Miss Aikin and Channing. Their brief exchange of words at Mrs. Barbauld's was continued by lively correspondence until Channing's death. He used Miss Aikin as a confidential sounding board for thoughts he was nursing but not quite ready to express publicly. She in turn served as his eyes and ears for developments in England and on the Continent.

Channing yielded to the blandishments of London friends and did some preaching to Unitarian congregations, receiving excellent notices for his exertions. When Thomas Lord Erskine sought him out, he had the pungent experience of hearing a peer advocate the downfall of monarchy. The sophisticated candor with which the English discussed politics continually amazed him.

The lionizing of the Channings reached its zenith in mid-June, when, by royal yacht, they were tranported to the Isle of Wight to be splendidly wined and dined. Their next junket was to the banks of the Wye for a last, long look at Tintern Abbey, after which they were soon aboard ship and sailing for Boston.

Driven to Europe by his desolate health, Channing returned home relatively unchanged in body, but with a marked toning-up of his temperament. In 1848, when the foremost philosopher-theologian of English Unitarianism, James Martineau, read and reviewed the first edition of *Memoir of William Ellery Channing,* he was struck by the "mystery" of Channing's European journey. It was a "strange blank" in terms of trenchant written observations by the traveler, yet it resulted in transforming an "anxious martyr-spirit, somewhat valetudinarian in mind as well as body, into [a] free, clear, and almost joyous servant of God."[47]

Was it breaking away from the stiff, decorous atmosphere of patrician Boston? Was it the horizon-expanding, ego nourishing experience of matching minds, as an equal, with Wordsworth, Southey, Coleridge, Aikin, and the others? Was it months in Italy's sensuous cities, or weeks among the liberating Alps? As a recorder of his experiences, Channing is no help at all. Yet, from the time he set foot again on native soil, he was an expanded man. "He [threw] himself," in Martineau's words, "with greater courage, upon his real feelings, and distinguishes, with greater ease, between the genuine convictions and the conventional judgments of his conscience. He had for years been reproaching himself, in a way familiar to many an earnest heart, for his 'timidity on the subject of religion,' in conversation; and for his inability to substitute for 'mere calls,' truly 'serious and ministerial visits.' He now felt that he had been striving after conformity with a mere professional expectation; that it was not possible to make more than a very subordinate instrument of 'what is sometimes called pastoral duty.' . . . he acquiesced accordingly in that work of meditation, apart from the disturbances of custom and passion, which enabled him, from time to time, to come down with something of a prophet's power upon a world not often reached so soon by the voice of retired wisdom. . . . But above all, his attention was more and more turned to questions of social reform; and he laboured at the direct application of his own lofty Christianity, to the correction of guilty usages and wrongful institutions."

On August 22, 1823, the Channings walked down a gangplank to a Boston pier, and two days later he was in his pulpit, rededicating his life to acting "upon other minds . . . through sympathy as well as instruction."[48] He served warning that for the "moral renovation of the world," to which he intended to devote the rest of his life, he would not lean on "political changes" or "public measures." From now on, his primary emphasis would be upon a participatory democracy of "moral change." His view of the Christian ministry was "more grand and solemn" than ever, but he could no longer restrict it to the profession. "*All* are called, in their various relations, and according to their power," he said, "to advance the cause of pure religion and of divine morality, to which the ministry is dedicated." The professional minister's sole distinction from the layman was in giving a more "concentrated care to this primary interest of mankind." Thus did Channing serve notice on his laity that henceforth he would expect their religious fervor to stretch from Sunday through all the days of the week.

Yet, with his characteristic aplomb, so maddening in later years to some of the younger firebrands, Channing bundled his family together and fled forthwith to Oakland. Anyone who has returned to his job after a long absence can guess at Channing's motivations. It *was* exhilarating, at first blush, to be back in the thick of things, especially as a beloved returnee. But a quick look around revealed a mound of waiting, impatient problems. One of the most depressing, as far as Channing was concerned, was Orville Dewey's acceptance of a call to the Unitarian pulpit in New Bedford. Looking over the great throng that hung on the words of his reunion sermon, Channing boggled at the prospect of going it alone.

Another disheartening development was the imminent departure from Boston of Bishop Cheverus. Their quiet but widely known friendship and mutual respect had done much to make Boston a model of ecumenical relationships. One of the most touching letters Channing received on the eve of his departure to Europe was from the Boston prelate. Cheverus wrote the letter in Latin, so that Channing could use it for purposes of introduction to Catholic circles if he wished. A paragraph read, "Although we cannot boast of having you as a colleague in the Catholic faith (would that we could!), still, in Christian charity and with sincere respect, we commend you to all Catholic pastors everywhere, and ask those to whom you show this letter to receive you kindly and hospitably." In addition, Cheverus placed in Channing's hands a warm letter of introduction, in French, to the vicar-general of the Paris archdiocese, M. Abbé Desjardins.[49]

In the strange manner of one thing leading to another, Channing's presence in Paris for reasons of health was a reminder that Cheverus's health had also suffered drastically from a combination of overwork and Boston winters. In addition, the French political situation had long since become congenial to his return. When the archbishopric of Montauban became vacant, Cheverus was summoned to fill it.

Channing's sense of personal loss was profound. The two were close neighbors, with the Cathedral of the Holy Cross just a few steps from Federal Street Church. Channing had watched with mounting admiration the effective labors of this cultured Catholic shepherd among the poor, and was anticipating years more of kindred effort. That hope was now blasted, along with his unexpressed fantasy of an associated ministry with Dewey. It was one of the high sentimental moments of Channing's career when Cheverus, about to leave for France, presented to his Federal Street neighbor a rare edition of Augustine's *City of God*.

Channing waited for six years to find the appropriate manner of expressing in print his assessment of Cheverus. It came in 1829, when he wrote his essay on the great Catholic mystic, Fénelon.[50] By that time, Catholic-Protestant relations in Boston had become considerably less comfortable; mutual suspicions were definitely on the rise. Channing used his Fénelon essay as a vehicle for reminding his readers that the Catholic church had consistently produced "some of the greatest and best men that ever lived," and that this was "proof enough of its possessing all the means of salvation." And it was not just a matter of past history. "To come down to our own times," Channing said, "has not the metropolis of New England witnessed a sublime example of Christian virtue in a Catholic bishop? Who among our religious teachers would solicit a comparison between himself and the devoted Cheverus? This good man, whose virtues and talents have now raised him to high dignities in church and state, who now wears in his own country the joint honors of an archbishop and a peer, lived in the midst of us, devoting his days and nights, and his whole heart, to the service of a poor and uneducated congregation. We saw him declining in a great degree the society of the cultivated and refined, that he might be the friend of the ignorant and friendless; leaving the circles of polished life, which he would have graced, for the meanest hovels; bearing, with a father's sympathy, the burdens and sorrows of his large spiritual family; charging himself alike with their temporal and spiritual concerns; and never discovering, by the faintest indication, that he felt his fine mind degraded by his seemingly humble office. This good man, bent on his errands of mercy, was seen in our streets under the most burning sun of summer, and the fiercest storms of winter, as if armed against the elements by the power of charity. . . . How can we shut our hearts against this proof of the power of the Catholic religion to form good and great men?"

From his Rhode Island retreat, Channing dispatched a letter to the Federal Street congregation. With Dewey about to leave for New Bedford, his need for assistance should be soberly considered, he advised. Though the improvement of his health was "encouraging," it did not warrant excessive trust. He believed that on most Sundays he could preach at one of the two services "without injury," but for the rest, some other provision should be made.[51] The response of the congregation was prompt. There was a unanimous vote "to settle a colleague with the Rev. Dr. Channing, provided it will meet with his concurrence, and provided that an arrangement can be made in relation to salaries satisfactory to the society and the pastors." Channing replied that he would welcome a colleague "with pleasure," and would "cheerfully relinquish" one fourth of his salary to help meet the added financial burden. With the problem neatly resolved, he returned to Boston, took the pulpit on the first Sunday of October, and preached on the text, "Oh sing unto the Lord . . . for he is greatly to be praised."

Channing was not, and could not be, a social reformer in the ordinary sense. He breathed religion as he breathed air, in and out, in an unconscious, indispensable rhythm. He measured everything by spiritual ideals. He looked out at the world with God-intoxicated eyes. His redeeming quality was that he fully understood the obsessive nature of his faith. He knew its limitations as well as its strengths. In the twilight of his life, he summed it up for Lydia Maria Child, who *was* a reformer in the most fundamental sense.

"I understand fully your language," he wrote Miss Child, "when you speak of *reform* as your 'workshop.' I fear I understand it too well, that is, I am prone to shrink from the work. Reform is resistance of rooted corruptions and evils, and my tendency is to turn away from the contemplation of evils. My mind seeks the good, the perfect, the beautiful. It is a degree of torture to bring vividly to my apprehension what man is suffering from his own crimes and from the wrongs and cruelty of his brother. . . . It is only from a sense of duty that I read a narrative of guilt or woe in the papers. . . . You see I am made of but poor material for a reformer. But on this very account the work is good for me. I need it, not, as many do, to give me excitement, for I find enough, perhaps too much, to excite me in the common experiences of life, in meditation, in abstract truth; but to save me from a refined selfishness, to give me force, disinterestedness, true dignity and elevation, to link me by a new faith to God, by a deeper love to my race, and to make me a blessing to the world."[52]

Had his fixation been differently directed, he could have been a formidable social revolutionary. Dewey, who not only knew him well, but had the analytical insight to make something of his knowledge, recorded a colorful collection of personal observations.[53] Channing's mind was, according to Dewey, "strained to the highest tension — he seemed not to know how to let it down to ordinary chit-chat.

"In a quiet and low tone, with little variety of intonation, without passion, without a jest, without laughter, without one common-place remark, he went on, day after day, either pursuing some one theme, as he often did for days, or, if descending to ordinary topics, always surveying them from the loftiest point of view, and always talking with such mental insight and such profound emotion as penetrated the heart through and through. There was a kind of suppressed feeling about him. . . .

"It was, indeed, altogether a most remarkable thing,— his conversation; and yet I do not know that I would have purchased it at the price he paid for it. He stood alone — I found him embosomed in reverence and affection, and yet living in a singular isolation. No being was ever more simple, unpretending and kindly-natured than he, and yet no such being surely was ever so inaccessible. . . . Even Henry Ware, possessing in so many respects a kindred nature, said,— 'I go to Channing, I listen to him; I go away; that is all.' It was long before I could lounge upon his sofa, as I talked with him, and say what I pleased. . . . Nobody, I imagine, ever said, on entering his study, 'How d'ye do, Channing?' "

With his arresting messianic presence, his single-mindedness, his overwhelming powers of concentration, Channing might have made even John Brown seem pale by comparison, yet such a turn in his life is unimaginable, not because he was physically infirm, not because he was a New England gentleman, but because he genuinely believed that every human soul, if it could but recognize it, was made in the image and likeness of God's universal love. A revolutionary must have a taste for destruction. But Channing's primary taste was for creation. He was convinced that man, in his likeness to God, is created as a creator; that he is formed not merely by his environment, his genes and his past behavior, but *by himself,* in response to ideas that perhaps never have been and are as yet nowhere realized. There is neither physical nor metaphysical necessity about these ideas: human beings have to choose them, thus man is free.

Freedom and creative power are, then, essentially one and the same. Their oneness composes the dignity of human nature, making man a sacred being. Creative dignity and development are the individual's birthright and society's responsibility.

"Bodily or material forces can be measured," Channing said, "but not the forces of the soul; nor can the results of increased mental energy be foretold . . . a community will tread down obstacles now deemed invincible, and turn them into helps. The inward moulds the outward. The power of a people lies in its mind; and this mind, if fortified and enlarged, will bring external things into harmony with itself. *It will create a new world* around it, corresponding to itself."[54] These lines are from Channing's address, "On the Elevation of the Laboring Classes," delivered to the Mechanic Apprentices' Library Association of Boston, and are typical of the soaring fluff of which Channing has been so often accused: a pre-Emerson "eyeball" transcendentalism, high-sounding, but hopelessly aloof from concrete social problems.

But it is always dangerous to take a Channing paragraph out of context. In virtually the next breath, he proposed a realistic, workaday, and for his time, ultraist, way of improving low-income housing: "In this city, how much health, how many lives are sacrificed to the practice of letting cellars and rooms which cannot be ventilated, which want the benefits of light, free air, and pure water, and the means of removing filth! We forbid by law the selling of putrid meat in the market. Why do we not forbid the renting of rooms in which putrid, damp and noisome vapors are working as sure destruction as the worst foods? Did people understand that they are as truly poisoned in such dens as by tainted meat and decaying vegetables, would they not appoint commissioners for houses as truly as commissioners for markets?"[55]

Channing knew that a proposal of this kind would call forth no groundswell of support from his well-housed laymen, who were gracious, kindly, benevolent, public-spirited, and charitable — to a point. But who were also narrow, unimaginative, and capable of considerable hostility toward intemperate new ideas affecting property. For this reason Channing felt moments of gnawing depression, and recurrent waves of feeling that his efforts were ashes. So he told his audience that remedies for slum problems would have to come from slum power: "The laboring people must require that the health of the city shall be a leading object of the municipal administration."

Many of his leading parishioners wearied quickly of this kind of Jacobin agitation, so he shrewdly appealed to their self-conscious feeling that on the whole they were capable of doing pretty well. In a document designed to nudge the Federal Street congregation toward the creation and funding of a social action committee, he softened up the parish's policy makers by reminding them that their personal possession of "ability, piety, good morals and human happiness" laid upon them the privilege of doing what they could for those less blessed. Accordingly, he proposed a multi-faceted program of services to the poor: improvement of educational methods, relief for debtors, investigation of prison conditions, a preventive approach to poverty, an attack on the causes of intemperance and "kindred vices," and a work program for the unemployed.[56] He also stressed that the committee should interest itself in "the education of young men of suitable qualifications for the ministry, especially of any belonging to this society and needing pecuniary aid"; and "support of missionaries in parts of the country destitute of a regular ministry."

The response did not sweep him off his feet. On June 6, 1824, an Association of the Members of the Federal Street Society for Benevolent Purposes was formed, which for a decade supported various charitable ventures, encouraged Sunday schools, missions, and ministries to the poor, and supported students at the Divinity School.[57] Channing was never able to transform his church into a social regenerator. But who has? He was not one to turn down half-loaves, however, so he took what his congregation, in its Franklinian sobriety, offered; sighed, and looked elsewhere for new horizons.

Though there were the same old aches and pains in his body, there was a better tone to his morale. On June 30, 1824, Ezra Stiles Gannett, remarkably mature for his years, was ceremonially installed as associate minister at the Federal Street

Church, with Channing preaching the sermon. Some of his more sensitive parishioners must have wondered a bit at his text: "Behold, I send you forth as sheep in the midst of wolves . . ." (Matthew 10:16). Who were the wolves into whose midst the trusting Gannett was being sent? The sermon was one of Channing's best, building stage by stage toward a peroration on the need for a reform-minded ministry in a corrupt age. The times, he said, were "obviously and grossly defective when measured by the Christian standard."[58]

Squeezed into the crowded congregation was George Ripley of the class behind Gannett's at the Divinity School. His later career as militant minister-reformer, transcendentalist, and principal founder of Brook Farm, was given wings by what he heard. Back in Cambridge, he wrote to his sister: "I would, but I cannot, enable you to form a conception of the infinite simplicity and apostolic meekness, united with the eloquence of an angel and spirituality of a sainted mind which characterize Dr. Channing. His sermon will be printed."[59]

From that moment, and for years to come, Channing was Ripley's practical religionist *par excellence*. Casting aside his family-acquired orthodoxy, he began to speak of himself as a "liberal" and "a child of Channing."[60] Henry Ware, Jr., a more seasoned and less impressionable observer than Ripley, was equally transported by the Gannett ordination sermon. "It is not possible for you to conceive of the excitement produced by Dr. Channing," he wrote. "I have never seen such enthusiasm equalled. To hear such a sermon is one of the memorable things in a man's life. It forms an epoch in his existence."[61]

Channing had been particularly eloquent in describing the soaring potential of the human mind. The times, he felt, were ripe for an "enlightened ministry . . . of imagination and reason." He for one (and he sensed the company of multitudes), wanted no more "dull, unsocial, melancholy" religion. Nor was he willing to wait "the slow pace of the great innovator, time." The new name of the game, he said, was "taking the work of reform" into one's own hands.

It was a brilliant performance, apparently stimulated by his ebullience at being able to turn so many pastoral chores over to so able and conscientious a young colleague. And his conscience was further purged by having officially diverted one quarter of his salary to the care and feeding of Mr. Gannett.

At this time, one part of Channing's mind was churning a great literary project — comprehensive philosophical work on the nature of man. It intrigued and goaded him because of his now solid conviction that moral revolution was utterly dependent upon proper appreciation of the noble attributes of the human soul. He believed that to dream of gutting the world of its corrupting influences, without first quickening men's consciences with religious inspiration, was nonsense. The crucial message was that moral perfectibility was as natural to man as eating and sleeping. It is greatly to Channing's credit that as long as he lived, he subordinated his yearning to write this magnum opus, and turned his attention instead to the tumults of life. When he died, the essay on man was still a pile of rough copy.

That he had an early inkling of this fate is evident in a letter he wrote to an English correspondent, Lant Carpenter, shortly before the Gannett installation. After telling Carpenter of his fond hopes for "a work of some extent," he commented on the frequency with which such "schemes of authorship prove abortive."[62] This one did, but for the last and busiest twenty years of his life, it was like a gray eminence, hovering over his shoulder, driving him to remember what social reform was all about, and to turn every experience inside out to determine what messages for man it really carried.

Virtually everything in the marketplace of daily living was grist for Channing's mill of man. Yet it was by sheer effort of will that he initially involved himself. By temperament, he was distant and aloof, and experienced the turbulent issues of his time as an unavoidable engulfment. Intellectually, he was a loner, a condition symbolized by the fact that the one public place where he felt free and comfortable was the pulpit. The clue to the reversal of Channing's usual course of life — he became more involved, more radical, more outspoken, with each of his last twenty years — is that he was an embodiment of his preachments. He believed that religious faith, properly conceived, built constantly stronger, deeper, wider bonds between man and man, between man and his Creator. So, he grew, he developed, he deepened.

But as faith permitted him riskier entanglements with the contaminations and confusions of political and social issues, his rationalism and self-reliance demanded sufficient detachment to remember that "we are all ignorant and erring."[63] By 1840, he became uninhibited enough to lend the enormous prestige of his presence to the Convention of Friends of Universal Reform in the Chardon Street Chapel, Boston — a gathering that gave most of his fellow patricians' apoplectic fits. This assembly received its lasting historical fame from Emerson's memorable description. It was composed, Emerson wrote, of "madmen, madwomen, men with beards, Dunkers, Muggletonians, Come-outers, Groaners, Agrarians, Seventh-Day Baptists, Quakers, Abolitionists, Calvinists, Unitarians and Philosophers."[64] Yet Channing, as reformer, had no intention of jading any of these with mere acquiescence to their crusades. "Some of us," he said, "stand out of the crowd and see the follies of all."[65]

Because he could not be a zealot, no matter how deeply he felt about a particular issue or event, Channing was forever being lashed by those in the grip of a passion. Knowing that he supported their ends, they gnashed their teeth at his insistence on being his own man as to means. He recognized the "great weaknesses" to which his moral independence exposed him, but what could a man do whose dependence on principles and general truths was as overpowering as his?

If his self-possession roused the bitterness of one-track radicals, his radicalism caused anguish and resentment among those who considered him a traitor to his class and calling. During Elizabeth Peabody's tour of duty as his volunteer amanuensis, she reported to him that one of his parishioners, after a sermon, had exclaimed, "We cannot allow Dr. Channing to say such things." To Channing it meant that he "must have said something worthwhile." He told Miss Peabody that the "sermon may be one worth printing."[66] In time, a portion of his congregation was in torment over him. He was virtually an avatar in their eyes, yet he was forever saying the most outrageous things, as in the preface to the third Glasgow edition of his works, in which, for *foreigners*, he prattled about "our present low state of civilization, the central idea of which is wealth," and then had the effrontery to predict that the time was at hand when the mass of men, "doomed . . . to the degradation of mind and heart in which they are now sunk," would rise "to remodel social institutions and manners."[67]

And he had problems not only with his parishioners, but also with his wife's family, the Gibbses. Prototypes of American nabobery, they squirmed as their celebrated clerical in-law inveighed against those "maddened with . . . boundless wealth," while multitudes writhed in "degradation and misery."[68] In the midst of President Andrew Jackson's war with Nicholas Biddle over the Bank of the United States, when most of Channing's more affluent parishioners were solidly with the astute but anti-democratic Biddle, and hysterically opposed to Jackson's class-conflict politics, Channing sided with the "rabble." His awesome congregant, Senator Daniel Webster, apparently without a twinge of conscience, captained Biddle's forces in the Senate at the same time that he was one of the bank's directors, and its debtor to the sum of many thousands of dollars.[69]

Channing blandly ridiculed Webster's jeremiads about how Jackson was ruining property, undermining law, and enthroning mob action. He asked Webster and the others why their nerves were not shaken by "the actual, present evil, the evil of that worship of property which stifles all the nobler sentiments, and makes man property."[70] Then, he really let himself go. "I have no fear of revolutions," he proclaimed. "We have conservative principles enough at work here. What exists troubles me more than what is to come."

The reaction of the Gibbses and their kind must have been violently critical, and if such was possible, his beloved dead brother Francis would have spun in his coffin. For it was not only among his wife's relatives that his outbursts rankled, but in certain quarters of his own family as well. Channing's crusade to end slavery was so repugnant to his early mentor, Uncle Henry, that he asked Dewey to avoid the subject when the old man was within hearing. "My anti-slavery labours have been very painful to him as well as to some other friends — I never name the subject to him — as I wish in no way to disturb his last days."[71]

Questions of wealth, affluence, and poverty were extremely close to Channing's heart, yet it would cheat his fallible humanness to neglect the moments when he succumbed to his intrinsic, privileged insensitivity to the real meanings of poverty. One of his most dismal pronouncements was made in 1835, in a sermon on "Ministry for the Poor":

"That some of the indigent among us die of scanty food, is undoubtedly true; but vastly more in this community die from eating too much, than from eating too little; vastly more from excess, than from starvation. So as to clothing, many shiver from want of defenses against the cold; but there is vastly more suffering among the rich from absurd and criminal modes of dress . . . than among the poor from deficiency of raiment. Our daughters are oftener brought to the grave by their rich attire, than our beggars by their nakedness. So the poor are often overworked, but they suffer less than many among the rich, who have no work to do, no interesting objects to fill up life, to satisfy the infinite cravings of man for action. . . . How many of our daughters are victims of *ennui*, a misery unknown to the poor, and more intolerable than the weariness of excessive toil."[72]

"Father" John Taylor, a talented Methodist pioneer of slum ministries, once told Elizabeth Peabody, "What a beautiful being Dr. Channing is! If he only had had any education!" When Miss Peabody twittered this news to him as if it was quite the most amusing thing she had heard in months, Channing responded very gravely. Taylor, he said, was right. "What I have needed is an education for my work."[73]

The "education" he could deeply sense he lacked was an understanding of how to make his honest, compassionate conviction of the primacy of moral reform relevant to the obvious necessity for reformed social and political institutions. Personal moral regeneration was *everything* to Channing. There could be no bad government, no virulence among the wealthy, no misery among the poor, when the people, as individuals, became wise, virtuous, and independent. How could the mass be reformed without reforming the individuals who composed it? And yet he could find himself taken in, spouting the Whig political line about the weary and harassed life of the wealthy in contrast to the purer lot of the poor. If one plunged below the surface of such pastoral myths, was not a social background, *a class* consciousness evident? Why shouldn't the poor struggle to change their conditions *as a class*, through political and economic action, and not merely as a collection of individuals striving for greater wisdom, uprightness, self-respect, trust in God and in one another? Channing was whiplashed continually by the seemingly irreconcilable conflict between the logic of internal reform and the logic of institutional reform.

Could the two somehow be synthesized? The career of Orestes Brownson seemed to say no. This rugged, brimming young man first took up Channing's reformist appeal to man's soul as a holy grail; then, more in sorrow than in anger, completely repudiated his mentor's thesis. As the panic of 1837 deepened into a nightmare of unemployment and near starvation, Brownson defected. The country's distorted and floundering financial system was patently too complicated for mere preachments of personal morality. With the terrible realities of human misery all about him, Brownson found his moral theories crumbling. He hurried to Channing to tell him that he was staggered by the hatred of the rich he found surging among his working-class congregation. But Channing passed it off as evidence of Brownson's inability to communicate properly with the poor.[74] Brownson responded by demonstrating that he could communicate his recantation of inner reform with considerable brilliance. He hacked at the roots of Channing's central theme: "This position is not tenable," he insisted. "If it were, it would be fatal to all progress, and be most heartily pleasing to all tyrants. The plain English of it is, perfect the individual before you undertake to perfect society; make your men perfect, before you seek to make your institution perfect. This is plausible, but we dislike it, because it makes perfection of institutions the end, and that of individuals merely the means. Perfect all your men, and no doubt, you could then perfect easily and safely your institutions. But when all your men are perfect, what need of perfecting your institutions? And wherein are those institutions, under which all individuals may attain to the full perfection admitted by human nature, imperfect?"[75]

At this point, Brownson believed himself to have turned from the impracticality of inner reform to the practicality of institutional reform. After several disillusioning years as a political activist, he took another swing, not back to Channing, but away from social reform altogether and into the arms of the Roman Catholic church. Channing did not swing. He endured the ambiguity of the contradictory claims of systems and individuals, and stuck to his guns that for him the human soul had to be the ultimate arbiter. On occasion he fell victim, as every man must, to the dominant myths of his own social class. This was certainly the case when he tried to portray the lot of comfortable lawyers and merchants as harsher than that of poor laborers.

But there is no conceivable way to write Channing off as a do-gooding salver of upper-class consciences. He was frequently inept, even naive, about grasping the intensifying complexities of political and economic struggle in America's headlong development, but his integrity as a prophet prevailed. His job was to look beneath the agitation, the convulsions, the bitter struggles, to discern the deeper foundations of an order in which the individual became more and more rather than less and less. For this reason he could pretend no love affair with panaceas for the masses. Neither would he deny, as his Whig friends did, that there was abundant cause for the savage political turmoil in American life.

"We must suffer and we ought to suffer," he cried out. "Society ought to be troubled, to be shaken, yea, convulsed, until its solemn debt to the poor . . . is paid."[76] Then he proceeded to do what he could, which was precious little, as he was the first to admit. Yet in retrospect it was nothing less than the engraving upon the American ethos of a permanent characteristic, namely that people open their eyes to discover great abuses, then do something about them.

The scope of Channing's awareness of these social abuses was phenomenal. With Tuckerman, he pushed hard for a new "humanitarianism" in welfare services to the poor, one that would attack the roots of poverty rather than satisfy itself with charity. The result was the birth in America of a social work profession. With Tuckerman, Dorothea Dix, and others, he set the forces in motion that finally persuaded public opinion to create hospitals for the mentally ill. With Bronson Alcott, Elizabeth Peabody, and Horace Mann, he beat the drums for new, progressive approaches to education, teaching methods, and school administration, paving the way for America's historically unparalleled educational revolution.

One of his lifelong interests, alcohol addiction, illustrated the degree to which he could divest himself of the moralizing typical of most religionists of his time. He saw in alcoholism not the evidence of sinful beings, but that of escape from various intolerable pressures generated by American life. Among the poor, he concluded, subsistence involved "a degree of labor exhausting to the spirits and injurious to health. Of consequence, relief is sought in stimulants."[77] In white-collar circles, as he figured it out, the rat race of "getting ahead," coupled with the inevitability of at least partially dashed hopes for most, drove many to find balm for their psychic wounds in liquor bottles: "Just as far as wealth is the object of worship, the measure of men's importance, the badge of distinction, so far there will be a tendency to self-contempt and self-abandonment among those whose lot gives them no chance of its acquisition."[78]

As superficial as this social psychology of alcoholism now sounds, it had the ring of revelation from another planet in Channing's time. His prescriptions for attacking the problem were, in his own view, eminently practical, though to many of his contemporaries they were laughably visionary. He began, as he always began, with the need for effort on everyone's part to cultivate greater moral strength. Then he turned to the recreationally impoverished lives of the laboring class. Other than drinking, brawling, and sex, what fun was available to them? Virtually none. Yet they were as capable as any of enjoying music, dancing, evenings of recitation, and libraries. So why shouldn't these be provided? Channing's prudishness surfaced when it came to theatre for the underprivileged — too bawdy, he felt. He rounded out his proposals with a plea for more responsible attention to the overall health needs of low-income groups.

Having lighted the way to healthy diversions and healthy bodies for the laboring classes, Channing turned to the need for cutting back the jungle growth of liquor distributors and retail outlets. He stopped short of advocating forced prohibition, which he was certain public opinion would not sustain (also he detested moral coercion), but it seemed obvious to him that with fewer stalls for the sale of intoxicants there would be less intoxication. Since it was men of substance who controlled the liquor traffic, they must be pressed to examine their consciences about the "great public evil" in which they were engaged. Moreover, the upper classes in general should set an example by banishing ardent spirits from their homes and tables.

Channing made few converts. His approach was shrugged off by the affluent, and repudiated by the more fanatical anti-liquor crusaders, setting the stage for America's long, acidulous prohibition controversy.

No claim can be made for Channing as an originator of concern for child labor, but he was one of the first Bostonians of stature to put his shoulder behind efforts to regulate the practice by legislation. It galled him to hear some of the men he knew and liked pontificate about leaving the conditions of child labor to the tender mercies of mill management rather than to bleeding hearts. His specific legislative proposals now sound bewilderingly mild — schoolrooms and teachers within factories, certain hours each week set aside for instruction, a five-day week for working children so that they might have Saturday for "relaxation," and not "be obliged to give up the Lord's day to amusement."[79]

Addressing himself to a committee of the Massachusetts legislature, he tried to persuade them that they would actually be doing a service to millowners by providing the factories with young workers whose characters had been improved by education.

Another of Channing's reformist concerns was stimulated by a letter and publication he received in 1825 from the English historian and reformer, William Roscoe, summarizing his conclusions on penal jurisprudence. "Beneficence, and not revenge, should be the motive of all criminal proceedings," Roscoe wrote, adding that "prisons . . . must be either places of vindictive . . . punishment, or places of instruction, industry, and reform."[80] In one of his frequent letters to Roscoe's daughter, Jane, Channing said that though he "inclined" to her father's views, he did not yet hold them with sufficient conviction to act upon them were he a legislator. But he made it his business to look further into the matter, even paying a lengthy visit to the experimental penitentiary in Philadelphia. He wrote Tuckerman that he was generally impressed. The harshest disciplinary punishment was the occasional withholding of a meal.

He was horrified, however, by the religious tracts furnished to the prisoners. "Truly," he wrote, "this plague of Calvinism, like the vermin inflicted on Egypt, finds its way everywhere."[81] He said that he had been toying with the idea of recommending to prison officials that each convict be assigned two full-time "intelligent and religious" counselors, the object being a concentrated effort at rehabilitation. But he was shaky about the idea, he told Tuckerman, when he considered that the counselors might be bearers of the Calvinist plague.

Channing worked closely with Tuckerman on new approaches to juvenile delinquency, lending his support to the establishment of the Thompson's Island Farm School in 1832, for boys seven to fourteen years old, many of whom were already addicted to alcohol. Bulfinch volunteered to design the main building. Channing rounded up financial backers, and gave businesslike advice about program and administration. Don't be satisfied with an "ordinary" superintendent, he wrote Tuckerman. And above all, don't let salary stand in the way of getting the man needed. "Make changes," he added, "till you find a man who can understand the young and reach their spiritual nature."[82]

At the same time, Channing decided to extend the aura of his influence in another direction. He was asked to draft a statement calling for repeal of the statutes under which debtors could be imprisoned. He accepted the assignment and penned a blunt message. It is no crime, he wrote, for a man to find himself in threadbare circumstances. Indeed, such a man deserved sympathy not punishment: "To imprison the prosperous man would be less an outrage on humanity and moral principles, because the prosperous has no claim on relief and can be imprisoned without depriving him and his family of the means of support, as is the case with the unfortunate debtor — I hold it then to be a plain duty to repeal the present law of imprisonment for debt."[83]

There is considerable significance in Channing's espousal of this cause. Abolition of imprisonment for debt was a primary plank in the platform of the Workingmen's movement, the closest thing America had in the 1820's and 1830's to a radical political force. The new industrial order created a new class of manual laborers who felt increasingly deprived of self-respect and status, to say nothing of the wherewithal to provide a decent living standard. Too many of those who benefited from the new order adopted views, infuriating to workingmen, that industrial poverty and degradation were either inevitable or nonexistent. Sometimes they said the one, sometimes the other, depending on circumstances.

In 1830, five out of every six prisoners in the jails of New England and the middle states were debtors, most of them owing less than twenty dollars.[84] Thus the law, for all practical purposes, was a class law. The "have-nots" detested it. But sturdy opposition to repeal came from the "haves," who somehow convinced themselves that repeal would undermine the sanctity of contracts and the safety of property. One of Channing's friends, John Quincy Adams, typified the irritable upper-class reaction to pleas of the type Channing had written. In 1831 he wrote, "I shall surely get no thanks . . . for pointing to the consequences . . . upon the security of property and upon fidelity to contracts, as well as upon credit."[85]

By identifying himself with a prop of labor agitation, Channing spelled out clearly where his central sympathies lay. Many of his intimates misunderstood. No matter. He knew that they were wrong, and would come in time to realize it. The only right relationship between men and the law was one in which the arbitrary exercise of power was reduced to its lowest possible limit. To imprison a struggling workingman for debt, at a time when food prices were doubling and a surplus of labor kept wages low and unemployment high, was a peculiarly cruel exercise of degrading power, he thought. It had to go, and it did.

Another opportunity to maneuver in the painful realm of being ahead of one's time was given Channing by Abner Kneeland, a colorful and cantankerous Universalist clergyman, who in 1829 asked to be defrocked, and announced to the world, via the press, that he had embraced atheism. Kneeland rented the Federal Street Theatre, close by Channing's church, and gathered unto himself a congregation of far-out freethinkers. He also started an enterprising and unconventional paper called the *Investigator*. His pulpit antics provided an astonishing contrast to his illustrious neighbor down the street. According to an eyewitness: "Mr. Kneeland would read portions of the Old Testament not designed for public-reading in a non-Jewish assembly; he would dramatically cast the Bible across the hall as a book not fit to be kept in decent company."[86]

Kneeland, who held the New Testament in equally low regard, quickly became the object of outraged demands all over Boston that the authorities "do something." Early in 1834, on the basis of his polemics in the *Investigator*, they did. A Suffolk County grand jury indicted him on three charges of blasphemy and obscenity: (1) he had quoted a scurrilous passage by Voltaire disparaging the virgin birth of Jesus; (2) he had published an article ridiculing prayer; and (3) he had proclaimed in a public letter to the editor of the *Trumpet*: "Universalists believe in a God, which I do not, but believe that their God, with all his moral attributes (aside from nature itself) is nothing more than a chimera of their own imagination."[87]

The case inched its way through the courts for four years. James Austin, the prosecuting attorney — a Unitarian, and a member of Channing's congregation — was determined to put the atheist behind bars. Kneeland was convicted and sentenced to three months' imprisonment.

Hosea Ballou, although one of Kneeland's oldest friends, was disgusted with his noisy crusade, and was not able to follow to its ultimate applications the church-state separationism he had earlier recommended to Channing during the constitutional convention. Instead, he felt that Austin, far from persecuting

Kneeland for his religious beliefs, had "ably vindicated the rights of conscience, the rational liberty of the press, and has in no instance overleaped the bounds of his duty." Kneeland promptly appealed his case to the Supreme Court of Massachusetts, where the charges against him were boiled down to willful denial of the existence of God (a violation of existing Massachusetts law), and his conviction on this count sustained. Finally, in June 1838, Kneeland was sentenced again, this time to a reduced term of sixty days.[88]

Ellis Gray Loring, who was frequently allied with Channing in good causes, felt that genuine free speech issues were involved. He wrote a rough draft of a petition for executive clemency and took it to Channing for support. Channing was at first cautious, for he abhorred Kneeland's views and he knew what a scandal the petition would brew. But he listened carefully to Loring, consulted others, then decided to let his name lead the list of one hundred and sixty-nine signers of the petition, which he pored over and revised extensively. A storm of abuse came, just as he expected, and the governor rejected the petition. Kneeland had to serve his sentence and Channing increased the number of his former admirers, but there was never likely to be another prosecution for atheism in Massachusetts.[89]

Channing was deeply chagrined by the jailing of Kneeland, but unruffled by the abuse directed at him. "In these cases," he told Tuckerman, "I feel that no man can harm me, but by impairing my love to him, by inspiring bad feelings. It is a comfort to me to find that I can be reproached without any desire to reproach. . . . As to human favor, I feel more and more that it must be given up. If I know Christianity, it is so at war with the present condition of society, that it cannot be spoken and acted out without giving great offense."[90]

During the early stages of the Kneeland affair, anti-Catholic bigotry, fed by the economic and emotional distresses of non-Catholic workingmen and fanned by segments of the evangelical Protestant clergy, produced a nasty incident, just short of a major catastrophe. Charlestown, known as an anti-Catholic stronghold and noted for its brawls between native-born Americans and immigrant Irish Americans, was the site of an Ursuline convent and school. During the long, hot summer of 1834, while Channing was sniffing the mild ocean breezes of Oakland, false rumors about a dissident nun being held in captivity in the convent swept through Charlestown and out across the surrounding area. Before cooler heads could convincingly spike the rumor, a mob gathered, lubricated themselves generously with alcohol, then set fire to the convent. The sleeping nuns and their pupils (some of them daughters of prominent citizens of the Boston area) barely escaped with their lives.

Three days later, a public meeting of sympathy with the Roman Catholic archdiocese was organized (with Unitarians in the forefront) and held in Faneuil Hall. That night an anti-Catholic mob paraded through the streets of Boston, threatening to burn the cathedral. It was dispersed by a strong show of force by armory guards.

Since the orthodox railers against Catholicism were equally incendiary in their attacks on Unitarians, it could be said that Unitarians had a special reason for alarm. But Catholic Bishop Fenwick, Cheverus's successor, did not see it that way. Knowing Channing and Tuckerman well as fellow servants of the poor, he was satisfied with the genuineness of their freedom from vulgar anti-Catholic bias, and of their equally genuine opposition to bigotry and persecution. Describing the anti-Catholic bitterness of Protestant sects in a letter to French friends, Fenwick wrote, "I must say that it is not the same with the Unitarians, and that on all occasions they show themselves favorable to the Catholics."[91]

Nestled in his Oakland retreat, Channing put in quite a summer of mental activity. Political and social agitation in England, following the Reform Bill of 1832, fastened him to his desk, where he pored over letters from his English correspondents and fired off answers. In addition, Jonathan Phillips was in England, and reporting on its tremors. "England must continue to be agitated," Channing wrote back. "Society will have no peace until reorganized by a higher spirit — nor ought to desire it."[92] But two days later, he was writing of his shock at a form of agitation he most devoutly did not wish. Proslavery mobs rioted in New York, attacking blacks and abolitionists with fierce impartiality. Channing was not surprised that such mob action could occur. "We know that materials for such explosions exist in all large cities," he said.[93] He was appalled, however, that "there was a toleration of the mob by the *respectable* part of the community," that the trials of the rioters were a "farce," and that he had not seen a single expression of "indignation" in the press. Then came the burning of the Ursuline convent.

Channing, characteristically, did not dash back to Boston. He let his thoughts sort themselves out and fall into place while the maples and elms of Oakland reddened. Early in October, he rose before his congregation and spoke his mind. With Europe in the throes of great social change and turmoil, it was more important to him than ever that America demonstrate the ability of free institutions to absorb stress, learn from failure, and vindicate the progressive hopes of mankind.[94]

He would not dignify the Charlestown mob, he said, by numbering himself among those who were moaning that society was "shaken to its foundations, all its joints loosened, all its fixtures about to be swept away." A mob, he went on, is horrible and detestable, and must be guarded against "efficiently," but no mob "springing from blind prejudices or passions" can tear down a society basically devoted to justice, sympathy with the oppressed, and zeal for the cause of human nature.

He expressed pride in the widespread "just and honorable" response to the Charlestown outrage, but noted that there were lugubrious exceptions right in their own midst — those who reconciled themselves with the notion that "Popery" after all was a provocative and irritating speck in Boston's eye. Channing classed this as earning spiritual parity with the mob itself.

To certify that his was not a holier-than-thou attitude, he spoke frankly of his own impatience with the "insolent and intolerant" infallibility doctrine of the Catholic church. But it was utterly indefensible, he continued, for presumed believers in religious freedom to rationalize the weapons of persecution and inquisition which Rome itself was in the process of "throwing down." In a barbed reference to the evangelical clerical col-

213

leagues whose fulminations had helped to soak the Charlestown torches, he said: "Nothing is so terrible as persecution. Human nature has never shown itself more fiendish than when it has cloaked its bad passions under the garb of religion, and let them loose. . . . Religion was given to bind together, refine, soften human hearts. Its great ministry is that of love."

Then Channing sounded again one of his great themes for the ingroup, his own prosperous "crowd." They wanted stronger laws for the prevention and control of street violence. "Let us have these laws," he said, but let no one believe that legislation alone will do the job: "Our mobs, though they have spoken in confused and discordant yells, have uttered one truth plainly; and this truth is that there exists among us — what ought to exist in no Christian country — a mass of gross ignorance and vice. They teach one plain lesson to the religious, virtuous, philanthropic, educated, refined and opulent; and that is, that these have a great work to do, the work of enlightening and lifting up a large portion of their fellow-creatures and their neighbors; that they have no right to spend their lives in accumulating wealth or in selfish indulgences, but that they are to labor, to expend time, thought, wealth, as their circumstances may permit, for the intellectual, moral, spiritual life of a multitude around them."

This was paternalism, and it was Channing's way of getting through to the Proper Bostonians he knew so well. By temperament, by background, by consciousness of the personal fortune brought him by his wife, he was one of them. But he had going for him a perception most of them lacked. He considered it his business to encourage the economically and culturally deprived to get solidly behind their own cause, to move in their own behalf, not to accept the status quo while waiting for the outstretched, charitable hands of the well-to-do. By appealing to the tainted philanthropy of his peers, he hoped to push what could be accepted and understood by the laboring classes as a *response*.

Channing did not pretend to be a sophisticate about the new economic and social forces that were creating unprecedented affluence and wretchedness in America. His voluminous correspondence shows few attempts to master the tough facts, figures, and conflicting theories behind the critical banking and monetary issues of his time. Occasionally, in personal letters, he would unburden himself of vacuous political comments, as in 1834, when he confided to Lucy Aikin that "the warfare of our headstrong, arbitrary President with our National Bank has turned our prosperity into commercial distress. . . . It is hoped that the usurpation of the President will be put down, and that he will be the means or occasion of introducing improvements into the Banking system, which, without a check, might have produced wide mischief."[95]

These words, if circulated, would have produced despair among Jackson's supporters and detractors alike. For his purposes as moralist-reformer, the glaring evils of a commercial society were enough, whether he completely understood them or not, and whether or not he could fully transcend his own class heritage. So he appealed to both the poor and the wealthy to do separately and together whatever was required to assure that all men learned and lived their basic equality and worth.

At times he floundered in his own contradictions. After years of touting the virtues of education, he awoke one morning feeling glum about the economic depression and scribbled a letter to William Rathbone blaming it all on "the spread of education."[96] Armed with a little learning, too many men, he said, decided to live by their wits rather than by their hands. They were rushing into trade, deluded with the notion that they "might grow rich with little toil."

It was the more plausible Channing who expressed himself in "Self-Culture" as angered by the charge, popular in high social circles, that schooling spoiled a good laborer by giving him ideas too big for his britches: "I reply, that a social order, demanding the sacrifices of the mind, is very suspicious, that it cannot be sanctioned by the Creator. Were I, on visiting a strange country, to see a vast majority of the people maimed, crippled, and bereft of sight, and were I told that social order required this mutilation, I should say, Perish this order."[97]

A man is to be educated, Channing said, "because he is a man," not because he is to make shoes, or run a business, or practice medicine. "It is the man who determines the dignity of the occupation, not the occupation which measures the dignity of the man."

One of his constant themes was a firm belief in the virtues of physical work. He had no wish, through reform, to relieve man of the necessity of it. Much as he admired Alcott the teacher, he admired Alcott behind the plow even more. Brook Farm appealed to him primarily because of its earthiness, the very aspect of the experiment that Hawthorne detested. Whether he glorified physical labor because he was able to do so little of it, or because he shared Jefferson's taste for hard-working agrarian yeomen, or because of the Calvinist ideals drummed into him in childhood, or because he had reasoned out a central place for physical exertion in the "elevation of the soul," it is impossible to say. What must be said is that Channing held hard, useful work in very high regard, and he refused to view education as a means of escaping it.

Conversely, Channing held in contempt the classical economic theory of his time — that of Smith, Ricardo, and Malthus — which insisted that in a free market, wages for laborers must be pegged at a subsistence level. Although it meant flying in the face of what others with wealth conceived to be their self-interest, Channing bluntly questioned the motives of those who claimed that the economic laws decreeing poverty were writ in the nature of things. These statements, he said, come "generally from men who abound, and are at ease; who think more of property than any other human interest; who have little concern for the mass of their fellow-creatures; who are willing that others should bear all the burdens of life, and that any social order should continue which secures to themselves personal comfort or gratification."[98]

The unvarnished truth, Channing went on, is that "no community has seriously set itself to the work of improving all its members, so that what is possible remains to be ascertained. No experiment has been made, to determine how far liberal provision can be made at once for the body and mind of the laborer. The highest social art is yet in its infancy. Great minds have nowhere solemnly, earnestly undertaken to resolve the problem, how the multitude of men may be elevated. The trial is to come."[99]

As a social reformer, Channing was perpetually in the toils of an inward trial. Strains of suspicion, prudence, and stoicism were deeply ingrained in his Newport-bred being. He lived amidst the embellishments and comforts of dowered wealth, half apologetically, half soothingly, with strong emotional ties to that segment of America which was inhospitable, to say the least, to radical ideas. Yet he was driven by a religious faith that insisted on *doing* something about injustice, about poverty, about everything that walled human beings off from their full fruition and development. He enjoyed enormous prestige, and he knew it, yet he was inhibited by the souring notion that it was more because of his clerical robes than because of his personal worth or wisdom.

Moreover, he was blessed and cursed with the kind of mind that could not lose itself in "causes"; a mind that was forever reminding that the people of this or that cause were, after all, people, just that, *people;* which meant that they were mixtures of big and little, good and bad, high and low. It would have been so much easier and clearer to stop thinking about people as individuals, to lump them all into one, into the cause, whatever it happened to be. But that he could not do.

What made it worse was that Channing's full emergence as a social reformer occurred precisely as Boston, and all other American centers of population, were transforming themselves into cities. It was in 1822 that Boston became, by corporate charter, a *city,* no longer a copy of an English town. It was not a change to be easily embraced by Channing, whose orientation was formed by the sense of citizen involvement, and the consensus of values that made a town meeting workable. Population growth, industrialization, immigration, economic class consciousness — these and other forces were blasting the old sanctions, creating disorder and disruption, and generally raising hell with the tight world of Channing's formative years. It was a time when multiple causes were inevitable, and because, above all, he had need to be a relevant man, he had need also to wrench himself into a posture of relevancy, to be a new kind of moral missionary to a new America. He could not only sympathize with the needed causes, but foretell and articulate them. Then came torment.

On the one hand, he saw that the forces loose in an expanding America drove people into contending parties, classes, associations, and movements, with unique interests and special needs. He was able to accept this, and to feel quite comfortable about using the terminology of "the commercial class," "the laboring class," "the rich," "the poor," and so on, when it was the fiction of affluent conservatives to treat all such distinctions as un-American. On the other hand, he was mortally fearful that whenever a good cause was organized, the organizers quickly became an oligarchy — the politicians and pros who ran things, while individuality in the ranks was progressively squeezed of its juice. He had a horrifying vision, for example, in acting as the "rouser" for Tuckerman's pioneering work among the poor, that a welfare bureaucracy could arise, so intense and dedicated in its bureaucratic practices that the poor would find themselves locked into a permanent caste status.[100] The radical scrutiny of America's bureaucracy-ridden welfare practices in the 1960's would not have surprised him.

If there was one central theme in his inner conflicts over causes, it was the necessity he recognized that individuals must be liberated so that they might determine their own lives. He could see all kinds of abstract good in abstract causes, but how could a cause, in the end, restore the individual's mastery and power over life and social enterprise? Surely not, as organized causes seemed inevitably to demand, by the individual surrendering his personal judgment to partisan policy. He was very clear about this, as he wrote in a letter to Charles Follen in 1834: "There is no need of what is called unanimity in . . . any . . . cause. Men are perpetually sacrificing their intellectual and moral independence to this idol."[101]

A misunderstanding of the nature of his concern led by a process of attrition to the crushing indictment of Arthur Schlesinger, Jr., published in 1945, that Channing's work "in sabotaging the liberal impulses of his day . . . has never been properly appreciated."[102] Schlesinger has since recanted to me personally. Channing did not sabotage, but neither would he offer up his intellectual and moral independence to a cause, whatever its credentials. This is not to say that he was a better man, or a worse one, for it. It was the way he was. He lived in a tension between a society that violated the free development of the human spirit, and reform *movements,* whose aims he shared, but whose means were often too fractional and too inflexible to make room for the very individuality they were supposed to allow.

But the one thing Channing could not do was to become a social dropout. He could give pioneer voice to a cause, he could support a cause, but he could become a homogenized part of no cause; he believed that a society, to be truly free, must be nourished by sufficient numbers of cause-conscious, inwardly reborn, outwardly independent men and women. His faith demanded a morally grounded participatory democracy; he preached that individual human judgments, when given the requisite chance, education, and inspiration, could be trusted to enter the crucible of social policy without first being hammered into monolithic shape by movements. He felt that everyone's vision, and particularly that of the dogmatically cause-minded, was necessarily partial. Democracy *had* to be a way of keeping partial visions open and flowing, even while it did away with injustice.

Channing was not blind, as has been claimed, to the effectiveness of regimented political action. On the contrary, he was well aware of its muscle and respected it, but he was certain that the results could never be what the sponsors predicted, because the powers of individuals in the process were weakened by too much dependence on group action. In his "Remarks on Associations" (1829), he reviewed his position with lavish thoroughness.[103] Men have learned, he said, that wonders can be accomplished "by the action of joint forces." As a result, an all-encompassing rationale arises to celebrate group action as the great and exclusive spring of improvement. The principle was so well established that no one dared lift a finger any more without first associating himself with a movement: "Would men spread one set of opinions or crush another? They make a society. Would they improve the penal code, or relieve poor debtors? They make societies. Would they encourage agriculture, or manufactures, or science? They make societies. Would one class encourage horse-racing, and another discourage travelling on Sunday? They form societies. We have immense institutions spreading over the country, combining hosts for particular objects. We have minute ramifications of these societies penetrating everywhere except through the poor-house."

He was bothered, he said, by where it would end. What would become of "individual action," "inward energy," "self-determination"? These, he felt, were the ultimate determinants of virtue, however virtuous great movements might be in their aims. He could foresee a time when the growing impersonality of a society, managed by combinations of power, would leave the individual feeling so small, so alienated, that he would forget what it meant to exercise "the sacred right of private judgment" and become a "passive, powerless recipient of whatever forms or impressions it may be thought fit to give him."

Now that virtually all of the reforms envisioned by the great movements of the nineteenth century have been entombed in the nation's public and private bureaucracies, Channing's disquiets seem remarkably prescient. Edgell's judgment is a reasonable one: "Much can be forgiven in a man who could see so clearly into the future, who was not taken in by the catchwords of reform, and who yet preserved faith in the possibilities of all men."[104]

What makes Channing's faith in the possibilities of all men considerably more impressive than it otherwise might be is how little it smacked of bemused-old-codger optimism. Between the need for muscular group action and the dangers of it, he toyed for a time with the utopianism of some of the transcendentalists — small, fraternal communities of choice specimens of humanity. He gave pats on the back to George Ripley's Brook Farm and to Adin Ballou's Hopedale Community in Milford, Massachusetts. But in the end, when Ballou tried to pin him down to signing the charter, Channing could not resist a realistic assessment of even the choicest collection of mortals. Ballou would find, he predicted, that his most formidable pitfall would be "the difficulty of reconciling so many wills . . . of preventing the interference, intermeddling, harsh-judging, evil-speaking, self-will, jealousies, exactions, and love of sway which scatter discord and woe through all our social relations."[105] When Channing spoke in this fashion, it was not an exercise of finger-pointing, for he was conscious of the bile of "harsh-judging" and "evil-speaking" that coursed so often through his own system. He knew what a jumble of opposites his own psyche contained; at one moment, pressing him to speak out against a mob howling for Catholic blood; at another, prompting him to write to Lucy Aikin in the meanest vein about foreign immigrants, especially the Irish — "ignorant hordes," he called them, who "cannot but abuse" the rights of citizenship granted them "on too easy terms."[106]

It was this kind of self-knowledge, a ruthlessly honest exposure of his whole mind, in all of its contradictory thrusts, that made his faith in human potential tough and potent. In his essay on Fénelon, he described why: "Nothing reveals to us the secrets of our own souls like religion; and in disclosing to us, in ourselves, the tendency of passion to absorb every energy, and to spread its hues over every thought, it gives us a key to all souls; for, in all, human nature is essentially one. . . . A man imbued with this spirit, alone contemplates vice as it really exists, and as it ought always to be described. In the most depraved fellow-beings he sees partakers of his own nature. Amidst the terrible ravages of the passions, he sees conscience, though prostrate, not destroyed, nor wholly powerless. He sees the proofs of an unextinguished moral life in inward struggles, in occasional relentings, in sighings for lost innocence. . . . We conclude with expressing our strong conviction that the human mind will become more various, piercing and all-comprehending, more capable of understanding and expressing the solemn and the sportive, the terrible and the beautiful, the profound and the tender, in proportion as it shall be illumined and penetrated by the true knowledge of God."[107]

Channing the reformer was, from beginning to end, Channing the religionist. Every problem in society finally reduced itself to how the human mind might more clearly come to be "illumined and penetrated by the true knowledge of God," which to him was synonymous with true knowledge of self, therefore true knowledge of all mankind. He saw this as the work of ages, not days. But each day presented its specific agenda of walls, barriers, evils, and injustices about which the religious man did something. Every man should know union and sympathy with every other man. But if affluence fosters arrogance in the house of Have, and poverty breeds self-contempt in the house of Want, how can this be? The walls must come down. If they do not, he warned, in a burst of prophetic insight, large cities become hostile camps of those who have made it and want to keep things as they are, and those who, having been locked into ghettos of poverty, seethe with fury and frustration — "two nations," he said, "understanding as little of one another, having as little intercourse, as if they lived in different lands."[108]

Channing believed that the walls could come down. He believed, as he said in 1835, on the first anniversary of the Benevolent Fraternity of Churches ministry to the poor, in "a series of operations for banishing from society" its poverty and injustice, and "for changing the face of the civilized and Christian world."[109] As the class lines grew tighter, some of his Beacon Hill neighbors, calling him a Locofoco — the emotional equivalent of "Commie" today — understood only too well what he was about.[110]

VI

"He Came Out into the Storm"[1]

CHANNING DECREED that the great right of a man is to use, improve, and expand his powers for his own and others' good.[2] The dictum was never better illustrated than in the contrast between his first and last public pronouncements on slavery. He had earlier mentioned slavery from the pulpit, but it was just that — fleeting citations in a wash of words flung over other themes. Then in June 1831, after six months of health cure amidst the slave economy of the island of St. Croix, he returned to his pulpit and used slavery as an undiluted topic. It was a "first" for him, and for his congregation. There were many present who hoped it would be the last; there were others — readers of Garrison's slashing, persecuted six-months-old *Liberator* — who nursed hopes that Boston's master spirit was about to cast himself headlong into the most venomous controversy of the century.

Both groups were wrong. Channing's maiden assault on slavery was labored and wooden.[3] His heart was in it, but his stylistic powers were not. His conviction of the "magnitude" of the evil grew "stronger and more painful," he told his congregation, yet he could not find the "power of conception" to express what he felt. As for the basic principles involved, he was not at a loss; as might be expected, they were "chiefly moral": "As far as the human soul can be destroyed, slavery is that destroyer. It is a direct war with the high powers and principles of our nature, and sinks man as far as possible into the brute. The slave is regarded as property, treated as property, considered as having no rights, subjected to another's arbitrary will, and thus loses all consciousness of what he is and what he should be. . . . That, under such an education, the sense of justice should be extinguished,— that they whose rights are every moment violated should not be alive to the rights of others,— that slaves should make lying and cheating their vocation, and should congratulate themselves on every opportunity of robbing the tyrant by whom they are robbed,— all this is a thing of course . . ."

Uncharacteristically numb of tongue, he described his remarks as having been "thrown out" to an audience with "little perception of the infinite evil of slavery," but from which "great results" might be produced, if only the right sentiments were given "clear, decided expression." Obviously, he was not yet uninhibited enough to be the supplier of such vibrant articulation, nor was he prepared to pronounce the name of the contumelious Garrison as the one the Lord had sent to preach the release of those in chains.

Eleven years later, in 1842, with death precisely two months away, but with his powers for his own and others' good singularly improved and expanded, Channing soared to his final antislavery peroration before a small, hastily assembled audience in the Berkshire town of Lenox, Massachusetts.[4] As he said, he had no business inflicting himself on his listeners, for in addition to his embarrassing frailness, he stood before them "unasked, uninvited." He knew, of course, that his Berkshire following viewed him as "the second coming" embodied, but the truth of the matter was that he could not permit the fourth anniversary of emancipation in the British West Indies to pass unmarked: ". . . Finding that no other voice would be raised, I was impelled to lift up my own."

"Were I asked," he said, "what strikes me as the greatest evil inflicted by this system, I should say it is the outrage offered by slavery to human nature. Slavery does all that lies in human power to unmake men, to rob them of their humanity. . . . Here is the master evil. Declare a man a chattel, something which you may own and may turn to your use, as a horse or a tool; strip him of all right over himself, of all right to use his own powers . . . and you cease to look on him as a man. You may call him such; but he is not to you a brother, a fellow-being, a partaker of your nature and your equal in the sight of

God. You view him, you speak to him, as infinitely beneath you, as belonging to another race. You have a tone and a look towards him which you never use towards a man."

Everything he said about the psychology of slavery applied to the white supremacist Northerner vis-à-vis blacks, and Channing knew it. Those of the free states, he said, "try to escape the reproach which falls on America by saying that this institution is not ours, that the foot of the slave never pressed our soil; but we cannot fly from the shame or guilt of the institution as long as we give it support."

Summarizing how it had always been with him, he wanted it known that his call for emancipation in the United States, as deliberate and as complete as in the West Indies, was representative of no feelings but his own. "I am giving you, not the ebullitions of new, vehement feelings, but the results of long and patient reflections; not the thoughts of others, but my own independent judgments. I stand alone; I speak in the name of no party. I have no connection but that of friendship and respect, with the opposers of slavery in this country and abroad. Do not mix me up with other men, good or bad; but listen to me as a separate witness, standing on my own ground."

In 1831, Channing could bring himself no closer to a discussion of emancipation than to predict its coming to the West Indies as a result of "the public feeling in England." By 1842, in Lenox, he gave emancipation top priority on the domestic agenda of the United States. Force, he said, must be avoided in the subversion of slavery, but the time had come for the free states to inform the South, in unmistakable terms, that constitutional support for the "deformity" must go, and that the free states would no longer act "as the slave holder's police": "For this end memorials should be poured in upon Congress to obtain from that body such modifications of the laws, and such propositions to amend the Constitution, as will set us free from the obligation to sanction slavery."

Once these goals were gained, Channing favored turning from political action to the creation of a moral atmosphere in which emancipation would become inevitable. Without support in the North, he felt, slavery could not stand; so it was crucially important to sell the feasibility of emancipation. "There are some people here," he observed, "more kind than wise, who are unwilling that any action or sensibility on the subject of slavery should spring up at the North from their apprehensions of the danger of emancipation. The danger of emancipation! this parrot-phrase, caught from the South, is thought by many a sufficient answer to all the pleas that can be urged in favor of the slave. But the lesson of the day is, the safety of emancipation. The West Indian Islands teach us this lesson with a thousand tongues."

Channing's eleven-year journey as an antislavery crusader really began, he told his Lenox friends, when as a boy of twelve he heard the venerable Rev. Dr. Hopkins bear "open and strong testimony against the slave-trade — a principal branch of the traffic" of Newport. But the impression was necessarily filtered through the ambiguous pattern of black-white relationships in his boyhood Rhode Island, a slaveholding state, and the slave market of the northern seaboard. His family owned, then freed, household slaves. Slave ownership was rejected, even detested, by his liberty-loving relatives, but the three-cornered slave *trade*, with Newport at its apex, was another matter — a business matter, something apart from what a man felt or did toward his black household help. Hopkins stood virtually alone in believing that the slave trade belonged in the same moral bundle.

But Hopkins was unique in a way that Channing did not catch at the age of twelve, and never completely grasped for the rest of his life. Hopkins was uninfected with the racialism which came to America with the first Englishmen. Channing was not similarly blessed. He learned early to abominate slavery and racial persecution, but it took a lifetime to move his psyche to the point where he could begin to see blacks as the natural equals of whites. Equal in the sight of God? He had no problem with that. Of course all men were equal in the sight of God. But from the first day he drew breath, Channing lived in a society that accorded the black man, whether slave or free, an inferior status. He absorbed it through his pores, and had a devil of a time exorcising it.

Hopkins, on the other hand, as early as 1774, prepared two young black men named Bristol Yamina and John Quamine for the unheard-of purpose of entering Princeton College.[5] Unfortunately, their college education was abruptly halted by the outbreak of the revolution. In his declining years, Hopkins's most intimate personal associate was the black sexton of his church, Mr. Newport Gardner. After a Sunday service, when the ailing Hopkins left the meetinghouse on Gardner's arm, he did so as on the arm of a son, not a servant.[6]

In the Channing household, the question of social equality simply did not exist. Particular black people were held in great affection, as servants, as professional cooks, as menials, as candy store keepers. They had their place, even an honored place. Personal relationships were warm, kindly, and protective. But the towering psychological wall between black and white was so taken for granted it was never noted.[7]

If the Channing household had its racial blind side, it also had its open side, where the meanings of black dignity could be felt. The Channing ire was kindled, for example, by the stratagem employed by the vestry of Newport's Trinity Church (the Gibbses' house of worship) to conceal the presence of blacks during services. A broad screen with pear-shaped slits was placed next to the organ, through which black worshipers could see the minister and congregation without being seen.[8]

Newport's most celebrated pastrycook, Duchess Quamino, whose sons Hopkins tutored for Princeton, was a School Street neighbor of the Channings, and regularly used the ample Channing oven for her more elaborate productions. She was an active (and unconcealed) member of the Second Congregational Church, and annually served tea in her small home to the three families she had served before gaining her freedom. Within a year after Channing began his Federal Street ministry, she died. He wrote a dignity-laden inscription for her grave:

In memory of
DUCHESS QUAMINO,
a free Black of distinguished excellence;
Intelligent, industrious, affectionate, honest, and of exemplary piety;
who deceased June 29, 1804, aged 65 years[9]

The taint of slavery was early removed from Channing's life, but except for these highly personalized gleams and flashes, the taint of racialism was not. The flawed pattern left him vulnerable in the years to come, when the hardest kinds of decisions had to be made, not only about slavery, but about the institutional racism of the North, without which slavery in the South could not endure.

In Virginia, as tutor to the Randolph children, he had been nauseated by the field-hand slavery he saw for the first time. "There is one object here which always depresses me," he wrote. "It is *slavery*. This alone would prevent me from ever settling in Virginia. Language cannot express my detestation of it."[10] Yet he was charmed by the warmth and graciousness of the slave owners he met, some of whom professed an abhorrence for slavery little less than his own, even as they kept themselves locked by economic interest to it. The Virginia experience was strangely unliberating for him, imposing upon him a cool silence that lasted for years.

In 1819–1820, when the country was swept by commotion over Missouri's request to be admitted to the union as a slave state, Channing was not sufficiently aroused to say anything publicly. Only in a private manner, bordering on secrecy, did he write in approval — a letter to Harrison Gray Otis, who saw in the Missouri question a chance to unite the northern states against the Virginia-dominated slaveocracy of the South.[11]

The European trip, which loosened Channing up in so many respects, also set him to conversing more freely about slavery. In 1826, one of his starchier parishioners, Mrs. S. P. Hale, fumed in a letter to Edward Everett that her beloved pastor had become "half mad on the subject of slavery"; had in fact made what her husband considered a "quite scandalous" reference to it in a recent sermon.[12] By 1828, he was able to spell out for his English correspondent, Jane Roscoe, what he had brooded about for years: "I rejoice in the zeal with which the cause of the Africans is espoused among you. On this subject I have had one fear, that too great stress had been laid on the physical sufferings of the slaves. I apprehend that the slaves of our country suffer less than the peasantry in some countries of Europe. The

228

true ground, I think, is, that slavery is a *wrong*, be the yoke lighter or heavier, and that, even where it provided sufficiently for the physical being, it destroys the intellectual and moral being, and utterly extinguishes the hope and capacity of progress. I trust your efforts are to prosper, for nothing can rid us of this curse in this country but a strong moral and religious feeling, and this will be aided by enlightened public sentiment in other countries."[13]

So unlike him! Channing approached the slavery issue with a deep and abiding despair. Those who opposed it did so, more often than not, for what to him was the least compelling reason: physical suffering, which was relative. Conceivably, the physical conditions of slaves could be improved. Then what? Slavery was a moral *wrong;* that was the beginning and end of it. But how could a nation so entangled in a vast, entrenched *system* of evil find the moral strength to extricate itself?

The question was put squarely to him that same year when Benjamin Lundy, a Baltimore abolitionist, paid a call, and Channing, caught between his caution and his despair, could not respond as his visitor wished. Yet he had to do something, so he posted a letter to Senator Daniel Webster in Washington in which his aching conscience plainly showed:

"A little while ago, Mr. Lundy of Baltimore, the editor of a paper called 'The Genius of Universal Emancipation' visited . . . to stir us up to the work of abolishing slavery at the South, and the intention is to organize societies for this purpose. I know few objects into which I should enter with more zeal, but I am aware how cautiously exertions are to be made for it in this part of the country. I know that our Southern brethren interpret every word from this region on the subject of slavery as an expression of hostility. I would ask if they cannot be brought to understand us better, and if we can do any good till we remove their misapprehensions. It seems to me that, before moving in this matter, we ought to say to them distinctly, 'We consider slavery as your calamity not your crime, and we will share with you the burden of putting an end to it. We will consent that the public lands shall be appropriated to this object; or that the general government shall be clothed with power to apply a portion of the revenue to it.' I throw out these suggestions merely to illustrate my views. We must first let the Southern States see that we are their *friends* in this affair; that we sympathize with them, and from principles of patriotism and philanthropy, we are willing to share the toil and expense of abolishing slavery."[14]

Channing's spiritual vision was forever blessed (or cursed) with a comprehensive perspective. To narrow one's perspective to a hatred of slavery was not enough for him, lest the power of that compact, single-minded rage end in sheer destructiveness. The federal union, for example. What would happen to it if North and South could not find a way to "share the burden" of abolition? As he told Webster, he could envision the day when the country would be shaken to its foundations by "sectional animosities" unless "wise men" could outflank "enthusiasts" with a constructive program for ending slavery.

What his comprehensive perspective lacked, however, was a stinging empathy with the *feelings* of slaves, a deficiency he soon afterward moved to correct. As the modest European restoration of his health crumbled, and Mrs. Channing's arthritis knotted, they decided on a half-year rest cure in the relaxed climate of St. Croix, amidst an economy based on slave labor, but doubled over by the body blow of the 1826 U.S. punitive tariff on sugar imports (for the protection of Louisiana's sugar economy, which was also based on slave labor).

Just before sailing in November 1830, Channing sat down to compose a few parting words to his congregation, and fell into one of his deep reveries, thought crowding on thought.[15] Boston was now a booming, changing city of sixty-one thousand, with twenty-seven thousand additional souls in the suburbs. In 1829, along with Ralph Waldo Emerson's advent as colleague pastor of Second Church, the city gained its first modern hotel, Tremont House, built at a cost of $300,000 with a facade of Quincy granite, one hundred and seventy guest rooms, ten public rooms, and a manager, Semeon Boyden, known as "prince of landlords." Here Jonathan Phillips would take rooms, where he and Channing and any other Harvard man who was not "indifferent," could enjoy an informal "Club of the Jacobins."[16]

Boston was a confusing mixture of culture and commerce. The

Boston Lyceum was born, and right after it, the Boston and Lowell Railroad. William Henry Channing, Oliver Wendell Holmes, and James Freeman Clarke graduated from Harvard, all three prime examples of the ability of the Boston mind to soar in the midst of grasping commercial interests, cramped prudence, and an excess of hostility toward flights of the imagination.

Thinking of his own congregation, so large and fashionable, and from whom he had gained additional independence by voluntarily surrendering still another two hundred dollars of his salary in 1829, Channing contemplated a strange compound of complacency and reformism; the decorous timidity of most, the belligerent conservatism of some, the unsubmissive idealism of a few. He knew that he was loved, that he was held in awe, that he was sometimes resented, and frequently seemed to be a fathomless conundrum. Considering the quaking state of his health, a lengthy absence could mean never seeing them again, so he decided to say what he would want them to remember as his last words.

He spoke to them as their friend, he said, not as their preacher; and with a freedom he did not usually permit himself in the pulpit. "It has been my duty to urge on you the real, deep, continued improvement of your character, as the only thing worth living for," he said. "That I have done this with imperfection I feel — oh how deeply do I feel." He told them how, in giving himself to "long and patient inquiry into the subject of religion," he had found reason to change many of his earlier views, for which he was grateful. Otherwise it would be plain that he had not used his mind "freely and fairly." Indeed the freest investigation had only confirmed his trust in "the great spiritual principles of religion," the most basic of which he described as "love toward all human beings." He hoped that whatever else his parishioners remembered of his efforts, they would recall his flat-footed rejection of the sectarian spirit, even when he was plumping most strongly for his "peculiar views." He had never considered himself a "better man" for escaping what seemed to him gross errors, simply a fortunate one.

In parting, he spoke what could serve as his epitaph, if such should be needed: "Respect those who differ from you and also respect yourselves. Do not feel as if you had monopolized truth or goodness. Treat none with derision. Esteem no man the more for thinking as you do, and no man the less for thinking otherwise, but judge all men by the principles that govern their lives."[17]

In St. Croix, surprisingly oblivious of his delicate condition, Channing plunged into a round of face-to-face discussions with slaves, filling pages of his letters with what he saw and heard. At last he again had slavery like a volume opened before his eyes, and, as was the case with him always, he learned quickly and thoroughly what he read. From his rented rooms in an old plantation house, he walked out each morning to mingle with slaves in their hovels, and at work in the sugar fields. Sweating and worn, he returned to the veranda to rock and fan, where he quietly observed the slaves coming slouched to beg redress for their personal grievances and wants, a charade, because kindly ol' massa, the resident clerk of the plantation house, no longer owned the plantation. Hard times, brought on by the American tariff, had mortgaged his fields and slaves and slave quarters to an absentee trustee, whose unapproachable manager was a West Indies version of Simon Legree. It struck Channing that "the mildest form of slavery might at any time be changed into the worst."[18]

He began to outline a major essay on slavery, to be addressed to the South in the form of an open letter. Five unforgivable years passed before he completed and published it. Even then, he suppressed the first edition's lengthy footnote, which passionately personalized his St. Croix experience, so hesitant was he to put the issue of slavery on other than a reconciliatory basis.

He had once passed a slave woman, the footnote recounted, who was singing as if she was the gayest of her work gang. He asked her why she found her work so pleasant. She answered decisively that she did not. "Supposing that she referred to something particularly disagreeable in her immediate occupation," Channing wrote, "I said to her, 'Tell me, then, what part of your work is most pleasant.' She answered, with much empha-

232

sis, 'No part pleasant. We forced to do it.' These words let me into the heart of the slave."[19]

He bumped into slaves who pleaded to be bought by anyone who would give them a chance to earn their freedom. He was revolted by an estate manager with a reputation for going easy with the lash, whose explanation of his success was that he persuaded slaves of the wisdom of doing their work without rather than with whipping, since they knew it had to be done one way or the other. "In other words," a nauseated Channing wrote, "the certainty and dread of chastisement were so impressed on them, that they never incurred it."

He ran on, giving personal testimony of slavery's dehumanization of slave and master alike, illustrating how the unwary could be deceived by shrewd blandishments about the paternalistic benevolence of the system. It is "next to impossible," he wrote, "to estimate precisely the evils of slavery. The slave writes no books, and the slaveholder is too inured to the system, and too much interested in it, to be able to comprehend it." Still, if even the most inexperienced observer would read the laws of the Slave States, the "barbarity" of them would be "decisive testimony against an institution which requires such means for its support." Yet he smothered these views once they were loose.

In a letter to Joseph Tuckerman he readily admitted that some of the slaves of St. Croix were probably better clothed, fed, and housed than many of Europe's free peasants, perhaps even subject to less drudging toil. But that was not the point, he insisted. What counted was their condemnation, "generation after generation, to a merely animal and unimproving existence."[20] With quick anger, he added that he did not blame the slaveholder alone. The prosperous classes everywhere, he said, were reprehensible in their willingness to let multitudes "live and die in . . . darkness."

After four months of observation, he wrote an essay-length letter to Jane Roscoe in which he summarized the state of his mind.[21] He was more satisfied than ever that the root evils of slavery were moral, that even its sorest physical sufferings could chiefly be traced to moral causes. It was a tactical mistake to dwell upon, and to exaggerate, the brutality of master to slaves, since most masters were not that brutal and resented the misrepresentation so deeply that they could not hear the rest of the antislavery message. It was undeniable that cruelty and suffering were widespread; indeed, the overseers of slave gangs "are generally uneducated, ignorant, undisciplined men, with little principle and strong passions, utterly unfit to be trusted with power." Yet the key to the wickedness of slavery was not to be found in physical cruelty except insofar as it was part of a "whole condition" that tends to degrade human beings "intellectually and morally, to make them little more than animals. . . . Here is the misery of slavery, nor do I think it can be expressed too strongly." It pained him that the "African race," which was "not characterized by the gloomy, ferocious, vindictive qualities of the North American Indian," was being corrupted by slavery into "mutual injuries and animosities."

It was these "corruptions," inseparable from slavery itself, that made emancipation both difficult and necessary, he concluded. Then, with a final sentence, he exposed to Jane Roscoe the pervasive chariness that he would carry back to Boston. "In this degraded condition of the negroes, their friends must proceed with the greatest caution. They are now incapable of self-government, and may bring the cause of emancipation into utter disrepute, if trusted at once with privileges which they must abuse."

Eleven years later in Lenox, when he memorialized the fourth anniversary of West Indies emancipation, one wonders if Channing recalled his wry words to Miss Roscoe: "We were told . . . that emancipation was to turn the green islands of the West Indies into deserts; but they still rise from the tropical sea as blooming and verdant as before. We were told that the slaves if set free, would break out in universal massacre; but since that event not a report has reached us of murder perpetrated by a colored man on the white population. We were told that crimes would multiply; but they are diminished in every emancipated island, and very greatly in most. We were told that the freed slave would abandon himself to idleness; and this I did anticipate, to a considerable degree as the first result. Men on whom industry had been forced by the lash, and who had been taught to regard sloth as their master's chief good, were strongly tempted to surrender the first days of freedom to indolent indulgence. But in this respect the evil has been so small as to fill a reflecting man with admiration. In truth, no race but the African could have made the great transition with so little harm to themselves and others. . . . The spirit of education has sprung up among the people to an extent worthy of admiration. We despise them; and yet there is reason to believe that a more general desire to educate their children is to be found among them than exists among portions of the white population in the slave States of the South. . . .

"Emancipation can hardly take place under more unfavorable circumstances than it encountered in those islands. The master abhorred it, repelled it as long as possible, submitted to it only from force, and consequently did little to mitigate its evils, or to conciliate the freed bondman. In those islands the slaves were eight or ten times more numerous than the whites. Yet perfect order has followed emancipation. . . . Emancipation conferred deliberately and conscientiously is safe."[22]

But Channing had a decade to travel before the moderation of his letter to Jane Roscoe would give way to the militancy of his Lenox address. Returning to Boston in the spring of 1831, he found the city's Establishment in a snit over Garrison's *Liberator,* the first numbers of which had been printed from *Christian Examiner* type, with Garrison and his assistant paying the rental charge by work on the *Examiner* itself. Channing subscribed, and scandalized Elizabeth Peabody by asking her to include it among the periodicals she regularly read to him. She could not understand his tolerance for what struck her as "the most unchristian and unreasonable violence and indiscriminate rage against the whole South and most of the North as well."[23]

Channing was also shaken by the verbal fury of a man determined to hammer the slave system to pieces with words. "Garrison knows he is right in the great principle," he told Miss Peabody, "he knows that it is of God; and so everything he thinks he regards as corollary to the unquestionable truth. The evil he has undertaken to fight is enough, you must admit, to craze the greatest mind. I can forgive the excesses of a generous humanity; they are rare."[24]

He could understand, and he could forgive — even when Garrison began to attack him — but he could not go along. Early in 1832, Garrison and others organized the New England Anti-Slavery Society, and it was believed, on the basis of Channing's willingness to put his exalted reputation on the line with the sermon he delivered after his visit to St. Croix, that he might join. When he offered no explanation of his refusal to do so, he deeply offended the Garrisonians in his congregation, just as he had earlier infuriated the anti-abolitionists.

Channing might have handled himself better. He might, for example, have sought Garrison out, to explain where he stood. He sympathized wholeheartedly with Garrison's demolition of the "colonization" dodge. He could accept "immediate emancipation" as meaning "the earliest practicable."[25] However, he could not deal with Southern slaveholders and moneyed Northerners as a mass of immorals, when to him they were individuals with widely varying moral capacities and potentials. He was not ready to dismantle the union. He could not, with his reservations, league himself with the Anti-Slavery Society, nor did he wish to criticize it publicly. His detestation of slavery was passionate, yet he was far from clear how it was to be done away with short of catastrophe.

Unable to bring himself to this kind of confrontation with Garrison, he ignored him personally and found himself between two fires. The anti-abolitionists were first alarmed then enraged by his moral harangues against slavery. Abolitionists, knowing him to be allied with their principles, were riled by his apparent determination to carry water on both shoulders. He was denounced by one side as an abolitionist, and derided by the other as spineless. Abolitionists did not give up on him; they yearned for his endorsements, and agonized over his criticisms. Anti-abolitionists soured on him in that special manner which is reserved for one who commits treason against his own set.

Channing, bolting for his shell, put aside his planned public essay on slavery, and earned one of the most grating judgments ever dealt him. His young parishioner, Maria Weston Chapman,

236

listened to her pastor's antislavery sermon after his return from St. Croix, and began rounding up abolitionist support within the Federal Street congregation. Channing discouraged her, but in 1834 she joined the Anti-Slavery Society anyway, becoming one of Garrison's most worshipful votaries. Her bitterness against Channing for rejecting her cause and its patron saint festered for years, unaffected by his later militancy.

Long after his death, when she edited Harriet Martineau's *Autobiography,* she let it all spill out. "Dr. Channing," she wrote, "between whom and Harriet Martineau a true friendship subsisted to the day of his death, was a good man, but not in any sense a great one. . . . He had neither insight, courage, nor firmness. In his own church had sprung up a vigorous opposition to slavery, which he innocently, in so far as ignorantly, used the little power he had to stay. He was touched by Brougham's eloquent denial of the right of property in man, and he adopted the idea as a theme; but he dreaded any one who claimed, on behalf of the slaves, that their masters should instantly renounce the right of ownership; he was terror-stricken at the idea of calling on the whole American people to take counsel on so difficult and delicate a matter in antislavery associations; and above all he deprecated the admission of the colored race to our ranks. He had been selected by a set of money-making men as their representative for piety, as Edward Everett was their representative gentleman and scholar, Judge Story their representative jurist and companion in social life, and Daniel Webster their representative statesman and advocate looking after their interests in Congress."[26]

In this brew of gall and quarter-truths, Maria Chapman finally paid Channing back for his unfortunate coldness toward Garrison, who with saintly patience went the second and third miles to win Channing's support. For two years after Channing's snub of the newly formed Anti-Slavery Society, Garrison plied him with antislavery publications, invitations to abolitionist meetings, and respectful appeals to speak out. No man to wheedle, he went to extraordinary lengths to elicit a fraternal response, and failed. With his patience finally worn out, he served warning in a letter that he would have to treat Channing as he found him.

Garrison considered trying once more to plead for help in delivering the country from "impending ruin." He wrote Channing on January 20, 1834: ". . . If the slaughter of two millions of victims who have gone down to their graves with their chains around them; if the cries of more than that number of tortured slaves now living; if a soil red with innocent blood; if a desecrated Sabbath; if a vast system of adultery and pollution, and robbery; if perpetuated ignorance and legalized barbarity; if the invasion of the dearest rights of man, and a disruption of the holiest ties of life;— and above all, if the clear and imperious injunctions of the most high God, fail to stimulate you to plead for the suffering and the dumb, it is scarcely possible that any appeal can succeed from [me]." He signed the letter, "Yours most affectionately and respectfully."²⁷

Channing could be forgiven for not responding, though he must have thought of sending Garrison copies of his recent exchange of letters with Ezra Stiles Gannett. The bind in which he found himself was clearly apparent. Writing from Newport, he confided to Gannett that his mind was stricken with the subject of slavery, and clouded by the widespread insensitivity toward the country's "greatest evil."²⁸ England was boiling with emancipation sentiment, he said, while privileged Americans were suppressing the abolition issue and talking nonsense about colonization. His suspicion of the Colonization Society was hardening: "I now fear that it is to extinguish the very, very faint sensibility which we have to this most tremendous and criminal of all forms of oppression — perhaps I may say — to the greatest outrage on humanity and Christian principles on the face of the earth — I refer to the opposition which it makes to the Anti-Slavery Societies — I presume from what I have heard that these societies are wanting in calmness and wisdom — but they adopt the *true principles,* the principles of humanity, justice and the gospel — it is a most fearful thought, that whilst these principles are gaining ground elsewhere, they should decline among ourselves."

Sooner or later, Channing continued, the true Christian spirit on slavery must break out, but the longer an unholy alliance of "respectable" Northerners with "the blind and guilty prejudices of the South" stifled a "solemn testimony against slavery which might transform the moral tone of Southern Christians, the likelier that the outbreak would be calamitously fanatical."

Gannett's answer was pinched and parsimonious — a fair example of what Channing could expect from most of his colleagues and congregation if he chose to wave an antislavery banner.[29] Gannett urged his senior associate to pursue a "prudent, *slow*, and solicitous" course; above all to avoid provoking the slaveholders. As for the abolitionists, they were best assessed by their patron saint, Garrison, whom he described as "one of the most dangerous citizens in our United States."

Gannett continued to fret over Channing's radical drift, and wrote a follow-up message a few days later; a clincher, he hoped.[30] One of his classmates, he said, was now living in Maryland where he had come to know and appreciate the Southern mind. Distaste for slavery was growing, according to this friend, but so too was fear of emancipated blacks. There was much favorable talk of the "removal of blacks" from the country.

Gannett had completely missed Channing's point — that colonization was a moral feint, a non-answer, a way of legitimizing suppression of the real issue. Hundreds of thousands of black *Americans* were in slavery! Why should they be more exportable than white Americans?

For relief from Gannett's obtuseness, he turned increasingly to Dr. Charles Follen, a German scholar, teacher, and Unitarian preacher, who had fled Europe in 1824 as a political refugee and settled in Boston where he won Channing's respect and sponsorship. The two became bosom friends. Follen, with his radical European background, was naturally attracted to the abolitionist movement. He now received Channing's active encouragement to join the Anti-Slavery Society and to push the English idea of compensated emancipation as a carrot for the slaveholders. The North, Channing felt, should be persuaded to accept this financial responsibility.[31] When Follen asked his advice-giving friend to come to the meetings and to do the advocating himself, Channing backed off, saying, "I have not bodily strength to attend their meetings, and strive with these stormy youths to act on Christian principles,— one of which is to hold an even balance, and do justice to every shade of good, even in the bad; to judge and condemn the sin unsparingly, but remember the sinner is our neighbor." Follen could accept this because he knew Channing's ability to play a unique role.

There were other zealous Garrisonians who recognized the potential value of his course as an antislavery loner. One of these, Lydia Maria Child, published in 1833 the first book to spring from Garrison's crusade, and with it she put her highly respectable career on the chopping block. She sent one of the early copies of *Appeal in Favor of That Class of Americans Called Africans* to Channing. He liked the title, sped through the pages, and set out on the long walk from Mt. Vernon Street to Lydia Child's house on Cottage Place, arriving frazzled from the hot sun, his cloak over his arm.[32]

It was their first private visit, and it lasted for three lively hours. Channing's admiration grew in a fashion his hostess hardly thought possible. He appealed to her to stand by the cause, to continue to speak out, even though it was certain that the literary fashion makers would try to annihilate her. (He was right about the vendetta that destroyed her career when she refused to desert the anti-slavery movement.)[33] Naturally he had certain reservations about her views. Channing without reservations would hardly be Channing. As Lydia Child described it: "He . . . entertained the idea, which he afterwards discarded, that slavery existed in a milder form in the United States than elsewhere. I was fresh from the bloody records of our own legislation, and was somewhat vehement in my opposition to this statement; and he sought to moderate me with those calm, wise words which none spoke so well as he."

From then on, the two got together frequently, with Channing taking the initiative because he considered Lydia Child to be a superior source of inside information on antislavery developments. "At every interview," she recalled, "I could see that he grew bolder and stronger on the subject, while I felt that I grew wiser and more just. At first I thought him timid, and even slightly timeserving; but I soon discovered that I formed this estimate from ignorance of his character. I learned that it was justice to *all*, not popularity for *himself*, which made him so cautious. He constantly grew upon my respect, until I came to regard him as the wisest, as well as the gentlest, apostle of humanity. I owe him thanks for preserving me from the one-sidedness into which zealous reformers are so apt to run. He never sought to undervalue the importance of Antislavery, but he said many things to prevent my looking upon it as the *only* question interesting to humanity. . . . Dr. Channing's interest in the subject constantly increased, and I never met him without being struck with the progress he had made in overcoming some difficulty, which, for a time, troubled his sensitive conscience. . . . Some zealous reformers did not understand this; and thus construed into a love of popularity what was, in fact, but a fine sense of justice, a more universal love of his species."[34]

One of the younger ministerial brethren for whom Channing had great affection was the Rev. Samuel J. May, a delicate, sensitive and impeccably certified Bostonian, who was "approbated" for the ministry at a meeting in Channing's home in 1820.[35] As a Channing protégé, he plunged into the temperance movement, advocated women's rights, worked for improved popular education, and generally made himself useful to liberal causes. On a preaching tour through the South, early in his career, he learned to abhor slavery and was therefore poised when Garrison's bugle sounded. He was also painfully acquainted with the North's white racism, for he was pastoring in Connecticut when Prudence Crandall opened her school for black girls, only to be forced by harassment and arson to close it down. May, virtually alone, stood at her side. By 1834, he was deep in the Anti-Slavery Society, and delighted with Channing's frequent invitations to drop by to chat about its affairs. Such opportunities were becoming exceedingly rare in fashionable Boston church circles. In that heartland of liberal thought, according to one chronicler, "not a single church could be obtained for a meeting or lecture on slavery; not a single minister, excepting Dr. Channing and the pastor of Pine Street Church would even read a notice of such a meeting, and no public hall of any size or commodiousness could be hired for such use."[36]

One autumn day, while May was listening to Channing's routine carping about the harshness of abolitionist language, his patience snapped. "Dr. Channing," he said, quite forgetting his usual reverence for the great one, "I am tired of these complaints. . . . It is not our fault that those who might have managed this reform more prudently have left us to manage it as we may be able. It is not our fault that those who might have pleaded for the enslaved so much more eloquently, both with the pen and with the living voice than we can, have been silent. We are not to blame, Sir, that you, who more perhaps than any other man, might have so raised the voice of remonstrance that it should have been heard throughout the length and breadth of the land,— we are not to blame, Sir, that you have not so spoken. And now, because inferior men have begun to speak and act against what you yourself acknowledge to be an awful injustice, it is not becoming in you to complain of us, because we do it in an inferior style. Why, Sir, have you not moved, why have you not spoken before?"[37]

The space between the two men became a void of silence. May, appalled at his own temerity, could scarcely believe that he had spoken so harshly to "the man, who had ever treated me with the kindness of a father, and whom, from my childhood, I had been accustomed to revere more, perhaps, than anyone living."

Channing's usually serene face was taut and tight-lipped. Then, all at once, it relaxed. In quiet, kindly tones, he said: "Brother May, I acknowledge the justice of your reproof; I have been silent too long."

In fairness to Channing, the months preceding Samuel May's autumn visit were made dismal by the loss of his mother. Her death on May 25, 1834, was, as he put it, a change in the very conditions of his life.[38] Their relationship had been remarkably close and sympathetic. He called her his "earliest, oldest friend." During the saddened summer at Newport, news of the bloody anti-abolitionist riots in New York piled shock upon his personal grief. As he had written earlier to Lucy Aikin, he wanted desperately to write and to act against slavery, yet he could not agree with "our abolitionists," had to work alone, but without the health to do so.[39] The New York riots bludgeoned him with the truth that whatever personal reservations he had about the fanaticism of Garrisonians, he could not stand by while their right of free expression was beaten to a pulp.

What happened in New York, he wrote Follen, filled him "with indignation and grief."[40] The duty of the abolitionists was clear. "Whilst they ought to review their principles with great deliberation," he said, "they ought not, at this moment, to *recant* any thing, because recantation will certainly be set down to the account of fear. I wish them to adopt a wiser course and a more benevolent tone towards their opponents; but not to abate their firmness one jot, not to use a wavering word, not to bring suspicion on their character and motives by the least appearance of timidity. . . . I wish them to give up their extravagance, and to pursue practicable objects, and such as consist with the principles of human nature, but to do this resolutely and from conviction, and not with the appearance of unwilling and forced concession to their foes."

Even as he wrote, Channing realized that what was shaping up in the country was a fearful rending of the social fabric. The agitation against slavery *must* go on. And as antislavery sentiment swelled, so too would the attack upon it. Moreover, there was a cleavage in his own feelings, which became evident when he entertained at Oakland, at May's urging, the English traveler and writer, Edward Strutt Abdy.[41] Harriet Martineau, who formed her close friendship with Channing a year later, was chagrined that Abdy felt compelled to publish so unsqueamishly the extent of Channing's ignorance of the plight of free blacks in America, and of his unexamined racialism.[42] But she was also convinced that Abdy's jarring visit did much to move Channing toward a major commitment to the antislavery cause, and to a significant change in his career. "Next followed the virtual accession of a great northern man to the cause," she stated in the *London and Westminster Review* of December 1838; "for though Dr. Channing continued to censure the abolitionists for two years after this, it was in the autumn of 1834 that his mind's eye was fixed upon the question on which he has since acted a brave part. It was at the close of this summer, in the parlour of his Rhode Island retreat, that the memorable conversation with Mr. Abdy took place, by which Dr. Channing's attention was aroused to the wrongs of the coloured race."

Channing had not been unaroused about the wrong of slavery, but Abdy's lacerating interview revealed to him, perhaps for the first time, the extent of his personal involvement in slavery's immorality by virtue of the racial stereotypes which undergirded it, and which he himself shared.

Channing had known only one black man on anything like an equal intellectual footing, a parishioner in his early days at Federal Street named Prince Saunders. Saunders went on to considerable fame as Christophe's right-hand man in Haiti, and before that rose to social prominence in England as a Boston delegate of the Masonic lodge of Africans.[43] In 1808, President John Wheelock of Dartmouth College had recommended him as a teacher for Boston's school of colored children, a project dear to Channing's heart, and, as pastor and parishioner, the two fell into a habit of regular visits at the parsonage on Saturday afternoons. When the parleys extended into the evening, as they frequently did, Channing's mother was not above showing her annoyance that so many of her son's precious hours were being spent on a black man,[44] who, among other presumptions, had founded a "Belles Lettres Society" for young white men. The brief experience with Saunders was not enough to uproot Channing's deeply ingrained racialism, as Abdy's merciless probing revealed.

Abdy was not impressed when Channing professed a complete lack of racial prejudice, remembering that Lydia Child had told him of Channing's resistance to social equality. Such a concession, he told Mrs. Child, would lead to amalgamation, an event which he was surprised she could contemplate without abhorrence.[45] Abdy was more impressed when Channing acknowledged and justified the fact that his black and white servants ate at separate tables.

When they began to discuss education, Channing expressed a firm conviction that it was best to have racially separate schools, and that abolitionists had hurt their cause by imprudently advocating integration. Abdy commented acidly that Channing seemed to believe in destroying a distinction "by continuing it."[46] So it went, through what must have been an extremely uncomfortable session, with Channing reverting continually, according to Abdy, to the theme that they were discussing the just claims of a race naturally inferior to whites.

That Channing was shaken was clear to Miss Martineau. In her *London and Westminster Review* article, she says that he began, as soon as Abdy left, to reexamine his position. By October, he was ready to make his strongest antislavery statements thus far, and "preached a thoroughgoing abolition sermon, as to its principles at least, though many months elapsed before he learned fully to recognize the merits of the men who were teaching and practicing them at the hazard of all that ordinary men most value."[47]

Channing returned to an autumnal Boston made edgy by the assault on the Charlestown convent, and drifting ever closer to the kind of rioting New York had already experienced. He dealt, as we have seen, with the anti-Catholic eruption, and then directed his congregation's attention to the reproaches the civilized world would heap "on a *free* nation, in which mobs pour forth their fury on the opposers of *slavery*." It was perfectly clear, he said, that there was widespread, weasel-like backing in polite society for what had happened. People were saying that while mobs are unfortunate, "they will put down *Anti-slavery*."[48]

How could anyone in his right mind so rationalize the putting down of antislavery, he wondered, except under a virulent spell of bigotry? Getting close to home, he probed with his congregation the reasons he as well as they could give to justify a distaste for abolitionists: "That they have carried good principles to extremes, have winked out of sight the difficulties of their object, have hoped to accomplish the work of years in a moment, have exposed their cause to suspicion by bitterness of language, by precipitancy, by needlessly outraging public feelings or prejudices, I certainly shall not deny."

He reminded his hearers that the real issue, however, was *slavery*, not the excessive zeal of its opponents, and that fueling the bitterness of abolitionists was the sullen indifference of the many to "this greatest calamity, scourge, curse, and reproach of our country." Ventilating some of the guilty passion he had stored up after Abdy's visit, he exclaimed: "Property in man! Property in man! You may claim matter to any extent you please as property,— the earth, the ocean, and the planets, but you cannot touch a soul. I can as easily conceive the angels of heaven being property as men."[49]

Some, Follen among them, hailed the effort as an out-and-out abolitionist sermon; others damned it as such. Several who sat in the Federal Street pews jointly asked permission to publish the manuscript, but Channing declined, pleading that he had not yet developed his ideas fully enough to let them loose on the general public. He was especially sorry to refuse, he said, because those who did not know him would undoubtedly attribute his reluctance to "selfish prudence."[50] He had preached the sermon, he continued, to free himself "from the painful consciousness of unfaithfulness to the interests of liberty and humanity," but, compared with what he hoped to do in the future, it was unfit for general circulation.

It was shortly after this that Samuel May came calling and stunned Channing with his outburst. May was about to take on an eighteen-month stint as general agent of the Massachusetts Antislavery Society, a role in which he would be five times mobbed, once in the company of John Greenleaf Whittier, who threw over his promising political career to campaign as an abolitionist. Channing, meanwhile, was still mulling over a major piece on slavery for sometime in the future, and piously hoping that in spite of abolitionist "extravagance," Boston would be spared mob action. May's flush of hot anger was understandable, and Channing understood. Yet he put off until spring, when he fled again to the seclusion of Newport, the punishing labor of writing his comprehensive indictment of slavery.

While he worked, the conservative gentlemen of Boston brewed a storm. Channing learned from the columns of the *Boston Daily Advertiser* that Mayor Lyman and numerous other worthies were to convene an anti-abolitionist meeting in Faneuil Hall on August 21. He hurriedly sent off an open letter, warning: "Any resolve passed at the proposed meeting, implying, however indirectly, that a human being can rightfully be held and treated as property,— any resolve intended to discourage the free expression of opinion on slavery, or to sanction the lawless violence which has been directed against the Antislavery societies,— any resolve implying that the Christian and philanthropist may not strive to abolish slavery by moral influences, by appeals to the reason, conscience, and heart of the slaveholder, any resolve expressing stronger sympathy with the slaveholder than with the slave, or tending at all to encourage the continuance of slavery,— will afflict me beyond measure. . . . That Boston should in any way lend itself to the cause of oppression will be a dark omen indeed."[51]

Channing was obviously warming to the idea of entering the public arena. His labors on the slavery pamphlet were not only renewing his sense of having something significant to say, but were performing wonders for his health, which he described as "uncommonly good."[52] Harriet Martineau arrived in Newport for the first of her lengthy visits with the Channings and found him "younger and pleasanter" than she had expected.[53] "The lower part of other faces is the most expressive of mirth," she said; "not so with Dr. Channing's, whose muscles keep very composed, while his laughter pours out at his eyes." Channing could not have been more distressed over what was happening in Boston, in the country, and in Congress over the slavery question, but when Miss Martineau arrived he was cresting as a man of his times. She sensed at once what it meant: "It appears a simple affair enough for an influential clergyman to declare his detestation of outrageous injustice and cruelty, and to point out the duty of his fellow-citizens to do it away. But it is not a very easy or simple matter on the spot. Dr. Channing lives surrounded by the aristocracy of Boston, and by the most eminent of the clergy of his own denomination, whose lips are rarely opened on the question except to blame or to ridicule the abolitionists. The whole matter was, at that time, considered 'a low subject,' and one not likely, therefore, to reach his ears. He dislikes associations for moral objects; he dislikes bustle and ostentation; he dislikes personal notoriety; and, of course, he likes no better than other people to be the object of censure, of popular dislike. He broke through all these temptations to silence the moment his convictions were settled; I mean not his convictions of the guilt and evil of slavery, but of its being his duty to utter his voice against it. From his peaceful and honoured retirement he came out into the storm, which might, and probably would, be fatal to his reputation, his influence, his repose."[54]

Entranced by Miss Martineau, and absorbed in his writing, Channing lingered at Oakland into the fall, analyzing the situation in which he would be fully immersed once his pamphlet appeared. Boston was becoming, he feared, a town of anti-abolitionist mobs. The city fathers, at their Faneuil Hall meeting, had done their work well, making it quite fashionable for gentlemen to break up abolitionist meetings and to howl down abolitionist speakers. On October 21, with Channing still in Newport, such a "broadcloth mob" seized Garrison, put a noose around his neck, stripped him of much of his clothing, and dragged him across Boston Common. Garrison, who barely escaped with his life, thanks to a heroic drayman, was clapped behind bars by Mayor Lyman as "the instigator of the mob." Plainly, a tremendous capacity for intolerance existed in the North, with blacks, abolitionists, and Catholics as available objects. But it was also clear to Channing that the ranks of those opposed to slavery were swelling rapidly, even if inchoately.

What about the South? Earlier, as Channing knew from his Richmond experience, the general attitude of the Southern planter was to apologize for slavery as a bad system he did not know how to get rid of. But for more than a decade, there had been a hardening of views, a brutalizing of the "black codes," and an elaboration of a nonsense-theory that slavery was not only essential for keeping blacks in their place, but was a positive good in itself, sanctioned by the Bible and necessary for the perpetuation of free institutions.

The progressive barbarization of Southern white attitudes can be traced from Denmark Vesey's insurrection at Charleston in 1822, the first of such seriousness since Gabriel's abortive attempt to capture Richmond in 1800.[55] From then on, blacks were brought under ever more repressive controls — curfews, night patrols, no assemblies except for worship. Whites were prohibited from teaching slaves to read and write in every Southern state except Maryland, Kentucky, and Tennessee.

The myth that most slaves were happy and contented was made an article of faith, with the countervailing belief that outside agitators could nevertheless stir up the exceptional malcontents like Nat Turner. Indeed, Turner's outbreak was blamed on Garrison's *Liberator*, though there is no evidence that copies of it were read by even a tiny percentage of literate Southern blacks. But white Southern gentlemen brought constant pressure upon white Northern gentlemen to suppress abolitionist publications and opinions, stressing the safety and honor of their womenfolk and children. Altogether too many Northerners, who were linked to Southerners by pocketbook as well as by prejudice, were responsive to these appeals.

The attempt to suppress drove moderates like Channing closer to the abolitionist zealots. He was convinced that the moral force of emancipation must be made to blow upon Southerners and Northerners alike with growing velocity, keeping them in a constant discomfiting encounter with the evil of slavery.

Early in November, he sent *Slavery* to the printer. "I have exhausted myself in writing my little book," he said. "The subject has been very painful to me, and I long to escape from it to more cheering views. However, we must learn to look evils in the face, and to bear the burdens of the suffering."[56] The "little book" ran to more than one hundred and fifty tightly knit, closely reasoned pages, most of which he confidently expected would "bring a storm" on his head.[57]

His introduction spelled out precisely what he intended to cover:

1. I shall show that man cannot be justly held and used as property.
2. I shall show that man has sacred rights, the gifts of God, and inseparable from human nature, of which slavery is the infraction.
3. I shall offer some explanations, to prevent misapplication of these principles.
4. I shall unfold the evils of slavery.

5. I shall consider the argument which the Scriptures are thought to furnish in favor of slavery.
6. I shall offer some remarks on the means of removing it.
7. I shall offer some remarks on abolitionism.
8. I shall conclude with a few reflections on the duties belonging to the times.[58]

Channing pounded out reason after reason why one human being cannot be the property of another human being. A man cannot be property, he said, because "he is a rational, moral, immortal being; because created in God's image, and therefore in the highest sense his child." Such a being, he went on, is "plainly made for an end in himself. He is a person, not a thing. He is an end, not a mere instrument or means. He was made for his own virtue and happiness. Is this end reconcilable with his being held and used as a chattel? The sacrifice of such a being to another's will . . . is the greatest violence which can be offered to any creature of God. It is to degrade him from his rank in the universe, to make him a means, not an end."[59]

Turning to rights, Channing described them as having a universal validity, grounded in nature, in morality, and in God. The right not to be someone's property is basic, he said. It cannot be reasoned away. It cannot be abrogated by man-made laws. It exists apart from any social contract.[60]

In his "Explanations," he credited the South with not being a monolith of moral depravity. Slave owners, he said, covered a spectrum from brutal tyrants, to those who feared poverty if deprived of their slaves, to those who fervently wished to be relieved of a system they detested but knew not how to end. He also wanted it understood that the North, "notorious for love of money, and given to selfish calculation," was on shaky moral footing in making demands upon the South. Both North and South must rise out of their corruption, he believed, to bring an end to slavery.[61]

In listing the specific evils of slavery, he packed his sentences with muscular language that was bound to infuriate slavers and to please abolitionists. From every conceivable standpoint, he found it unmitigatedly ruinous to master and slave alike, a license to cruelty, an invitation to depravity, an unbearable stench in the nostrils of free institutions. Before turning to the celebrated "Scriptural" defense of slavery, he took the other rationalizations for it and demolished them one by one: that the slave is better off than many a free laborer or peasant, that the slave is happy in his dependence on superior white masters, that the slave is taught religion.[62]

It was the argument from Scripture that appalled him most. Because it was put forward with a straight face, he answered it in the same manner. The Pauline text commanding slaves to obey, and commanding masters not to release their slaves but to treat them justly, he ruled out as having no validity "in this age of the world, and amidst the light which has been thrown on the true interpretation of the Scriptures." Yes, Biblical passages could be found to justify slavery, but others justified polygamy. "Why may not Scripture be used to stock our houses with wives as well as with slaves?" Channing asked. The plain rule of Scriptural criticism, he insisted, was that "particular texts should be interpreted according to the general tenor and spirit of Christianity. And what is the general, the perpetual teaching of Christianity in regard to social duty? 'All things whatsoever ye would that men should do to you, do ye even so to them; for this is the law and the prophets.' Now does not every man feel that nothing, nothing could induce him to consent to be a slave? . . . Can he pretend, then, that in holding others in bondage, he does to his neighbor what he would that his neighbor should do to him? Of what avail are a few texts, which were designed for local and temporary use, when urged against the vital, essential spirit, and the plainest precepts of our religion?"[63]

Moving on to the "Means of Removing Slavery," he placed the burden squarely on the shoulders of the slaveholder, to whom he naively (and outrageously, from a black man's standpoint) attributed a uniquely "intimate knowledge of the character and habits of the slaves." He was not consciously trimming, for he demanded that slaveholders accept unqualifiedly the principle "that man cannot rightfully be held as property." But he was his most typically cautious self in urging that the South be left to work out its own program of gradual emancipation.

In words he was happy enough to eat seven years later in

Lenox, he warned of dire consequences in the West Indies, on account of emancipation being forced by "a foreign hand." He warmed the hearts of black and white abolitionists, however, by describing colonization as "equivalent to a resolution to perpetuate the evil without end." Anticipating the howls of anguish from Northern antislavery zealots who would feel cut off by his approach, he exhorted them to continue spreading "enlightened opinion" on slavery, and not to become depressed by the gradualism of their influence, nor intimidated by scare headlines about intermarriage and incitement to slave revolts. As for "amalgamation," he asked how it could go on "faster or more criminally than at the present moment." Slaveholders ought to blush every time they used the word, he said. While it was unlikely that illiterate and carefully guarded slaves would read antislavery literature, the entire argument for suppressing it was absurd anyway, he reasoned, for it meant blotting out much of the world's noblest literature, to say nothing of the history of the American Revolution.[64]

Next Channing launched into his familiar cautions and chidings for abolitionists. He did so unwillingly, he said, because he honored them for their "strength of principle" and "active goodness," and sympathized with them in the persecutions they continually suffered. Nevertheless, he was distressed by their harangue for "Immediate Emancipation" — a motto which, without sufficient explanation, was counterproductive, he claimed. He attacked also the "showy, noisy mode" of abolitionist agitation, demonstrating that he still held the notion that it was the form rather than the substance of abolitionism that enraged the Southern masters and their Northern apologists. Getting past that hurdle was still ahead of him.

Finally, he addressed himself to the duties of the free states as the country moved inexorably into a crisis over slavery — "a question not of profit or loss . . . but a question involving the first principles of freedom, morals, and religion." The first duty, he said, was to wake up to the "solemnity" of the crisis, and to take hold of the "great fundamental truths by which private efforts and public measures are to be determined." The North, he said, had a duty to frown on any attempt to excite insurrection or violence in the South, but since there was no inclination among abolitionists to do this, the duty was not a pressing one. Much more pointed was the duty of all in the North to use "every virtuous influence for the abolition of slavery . . . to encourage . . . continually increasing opinion . . . in favor of personal freedom."

Because he saw many in the North giving way to the flattery and intimidation blowing out of the South, he urged the free states to gird themselves for a struggle of the soul. He yielded to none in his love of the Union, he said, and would sacrifice anything but truth, honor, and liberty to preserve it: "Still, if the Union can be preserved only by the imposition of chains on speech and the press, by prohibition of discussion on a subject involving the most sacred rights and dearest interests of humanity, then union would be bought at too dear a rate; then it would be changed from a virtuous bond into a league of crime and shame."[65]

The appearance of *Slavery* thrust Channing onto center stage. In Harriet Martineau's words, he was "wondered at and sighed over in private houses, rebuked and abused in Congress, and foamed at in the South."[66] Abolitionists alternately praised and scalded him. Garrison first went publicly in one direction, hailing *Slavery* for its "luminous expositions of many of the principles for which we have long been contending. They will thus be made acceptable to very many who have not condescended to receive them from us."[67] Privately, however, he fumed at Channing's insipid dependence upon gentle moral suasion to melt hard slaveholder hearts, then vented his spleen in the columns of the *Liberator,* documenting under twenty-five headings his conclusion that *Slavery* was "utterly destitute of any redeeming, reforming power," was "calumnious, contradictory, and unsound"; and as such, "ought not to be appropriated by any genuine abolitionist."[68]

Follen took Channing to task for defects of logical arrangement in the first two chapters, but otherwise found much to applaud.[69] Ellis Gray Loring regretted the barbs at abolitionists, but judged "nineteenth twentieths" of Channing's pages to be "sound."[70] A scholarly abolitionist indictment came from the pen of Elizur Wright, Jr., editor of Anti-Slavery Magazine, a quarterly published in New York by the American Anti-Slavery Society. He relegated Channing to pre-eminence among "clerical opposers of active measures for the abolition of slavery," and added that "the ingenuity which they manifest in fencing and fettering their principles, so as to prevent any efficient action, till such time as slavery shall please to abolish itself, is really worthy of a better cause. They have the most exalted conceptions of the power of truth, but seem to despise all vulgar and physical means, and extended arrangements, for bringing it to act upon the public mind."[71]

When he wrote, Wright was not aware of the extent to which Channing's "fencing and fettering" struck Boston society and Boston's respectable clergy as something quite different. John Quincy Adams saw at once that while Channing had thrown sops to slaveholders, and had slapped abolitionist wrists, he had produced "in fact an inflammatory if not incendiary publication."[72] Adams admired Channing for it, for he knew how scandalized the conservatives of State Street, Beacon Hill, and the American Unitarian Association were.

Old-line members of Federal Street stopped calling at the Channing home; some even refused to speak when passing Channing on the sidewalk. He who had been an object of almost mystical adulation was suddenly a pariah.[73]

Channing had expected the kind of denunciation Representative Waddy Thompson of South Carolina spewed out on the floor of Congress: "I venture to say that no book of the same number of pages in any language contains libels more foul and false."[74] But one of his own parishioners, Massachusetts Attorney-General James T. Austin, struck the kind of blow he did not anticipate. Austin charged his pastor with an appeal to the prurient interest by dwelling on slavery's encouragement of licentiousness, then went on to indict Channing for proclaiming *"the doctrine of INSURRECTION."* Austin claimed that Channing's assault on slavery was an open invitation to every slave to "rise in his strength or his madness, and shake off his chains." Since Channing had no practical solution to slavery, why did he pontificate? Austin asked — then concluded sarcastically that Dr. Channing apparently gleaned his insights "from a refined and elaborate metaphysical subtlety wholly incomprehensible to a great part of mankind — from new light in the recesses of his study, from some double distillation which by a novel process of alchemy he has been able to effect on the dry bones of ancient history."[75]

If many of his ministerial colleagues chilled toward him, there was compensation in the appreciative comments of trusted friends like Noah Worcester and Samuel May. Worcester's letter he answered on the same day, expressing his "great pleasure" in a commendation he considered "very precious."[76] He assured Worcester that he had been prepared for "fierce opposition at a distance," and "not a few opposers at home." He was grateful that many "who were grieved when they heard of my purpose to write on this subject, have expressed their satisfaction in the work."

It was painful to absorb Austin's venomous attack, a totally new experience, and to see a widening gap between himself and the congregation he had served for a third of a century, yet he could not help being aware that his influence had taken a giant stride. May's assessment confirmed this. He found that Channing's foray greatly broadened the base of interest in the slavery question, not only because of what he wrote, but because he, "with the highest reputation as a writer and as a divine," was willing to write it.[77]

Harriet Martineau recounted a conversation between herself and a Boston lady shortly after *Slavery* appeared.

"Have you seen Dr. Channing's book?" the lady began.

"Yes. Have you?"

"O no. Do not you think it very ill-timed?"

"No; I think it well-timed; as it did not come out sooner."

"But is it not wrong to increase public excitement at such a time?"

"That depends upon the nature of the excitement. But this book seems to have a tranquillising effect: as the exhibition of true principles generally has."

"But Dr. Channing is not a practical man. He is only a retired student. He has no real interest in the matter."

"No worldly interest; and this, and his seclusion, enable him to see more clearly than others, in a case where principles enlighten men, and practice seems only to blind them."

"Well: I shall certainly read the book, as you like it so much."

"Pray don't, if that is your reason."[78]

The furor over his book piqued Channing's curiosity about the abolitionists, with whom he was now, willy-nilly, identified. Follen alerted him that Governor Everett had laid before the Massachusetts legislature a proposal that abolitionists be made indictable at common law. A legislative committee was to hold hearings on the question in the Senate chamber on March 4, and Follen urged Channing to lend the prestige of his name and presence as the case for the Anti-Slavery Society was presented. Channing made no promises, but, despite a chill day, he showed up, muffled in cloak and shawl-handkerchief. As he darted across the chamber, he passed and shook hands with Garrison, causing a rustle in the crowded gallery. He admitted that he had not been certain whose hand he was shaking,[79] but Garrison was unaware of this and told Miss Martineau the next day how pleased he was with Channing's greeting. She asked him how he could care, after what he had been writing about Channing.

"The most difficult duty of an office like mine," he replied, "is to find fault with those I love and honour most. . . . Dr. Channing, while aiding our cause, has thought fit to say that the abolitionists were fanatical; in other words, that we set up our wayward wills in opposition to the will we profess to obey. I cannot suffer the cause to be injured by letting this pass; but I do not the less value Dr. Channing for the things he has done."[80]

Apparently encouraged by his first public venture in the company of abolitionists, Channing decided in May to test the waters again. By this time, *Slavery* was a national best seller, so that when Channing rounded off the annual meetings of the American Unitarian Association by going immediately to the New England Antislavery Convention, it was a matter of moment and an entrancing experience for him.[81] There he was, he wrote, "surrounded by plain people," a surprising number of whom possessed striking powers "of speaking in public." He could not admit that he had overemphasized in the past the abolitionist penchant for "bitterness and intolerance of feeling," but he acknowledged that he heard nothing to compare with the "vituperations" that were normal fare in Congress. The abolitionists might not be good politicians, he said, but when tried by the common standards, he did not find them "wanting."

His greatest satisfaction of all, he wrote, was an address by a black man. His description illustrates the guilelessness of Channing's racial stereotypes: "His complexion led me to think he was of pure African blood, and his diction, his countenance, his gestures, his thoughts, his whole bearing, must have convinced every hearer that the African is a man in the highest sense of that word. I felt that he was a partaker with me of that humanity for which I unceasingly thank my Creator. I felt on this occasion, as I perhaps never felt before, what an amount of intellectual and moral energy is crushed, is lost to the human race, by slavery."

It had apparently not crossed Channing's mind that there were black men in the vanguard of the antislavery movement, that ever since the Revolutionary War free blacks had regularly petitioned Congress for an end to slavery, that for a decade before Garrison's arrival on stage, Northern blacks had agitated against colonization schemes, that two years before *Liberator's* birth, and five before Channing's *Slavery*, a Boston black man, David Walker, had published *Walker's Appeal*, one of the great abolition pamphlets.[82]

Though he had no intention of becoming a card-carrying member of the Antislavery Society, he was deeply moved by what he saw and heard. "You know by instinct," he wrote, "whether you are surrounded by life or death. This body was alive. I am sure, that, if the stirrers up of mobs could have looked into the souls of the Abolitionists, they would have seen the infinite folly of attempting to put them down by such persecutions as they can bring to bear on them."[83]

Channing bristled at the absence from the meeting of "the influential part of the community . . . men of standing, as they are called."[84] Where were his leading parishioners? Like others of their type, they were at their desks, or in their drawing rooms, hoping that antislavery agitation, like a bad dream, would go away. The "harvest of Abolitionism" was to be reaped, he mused, from the middle classes, and from the "farmers, mechanics, and other working men," who were already well represented in abolitionist ranks, and whose numbers would surely swell as the latest foray of Southern politicians sunk in. How many had yet heard that the current instruction from Dixie influentials to Northern men of substance was that if they wanted to hang on to their property and their privileges they'd better begin thinking about fastening slavery on their own laboring masses?[85] Abolitionist leaders, Channing felt, had both the zeal and the shrewdness to make the most of that plum.

Still he worried. Even though antislavery rode the wave of the most powerful moral principle of human nature — possession of one's own body and soul — there existed a monumental skepticism about progress and reform. And nowhere did he find this skepticism more overbearing than in Boston, where opposition to antislavery speech and action was at an all-time high. That he himself might have been lynched had he shown up in a Southern city paled in his estimation beside the indignities heaped by Proper Bostonians on his distinguished houseguest Harriet Martineau for appearing and speaking at a meeting of the Women's Antislavery Society.

Struggling to comprehend, Channing delivered himself of one of his most scalding analyses.

"The people at large," he said, "are swallowed up in gain, are intoxicated with promises of boundless wealth, are worshipping what they call prosperity. It concerns them little who is slave and who is free, or how the battles of liberty and truth are fought at home and abroad, provided they can drive some enormously profitable bargain, or bring some vast speculation to a successful issue. Men are too busy to think of Abolitionism, and will be apt to forget it, unless forced on their notice by violence. . . .

"The people of this city repel indignantly the charge of being friends of slavery, but, on the whole, they are altogether indifferent to it. A great part of them care no more for the slave of the South than for the Pariah caste of Hindostan. This indifference very easily takes the form of opposition to any efforts which

258

may offend the South. In truth, we have many elements of a proslavery spirit, which only wait for occasion to be unfolded. In the first place, the class here, as in all Free States, which holds the same social rank with the Southern masters, very naturally sympathizes with them, and shrinks from a class so fallen and abject as the slaves. Then we have a considerable body of conservatives, who live in alarm at the instability of the times, and who see no security but in keeping things, good or bad, just as they are. To these must be added . . . the men of business . . . who hold profitable relations with the South, and frown on any man, be he who he may, whose inconsiderate philanthropy would rob them of a customer or diminish their gains. The politicians, of course, inquire how the agitation of the subject will affect their party and promotion."[86]

Yet it was undeniable that his book on slavery was enjoying a far more enthusiastic reception than he had expected. He toiled on, and the fall of 1836 brought him his chance to speak out again. James G. Birney of Danville, Kentucky, freed his slaves, then scampered across the Ohio River to avoid the reprisals of his neighbors. In Cincinnati, hoping for a warmer reception, he launched an antislavery paper, the *Philanthropist*. Cincinnati gentlemen of the type Channing moaned over in Boston promptly organized a mob. Birney's press was smashed and he himself hounded out of town.

Channing wrote a twenty-six-page open letter to Birney, defending the right of antislavery speech with a considerably earthier eloquence than he had used in *Slavery*. Birney, contrary to Channing's view (and Garrison's for that matter), believed that the key to abolitionist success lay in political action. Indeed, in 1840 and again in 1844, he would be the presidential candidate of the short-lived Liberty party.[87] But whatever his differences with Birney, or Birney's with Garrison, Channing was thoroughly aroused by "the spirit of violence and persecution which has broken out against the abolitionists through the whole country."[88] Abolitionists, he said, "rendered to freedom a more essential service than any body of men among us" by persevering "amidst menace and insult." Even he, perhaps, would not now be writing in safety, had abolitionists knuckled

259

under to their ferocious assailants. "From my heart I thank them," he continued.[89]

Having blasted one by one the arguments and fears of anti-abolitionists, Channing could not resist reading another lecture to the abolitionists themselves on their verbal violence and intolerance. Garrison responded, typically, by running the entire letter in the *Liberator,* adding that "a million letters like this would never emancipate a single slave, but only rivet his fetters more strongly."

Nevertheless the letter carried Channing another fateful step into the national tumult, identifying him more and more closely with the abolitionist cause, stripping away still more of his aura of untouchability.

Interestingly, Channing and Garrison saw eye to eye on the dangers of politicizing the emancipation struggle. "Anti-slavery," he wrote in the midst of John Quincy Adams's bitter struggle in Congress to preserve the right of petition, "is to triumph . . . by becoming a living part of the public conscience and religion [precisely Garrison's opinion]. Just in proportion as it is complicated with political questions and feelings, it is shorn of its strength."[90]

In the same letter, written to Ellis Loring on March 11, 1837, Channing once again echoed Garrison: "There is a class of politicians who will use Abolitionism to rise by, but will disgrace it by want of principle."[91] With disarming frankness, he advised Loring, who had adopted the Birney rather than the Garrison approach: "I hear less said now of your fanaticism, and more of your want of moral purity. I ascribe the change to your political action."[92]

Resolution of the political action conundrum forever eluded Channing. He died still believing that moral passion and the individual, admonitory approach had to be preferred to political action. Yet he found himself drawn steadily and inevitably into collective action and political involvement.

On August 1, 1837, Channing completed and signed an eighty-page open letter to the formidable Henry Clay on the "Annexation of Texas," as political a question as could be found. It was the most explosive piece he had ever done; a genuine excursion into pamphleteering. Even Mrs. Chapman, one of his unforgiving critics, admitted that it probably fended off the annexation of Texas for some years. Channing had approached his task with characteristic thoroughness, draining the brains of Joseph Tuckerman, Horace Mann, Jonathan Phillips, Judge Story, John Quincy Adams, and Samuel Sewell before trusting his pen to paper. He was convinced that in the Texas question, the long, tragic drama of slavery and freedom came to a head. To every American it held up a mirror. What kind of people are we?

Channing reviewed the Texas insurrection and the broader plot to dismember Mexico, then embarked on a scorching denunciation of annexation as the first step on a bloody national career of "encroachment, war, crime," and unlimited slavery. Weep though he would over the dissolution of the Union, he would prefer it "to an act which is to pledge us as a people to robbery and war, to the work of upholding and extending slavery without limitation or end."[93]

Channing was not simply blowing hard for effect. Unlike Parker later, he did not underestimate the sincerity of the South in its recurrent secessionist threats. "On this point the South does not merely bluster, but is in earnest," he said. It was time for the free states to indicate an equivalent earnestness. "To me," he informed Clay, "it seems not only right, but the duty of the Free States, in case of the annexation of Texas, to say to the Slaveholding States, 'We regard this act as the dissolution of the Union. . . . We will not become partners in your wars with Mexico and Europe, in your schemes of spreading and perpetuating slavery, in your hopes of conquest, in your unrighteous spoils.' "[94]

At this same time, news of a martyr reached Boston. Elijah P. Lovejoy, on November 7, 1837, had been shot and killed while defending his antislavery press in Alton, Illinois. Increasingly stimulated by his involvement as a self-consciously controversial public prophet, Channing urged his friend Sam Sewell to organize a Faneuil Hall rally to protest the lynching of Lovejoy. To underline his commitment, he placed his name first on a list of one hundred petitioning the mayor and aldermen for use of the hall. When a backlash counterpetition was rushed to the city fathers, they turned down Channing and his friends. An aroused Channing decided to "give a practical manifestation of opinions which might otherwise have been considered merely theoretical."[95] In the *Boston Daily Advertiser* of December 2, he published an open letter "To the Citizens of Boston," appealing once again for the use of Faneuil Hall. "Is the whole country to sleep?" he asked. "A martyr to the freedom of the press has fallen among us. A citizen has been *murdered* in defense of the right of free discussion," he went on. "Has Boston fallen so low? May not its citizens be trusted to come together to express the great principles of liberty, for which their fathers died?"[96]

Bowing to renewed pressure and uncomfortably conscious of the imminent municipal election, the Board of Aldermen suddenly agreed to open Faneuil Hall on the morning of December 8. Channing, as keyed up as any of the more than five thousand who crowded in, sat on the platform as his friend Jonathan Phillips opened the meeting. The Rev. E. M. P. Wells knelt and offered prayer, then Channing spoke. His words had been carefully composed and committed to memory. "It is not . . . without reluctance, that I . . . speak in a place and under circumstances to me so new and unusual; but I am commanded to make this effort by a voice which I cannot disobey, by a sense of what I owe to myself, to this community, and to the cause of freedom." Applause billowed up, but Channing choked it with a plea for silent attention.[97]

Acknowledging that the finicky resented a man of God meddling in secular tumult, he insisted that churches were not the only "holy temples of religion." As a "man, a citizen, and a Christian," he found Faneuil Hall a holy place "when a great question of humanity and justice is discussed here."[98]

Benjamin F. Hallett then introduced the resolutions which Channing had drafted to reaffirm freedom of speech and the press, to condemn lawless violence, and to assert the Christian obligation to attend zealously to public affairs.

"Resolved," began a passage so typical of Channing, "that when a fellow-citizen has been destroyed in defending property and the press, it is alike weak and criminal to reproach him as

responsible for the deed, because he refused to surrender his undoubted rights at the command of his murderers. . . . And even if our fellow-citizen . . . was driven by the violence which assailed him into rash and injudicious deeds, we are bound so to express our grief as in no degree to screen his lawless assailants from the reprobation which is their due."[99]

George O. Hillard spoke for the resolutions and appeared to have the crowd with him until Channing's parishioner and old nemesis, James T. Austin, the attorney general, delivered a scathing denunciation of the meeting, of the resolutions, and of Lovejoy himself, whom he accused of inciting slaves to rise against their masters as wild beasts thirsting for blood.

The old hall rocked as the crowd, suddenly polarized, began to cheer and boo. Phillips turned to Channing and found him watching the uproar with studied serenity. "Can you stand thunder?" he asked, smiling. "Such thunder as this, in any measure," Channing answered, his eyes smiling back.[100]

The audience quieted down when young Wendell Phillips strode to the platform to invoke the spirit of the Revolutionary Fathers whose portraits studded the surrounding walls. In an extemporaneous oration that launched his extraordinary career as abolitionist and reformer, Phillips gradually worked most of his hearers into an emotional burst of righteousness. Then he laid it onto Austin: "Sir, for the sentiments he has uttered, on soil consecrated by the prayers of the Puritans and the blood of patriots, the earth should have yawned and swallowed him up." There was deafening applause.

Channing was impressed. So too were most others. The resolutions were passed by a substantial majority, and Boston became an even more divided city. Channing's role widened the split among his own parishioners. The *Liberator* rhapsodized over his connection with the meeting, quoting his statements verbatim, and Channing, typically, recoiled. Within a week, he sent a letter to Garrison for publication in the *Liberator*, scolding abolitionists for their failure to condemn Lovejoy's resort to weapons, and scoring again the violence of abolitionist language.[101]

Garrison, the Christmas spirit notwithstanding, was disinclined to turn the other cheek. Channing's letter, he replied in his editorial, was "defective in principle, false in its charity, and inconsistent in its reasoning." The great preacher's motives were pure as always, Garrison went on: "Dr. Channing, if he is sometimes cautious, even to criminality, has no duplicity." But how sad that just as Channing seemed to be showing a "more intrepid spirit," he should succumb to his old infirmities. Channing was simply wrong, Garrison continued, to press the doctrine of nonresistance on others when he himself had repeatedly rejected it in favor of legitimate self-defense.[102]

Channing felt he could understand Garrison's pique, though disagree he must. In a letter to Follen, he pointed out that his increasing identification with the abolitionist cause compelled him more than ever to express his conscientious agreements and disagreements.[103] To Miss Martineau he wrote that it was the misfortune of his position "to satisfy no party."[104]

If Garrison fumed, the controlling conservative faction at Federal Street Church did some fuming of its own. Channing's long-standing practice of having antislavery meeting notices read from the pulpit was overruled.[105] He responded by seeking "the holy" beyond the walls of the Federal Street meetinghouse, lending his name and prestige to petitions seeking abolition in the District of Columbia, and congratulating Levi Lincoln for breaking in Congress the "silence with which our representatives have so long listened to the men of the South."[106] John Quincy Adams, locked in his bitter struggle for the right of petition, informed Channing that his support was "one of the most precious rewards of my trials and one of the most powerful incentives to perseverance."[107]

Meanwhile, divine justice, if stalled in the United States, was prospering in the British West Indies, where emancipation was proclaimed and implemented. When the Massachusetts Antislavery Society sponsored in Fall River a gala celebration of the event, Channing, accompanied by Jonathan Phillips, deserted his beloved Newport to attend. The affair, he told Joseph Tuckerman, filled him with "more cheering hope than ever."[108]

With eight hundred thousand free blacks already loose in the West Indies, and with abolitionist agitation frothing across the

United States, Henry Clay decided in January 1839 to train the biggest guns of his oratory and eminence on the antislavery movement. Channing was genuinely alarmed as he read the first reports of Clay's powerful assault. Skillfully, Clay had assembled every conceivable justification and rationalization for the perpetuation of slavery. When the arguments were coupled with the Whig leader's enormous prestige, it was obvious that the cause of emancipation was in the fight of its life.

Channing huddled with Jonathan Phillips to discuss a response. He was still smarting from a product of the Boston rumor mill that he lived in luxury on his dead father-in-law's proceeds from past rum-selling and slave-trading. Tittering over this had been as prevalent among abolitionists as among his conservative acquaintances. Had the gossip undercut his effectiveness? Only once had he tried to set the record straight, and that in a letter to Elizabeth Peabody. He told her that he was willing to take note of the rumor-mongering because it affected "the reputation of those who had gone." It was true, he wrote, that forty years earlier his wife's father had owned a distillery which sold its products to those "who wanted it, without asking questions about its use," and that among the customers were undoubtedly some engaged in the slave trade. This distillery, however, was a "trifling item" in his father-in-law's "vast concerns," and the profit from it "a drop of the bucket compared with what he gained from a commerce spread over the globe." Channing reckoned that he had "paid the debt, many times" by his labors in the cause of antislavery. The charges, he said, would make him smile, "if they did not indicate unprincipled malice." He resented that "for the sake of giving me a stab, a man is dragged from his grave."[109]

Trusting that as was her wont, Elizabeth Peabody would spread the word extensively, he concerned himself solely with the question of whether or not his antislavery muscle had been weakened. He and Phillips decided that a response to Clay from Channing was clearly indicated. The next morning, he began to write, using an open letter to Jonathan Phillips as his vehicle.[110]

He would waste no time on Clay's vitriolic descriptions of the abolitionists. "They must fight their own battles." Clay had constructed a premise that slavery was a permanent feature of the Southern landscape; let the North keep hands off. "Does sympathy stop at a frontier?" Channing asked. Not if Christianity, with its grand truth of brotherhood, is taken seriously. The doctrine of human rights knows no geographical boundaries. For barring his black brother from the "recognized privileges and immunities of a man," the slaveholder must face the "tribunal of the civilized world and the higher tribunal of Christianity and of God."

The states of the Union are responsible to and for one another. The free states, personally contaminated by continued slavery in the District of Columbia and by the strictures of the fugitive slave laws, are duty bound to resort to a "higher law." Anticipating the arguments Parker, Thoreau, and Martin Luther King would later use, Channing declared, "No charter of man's writing can sanctify injustice, or repeal God's eternal law."

Satisfied that he had confirmed the duty of agitation against slavery, he went at Clay's case against emancipation point by point. Was emancipation inconceivable, as Clay claimed, because it would either generate race war or lead to amalgamation? Channing marshaled evidence to the contrary. "Can any impartial man fear that amalgamation will, in any event, go on more rapidly than at the present moment?" As for emancipation resulting in racial bloodshed, what of the "experiment of the West Indies"? There the slaves outnumbered the masters eight or ten to one, "yet the gift of freedom has not provoked an act of violence."

As for Clay's claim that the Union could not survive further shocks of abolitionism, Channing countered that "were the Union as weak as these clamors suppose, were it capable of being dissolved by any of the hundred causes which are said to threaten it, then it would not be worth the keeping." The Union, he concluded, "is not so weak as our alarmists imagine."

Though obviously not his intent, Clay's speech "will but aid" the antislavery spirit, Channing felt, for this spirit must and will prevail. "Strange," he said, "that in an age when great principles are stirring the human soul, and when the mass of men, who have hitherto slept, are waking up to thought, it should be imagined that an individual, a name . . . can arrest the grand forward movements of society! When will statesmen learn that there are higher powers than political motives, interests, and intrigues? When will they learn the might which dwells in truth? . . . Slavery must fall, because it stands in direct hostility to all the grand movements, principles, and reforms of our age, because it stands in the way of an advancing world."

Altogether, Channing had succeeded in putting together quite a potpourri, and in the process he had denounced slavery more vigorously than in his earlier writings. Yet his inevitable carping at the excesses of abolitionists had become milder. He was obviously, no matter how reluctantly, embracing the need for more direct action against the slave system. Understandably, his latest efforts warmed abolitionist hearts, even Garrison's, who found little to criticize. There was an unexpected plum in a review by Henry Ware, Jr., in the *Christian Examiner*. Channing had complained sourly that he found no sect "more indifferent" to the antislavery conflict than Boston Unitarianism, which he described as the virtual prisoner of the "more prosperous and fashionable."[111] Ware, however, was lavish in his praise, lauding Channing for demolishing Clay's "monstrous claim" for "the perpetuation of slavery."[112]

James T. Austin ran true to form, blistering his pastor unmercifully for doing abolitionism's dirty work while hiding outside the movement. Channing, he said, had become the dupe of his wild young friends, the transcendentalists, who were deranging "the conduct as well as the faith of the world."[113]

No one noticed, except literate blacks, who had learned to keep such insights to themselves, that Channing, for all his growing militance against slavery, uncritically accepted racial stereotypes. In the course of refuting Clay on the terrors of emancipation, he spoke of the "characteristics of the colored race" that were "particularly fitted to keep them harmless." "I refer to their passion for imitation of their superiors, and to their love of show and fashion, which tend to attach them more to the white race than to their own."

Channing was steadily radicalizing himself, however, and was well aware of the cost. Any lingering illusions of Boston's Whigs that he was their unofficial chaplain were gone, and so were lots of the old friendships. Colonel Stephen Higginson, who had loaned a Federal Street Church pew to Maria Weston Chapman, icily revoked the privilege when she invited Garrison to attend service with her.[114] The shaft was aimed more at Channing than at Garrison. John Quincy Adams, who somehow found time to keep tabs on all kinds of things, recorded a diary account of two long discussions with Channing on the slavery issue in November 1838. "The Doctor," he wrote, "was heretofore an idol of the party now calling themselves Whigs, but has become very obnoxious to them. They had almost worshipped him as a saint; they now call him Jacobin."[115] Adams felt that Channing was much more deeply troubled by "this change in his worldly fame" than showed on the surface.

Channing's wish for at least partial escape from his increasingly exposed involvement cropped out in a sudden decision to begin work in earnest on the masterwork he had been contemplating since 1824 — his treatise on man. His old nemesis, illness, was also a factor. He had been feeling so wretched that he found it necessary to cancel delivery of his charge at the ordination of Robert C. Waterston as minister at large to Boston's destitute.[116]

Events swept him on. As John Greenleaf Whittier expressed it to Channing's son William Francis many years later, his father "threw upon the altar [of antislavery] the proudest reputation in letters and theology of his day."[117] How deep the cuts were became apparent when Channing's beloved Charles Follen died aboard a burning New York-to-Boston packet on Long Island Sound in January 1840. The usually stoical Channing buried his face in his hands when told the news. It was decided to pay a suitable memorial tribute to Follen, and at Federal Street Church, with Channing participating. The Rev. S. J. May, in behalf of the Massachusetts Antislavery Society, requested the use of the church. Channing seconded the request, and the standing committee agreed. Within forty-eight hours, and without consulting Channing, the standing committee unanimously reversed itself. Yet every member of the committee knew that

Follen had been one of Channing's dearest friends! Channing, wrapping himself in the splendor of desolation, questioned the usefulness of his entire ministry to the Federal Street flock. Like it or not, that flock would hear him preach on Follen, after which the standing committee could do what it pleased about his continuing relationship. From the pulpit he had made famous, he memorialized his friend as one to whom "the most grievous sight on earth was the sight of man oppressed, trodden down by his brother. To lift him up, to make him free, to restore him to the dignity of man . . . this seemed to him the grandest work on earth, and he consecrated himself to it with his whole soul."[118]

Follen, he noted, had many dear friends among the congregation. He left unspoken the implication that such friends were neither numerous enough nor powerful enough to stop the church from officially humiliating Follen by insulting his memory. But he had his say about Follen, not only for his friend's sake, but for the sake of pulpit freedom as well. Then he addressed a letter to the standing committee relinquishing what little salary he still took, and announcing his "wish and purpose" that all of his "public functions" as pastor "should cease."[119] Strangely, he did not want a "formal dissolution," and none took place. His ministry, nearly forty years of it, simply petered out. He preached no more at Federal Street that year, nor in 1841. In 1842, the last year of his life, he preached but once, on his sixty-second birthday. Such time and energy as were his would be spent elsewhere.

In one of his infrequent appearances as a public guest, in Philadelphia in May 1841, Channing revealed his promptings: "A minister deriving power from his intellectual, moral, and religious worth is one of the chief elements of a true and quickening church. Such a man will gather a true church around him; and we here learn that a Christian community is bound to do what may aid, and to abstain from what may impair, the virtue, nobleness, spiritual energy of its minister. It should especially leave him free, should wish him to wear no restraints but those of a sense of duty. . . . He must follow his own conscience and no other. How can he rebuke prevalent error without an unawed spirit? Better that he should hold his peace

269

than not speak from his own soul. Better that the pulpit be prostrated than its freedom be taken away."[120] Channing shared with Philadelphia his painful Boston lesson that virtue is "no local thing," and he defined the one church to which he belonged, "the universal church." No man could be excommunicated from it, he said, "but by himself, by the death of goodness in his own breast."

It was an emancipated Channing who turned again to the slavery question. He proudly informed Follen's widow, Eliza, that he was writing a piece to be called *Emancipation*, based on Joseph Gurney's *Familiar Letters to Henry Clay of Kentucky*, describing a winter in the West Indies. He was expressing some thoughts, he said, not touched in his previous writings.[121] One of the new thoughts, as it turned out, was a special word for the women of the country, to whom, according to Channing, "slavery should seem an intolerable evil, because its chief victims are women."[122] Women, he said, should be about the business of arousing their husbands to "manly indignation" against slavery.

Having identified himself with a more militant feminism, he adopted a more aggressive attitude toward the role of the free states. They must liberate themselves from all acts in support of slavery! He listed a set of indicated constitutional amendments: abolish slavery in the District of Columbia; free the free states from the obligation to return fugitive slaves; end federal responsibility to support the claims of slaveholders for protection against foreign countries. It was clearly Channing's most positive program of action thus far. Two poles of the abolitionist cause, Garrison and Birney, were equally impressed. *Emancipation*, published by Elizabeth Peabody, became a best seller. So far had Channing progressed that rumors spread about his deserting his profession to become a politician. "Some wise ones," Channing wrote to Ferris Pell, were intimating that he "had an eye on a seat in Congress!"[123] To Channing this was sad proof of "the obtuseness of too many of my readers."

"Obtuseness" alone did little justice to the complicated attitudes amidst which Channing was striving to define his new role. For years he had witnessed his electric effect on congregations.

Instead of ladies fanning themselves, and gentlemen napping, they looked at Channing and listened to him, as if doubting the possibility of so extraordinary an effort. Of course he was flattered. But his restless mind also rebelled. He knew only too well that what attracted so many of the genteel and fashionable to the pews was the conviction that religion was a powerful means of repressing the vices and passions of the multitude. It was the duty of the best people, therefore, to encourage religion, and to enjoy it — in its more palatable forms. And not only to enjoy it, but to spend Sunday afternoons discussing it.

Channing knew that the Sunday afternoon chatter increasingly made a politician of him, a politician trying to cram everything under the head of morality. To imagine the conversations was enough to make his skin crawl. Indeed, he had only to read a sketchbook like *Aristocracy in America*[124] by the German nobleman, Francis Grund, to confirm what some of Boston's most solid gentlemen were saying. "Channing's heart bleeds for the slaves. Why is he so strangely silent about the condition of free blacks amongst ourselves?" "Some clergymen really have exposed themselves to mob action by their anti-slavery preaching, but not Channing, not in Boston, where he can preach and publish in the greatest possible security." "Channing contradicts himself every third or fourth line, preaching union on the one hand, and the dissolution of it on the other."

Channing could ponder as few others, because he was so much a part of it himself, the remarkable Boston resistance to attacks of tender passion. He could appreciate why his growing tendency to speak and act "out of season" roused confusion and contempt. As was well known, an educated Bostonian, even when he fell in love, did so only because he was quite ready to get married, and found the object of his affections a socially acceptable and legitimate one. Sentiments were not to be thrown away on unattainable objects. Feelings were to be husbanded as property. Compared with prudence and calculation, faith, hope, and love were of small account. If this meant a degree of hardness and severity, it also meant a unique capacity for self-government.

271

He might have run off to Newport to dissolve into sardonic bitterness. Instead he seemed determined to put together new combinations of a New England self, and to encourage others, especially among the young Transcendentalists, to do likewise. His protégés, Emerson, Parker, Ripley, and Clarke, were reaching for a new religion, for new men and women, in a new world. In January 1841, James Freeman Clarke returned permanently to Boston after a seven-year pastorate in Louisville, Kentucky, determined to foster church renewal and expecting to find there, as the fruit of Channing's labors, an audience open to the Christian Transcendentalism he wished to preach. Channing found in Clarke a unique ability to define the philosophy which undergirded his programs of reform — God is *now* in the world. He is *now* in our hearts. He is ready *now* to inspire by his spirit. He is uniformly near, the light within us, the life of our life.[125] On what other basis could antislavery make sense? Or the banishment of poverty? Or the renewal of the church? All were bound together, as Channing had spent a lifetime pointing out, and as Clarke was now bent on embodying in a new kind of church, a genuinely catholic church, a "Comprehensive Church" he called it, combining the best elements of all former religious systems. These would embrace, as "independent but harmonizing elements," the Catholic principle of universality, the orthodox Protestant understanding of sin, Unitarian liberality, Transcendentalist emphasis on immanent Divinity, and a radical approach to social justice. Channing could see his entire life encapsulated in the Clarke prospectus. Naturally he responded.

When Clarke put it together in his Church of the Disciples, calling for lay members, men and women, who wanted active not passive roles, Channing plunged in and took part in many of the preliminary meetings. His two brothers, his son, and several members of Federal Street became members of the Church of the Disciples, with his blessing.[126] When the question of composing a declaration of faith arose, it was Channing who took the more radical line. Clarke preferred the traditional wording: "Our faith is in Jesus, as the Christ, the Son of God." Channing advocated "in Jesus as the divinely appointed teacher of truth." Clarke appreciated the irony of cautious old Channing lecturing him that he must constantly be more fearful of conformity than of eccentricity.

The year 1841 was one of the most absorbing, active years of his life. He was busy with the preparation of a complete edition of his works, serving posterity and family at the same time. To his brother George, just then entering the publishing field, he gave the copyright of the edition. From his brother George, he extracted the promise that after a few years a much less expensive edition would be published for the less affluent. He was fascinated by George Ripley's drive to found "the church of the future" in the communal living and manual labor of its members. He was stirred by Orestes Brownson's advocacy of the abolition of the "priesthood" throughout Christendom. Out came Emerson's first series of essays. On May 19, at the Hawes Place Church in South Boston, Theodore Parker bombed the religious establishment with his *The Transient and Permanent in Christianity*, a manifesto of Transcendentalist Unitarianism. Each of these young men had sat at his feet, invaded his privacy, mined his brain, taken great lodes of his thought off to refine and radicalize. Now they were creating the new, genuine American spirit and culture of which he had dreamed. As an old man near death's door, he flinched at their flamboyant frankness. Yet he felt as never before a youthfulness and ardor in his own thoughts.

Off to Philadelphia he went to address the Mercantile Library Association on "The Present Age,"[127] to demonstrate that he too, along with the young Turks of Boston, found a commanding tendency at work toward "expansion . . . diffusion . . . universality." The grand idea of humanity, he said, was "the importance of man as man," and this idea was spreading "silently, but surely."

With newfound amiability toward "associations," he declared: "Benevolence now gathers together her armies. Vast associations are spread over whole countries for assailing evils which it is thought cannot be met by the single-handed. There is hardly a form of evil which has not awakened some antagonist effort. Associated benevolence gives eyes to the blind and ears to the deaf. . . . Benevolence now shuts out no human being, however low, from its regard. It goes to the cell of the criminal with words of hope, and is laboring to mitigate public punishment to make it the instrument, not of vengeance, but reform. It remembers the slave, pleads his cause with God and man, recognizes in him a human brother, respects in him the sacred rights of humanity, and claims for him, not as a boon, but as a right, that freedom without which humanity withers and God's child is degraded into a tool or a brute."

The Channings remained in Philadelphia until the end of May, when he preached to the First Congregational Unitarian Church, which he had earlier helped to establish. Returning by way of New York, he received there a letter from W. H. Furness, Philadelphia's Unitarian minister, telling him that several Jews had been in the congregation when he preached and understood him to mean that by his definition of the Church, Jews were not excluded. Would Channing comment further?[128] Back in Newport, ill with travel fatigue, Channing was nursed by his son, William Francis, now twenty-one, who had become more and more a companion and confidant. The two discussed Furness's letter, William Francis wanting to know just how his father did view Christ these days. According to William Francis, Channing answered that he was "more and more disposed" to emphasize the "simple humanity" of Jesus.[129]

The relationship of father and son had moved restlessly through the years. "I understand the play of Mary's mind," Channing told Elizabeth Peabody in the days when she was tutoring the Channing children, "but cannot get a clue to William's."[130] William Francis went through years of open rebellion against his father's taste for classical study. He flaunted his own exclusive taste for the natural sciences. When William Francis became virtually a school dropout, Channing shipped him off to Fellenberg, Switzerland, "hoping for the good effect of change of climate and all surroundings."[131] There the boy got caught up in the equalitarian rebellions of the time, taking the democratic side. He returned, much to Channing's satisfaction, full of fire on social and moral issues, and ready to line up with the antislavery cause. Less to Channing's liking, it was apparent that Europe had done nothing to sharpen his son's appetite for the classics, and had only deepened his interest in physics. Accepting fundamental differences in the way their minds worked, the two grew steadily closer. The love and companionship of his son was much in Channing's mind when he wrote: "What mysteries we are to ourselves! Here am I finding life a sweeter cup as I approach what are called its dregs."[132]

Channing moved into the last year of his life roused to add still another elaborate essay to his antislavery writings. The *Creole*, a brig out of Richmond, Virginia, set sail on October 27, 1841, from Hampton Roads, destined for New Orleans with a cargo of tobacco and one hundred and thirty-five slaves. At sea on November 7, several of the slaves seized the ship, killed a slave dealer named Hewell, and forced the crew to steer for Nassau. There the vessel was impounded by the British attorney general, who held nineteen blacks on charges of mutiny and murder, but gave sanctuary as freed men to the rest, despite the vigorous protest of the American consul. Back home, Southern senators and representatives fumed in Congress, causing Secretary of State Daniel Webster, on January 29, 1842, to address a letter of instruction to Edward Everett, minister to England.

Webster gingerly sidestepped the fugitive-slave issue, basing his claims instead on the theory that when vessels are carried by accident or violence into a foreign port, there should be no interference with the cargo. Great Britain responded that in this case as in others, the slaves were automatically freed by touching British soil. As the negotiations between Webster and Lord Ashburton churned on, slaveholder tempers and rhetoric rose, but antislavery people in the North were for the most part surprisingly indifferent. Not Channing. From the beginning he was convinced that vital issues were involved. After consulting with his young friend Charles Sumner, he resolved to write a broadside to be titled *The Duty of the Free States* and calculated to put steel in the backbones of Northern congressmen.[133] England, he was certain, would hold the high ground she had taken, but he was determined to rescue Webster from the humiliation of a conflict based on Great Britain's simple declaration that no human being touching her soil could continue to be a slave. "We are called," he wrote in the peroration ending part II of his pamphlet, "to be witnesses to the world of a freer, more equal, more humane, more enlightened social existence than has yet been known."[134]

As for Webster's nationalistic rationalization that men derived their status and identity from the nation to which they belonged, Channing, in refutation, poured the foundations of a more universal citizenship: "Man is not the mere creature of the state," he said. "Man is older than nations, and he is to survive nations. There is a law of humanity more primitive and divine than the law of the land. He has higher claims than those of a citizen. He has rights which date before all charters and communities; not conventional, not repealable, but as eternal as the powers and laws of his being. This annihilation of the individual by merging him in the state lies at the foundation of despotism."[135]

Not only are the free states free from obligation to protect slavery abroad, Channing stated, but they are duty bound to free themselves from all complicity with slavery whatsoever, free indeed to withdraw from the Union should Texas be annexed.

The *Creole*-inspired pamphlet to some extent embodies Channing's earlier hope that a legal compromise could be worked out which would enable the free states to disengage themselves entirely from the slavery issue, so that they could avoid any responsibility for the perpetuation of slavery, while at the same time doing everything possible, short of war, to bring it to an end. He had expressed this hope in a letter to his congressman, Robert C. Winthrop, as follows:

"Can no compromise or arrangement be made by which the subject of slavery may be taken out of Congress, or detached from national politics? The free states, I think, should give every pledge that they will not exert the power of the general or state-governments for the purpose of abolishing or acting on slavery in the slave states, any more than in foreign countries, and on the other hand, they should insist on being relieved from all obligation to give support to slavery. Let them leave the subject wholly to the action of the slave states, interfering neither to uphold or destroy."[136]

Channing's broadside was avidly bought, read, discussed, praised, and scolded. The *Creole* affair was no longer a small matter in the North. Though the subtleties of his pages were not necessarily appreciated, he had succeeded in his intention of stirring the public mind. On September 4, hardly dreaming that Channing had a month to live, Sumner wrote to his brother: "Who excels, who equals, Webster in intellect? I mean in the dead weight of intellect. With the moral elevation of Channing, he would become a prophet. Webster wants sympathy with the mass,— with humanity, with truth. If this had been living within him, he could never have written his Creole letter. Without Webster's massive argumentation, Channing sways the world with a stronger influence. Thanks to God, who has made the hearts of men to respond to what is elevated, noble, true! Whose position would you prefer — that of Webster or Channing? I know the latter intimately; and my admiration for him grows constantly. When I was younger than I am now, I was presumptuous enough to question his power. . . . I am glad that I am wise enough to see him in a different light. His moral nature is powerful, and he writes under the strong instincts which this supplies; and the appeal is felt by the world."[137]

On his sixty-second birthday, which fell on a Sunday, Channing preached for the last time in the Federal Street Church, choosing as his text: "While we look not at the things which are seen, but at the things which are not seen: for the things which are seen are temporal; but the things which are not seen are eternal." (2 Cor. 4:18.) In consideration of the gulf that had opened between him and his congregation, it was a conciliatory text and a conciliatory message. What could be "seen" of his thirty-nine-year ministry was not much, but "the one sublime idea" of that ministry — the greatness of the soul — was not, and could not be, lost.

The Channings had long hoped to see something of rural Pennsylvania. Having paid birthday respects to the people of Federal Street, they left soon afterward for a brief visit with friends in Philadelphia, then headed northwest. The lush, rolling farmlands thrilled Channing: so different, he wrote Jonathan Phillips, from the "sterility of New England."[138] The life of the mind and spirit, however, was something else. He confided to

Phillips that he found the people of his home state much more "thriving" in their ideas, much less burdened with political corruption, and considerably less victimized by the excesses of party spirit.

By June, Channing was confined to a Wilkes-Barre inn, suffering from what a local physician diagnosed and treated as inflammation of the lungs. To Harriet Martineau he confided that convalescence was something of a delight, what with his window overlooking the lazy Susquehanna.[139] Moreover, he told her, he flourished on news that his books were circulating freely and getting enthusiastic responses among English working-class readers.

Charles Sumner had been writing about the progress of part II of the *Creole* piece, so Channing sent him a letter describing his general satisfaction with the revised proof sheets he had seen, but asking that a missing one be rushed to him.[140] Illness, Channing wrote, had not improved his pages, "but they will fall into the hands of people in health." "Happily the children of our brain need no care or nursing" after they have been given to the world, he added. As for the cause of his temporary health setback, he told Sumner: "Sleeping on board the canal boat, a thing which I had resolved against is the only imprudence for which I cam blame myself." He asked Sumner to relay the news to his physician brother Walter.

By plodding stages the Channings made their way to Albany, then on to the Berkshires, where by early July they settled into the Lenox Inn. To the delight of the Sedgwick clan and other friends, they indicated an intention to enjoy the invigorating Berkshire air for most of the summer. As relaxed as he had ever been, Channing found the inn's piazza much to his taste. Looking out at the quiet hills, he could still hear, he wrote Phillips, "the distant roar of the world."[141] He felt a twinge of guilt at not being more troubled by it, but concluded, "When in our pilgrimage, we reach a verdant sunny spot, it is not wrong to sit down and refresh ourselves."

The Sedgwicks, who had thought of Channing as the feeble contemplative recluse so familiar to Boston, could hardly credit what they saw of him now. He was free, happy, and apparently in glowing health. Whether on an excursion to Bashpish, or a week at Stockbridge, or on the garden-party circuit, he exuded informality. Children, no matter how many or how noisy, could count on his playful forbearance. Catharine Sedgwick described her astonishment in a letter to Dewey, who knew better than to be astonished at Channing's easy participation in their local Berkshire style of "anti-conventionalism," their "free way of going on."[142] During one particularly lively parlor conversation on the best age of a person's life, Channing smiled and declared that he thought it to be about sixty.[143]

Something approaching a newfound facetiousness showed in a letter he penned to Catharine Sedgwick after she left Lenox on a brief trip to Saratoga. "You do not treat us fairly," he said. "First, you took yourself away. That was wrong enough — & now you allure your brother from us. We consented to the first injury, but you have no warrant for the last. We seem to have nothing to do, but to revenge ourselves by being as happy as we can in spite of your absence. Your gentle nature cannot well understand this being happy out of *spite;* but you can comprehend that there must be something *piquant.* You can make us one expiation. You must attract great admiration where you are, & in the midst of the incense must look towards Lenox & say, *There* after all is the feast of reason & the heart."[144]

The "piquant" Channing of 1842 had moved an immense distance from his tormented youth in Richmond. Indeed, in a letter from Lenox to his inveterate English correspondent Lucy Aikin, he was moved to expand on his tranquil autumnal attraction to the likes of Miss Sedgwick: "Hardly anything can exceed the delicacy and loveliness of our young women. The sight of them is one of my pleasures as I walk in the streets."[145] He bemoaned the unhappy fate of these "frail flowers," however, in comparison with the sturdier breed of English women: "Whether from climate or wrong modes of living, or from the burden of toil which motherhood in this country lays on your sex, our young women fade at an early age."

Miss Aikin, in an answer Channing must have received just before departing Lenox, couldn't resist the temptation to straighten her old friend out a bit: "As to the delicate subject of comparative beauty, our travellers attest that you have many very pretty girls; so have we: and even Miss Sedgwick pronounces that 'the Englishwoman is magnificent from twenty to five-and-forty.' We are satisfied; so let it rest."[146] But Miss Aikin could not let it rest. Seething apparently over Channing's sniffy description of the Englishwoman's masculine gait, she poured it on: "With respect to our . . . *stride,* as you say, I have a little history to give you. Down to . . . fifty years ago, our ladies, tight-laced and 'propped on French heels,' had a short mincing step, weak nerves, much affectation, a delicate helplessness and miserable health. Physicians prescribed exercise, but to little purpose. Then came the event which is the beginning or end of everything — the French Revolution. The Parisian women, amongst other restraints, salutary or the contrary, emancipated themselves from their stays, and kicked off their *petit talons.* We followed the example, and, by way of improving on it, learned to march of the drill-sergeant, mounted boots, and bid defiance to dirt and foul weather. We have now well-developed figures, blooming cheeks, active habits, firm nerves, natural and easy manners, a scorn of affectation, and vigorous constitutions. If your fair daughters would also learn to *step out,* their bloom would be less transient, and fewer would fill untimely graves."

Channing, in his jolly Berkshire mood, must have smiled with more than his eyes as he absorbed Miss Aikin's brand of feminism. Shifting to politics, she thanked him for his "Duty of the Free States," and encouraged him to press his demand for emancipation in the District of Columbia "at *all* risks." As for the English temper on the *Creole* dispute, she advised that the South's "man-owners may as well give up all hope of our lending our hands to the recovery of their chattels; we shall go to war sooner, I can tell them."

Channing had indeed been pressing the antislavery cause, using as his peg the eighth anniversary of the beginning of West Indian emancipation, the fourth anniversary of its completion. On August 1, a refulgent Sunday, he asked use of the Lenox meetinghouse pulpit to deliver what proved to be his last public utterance. By and large, the Berkshire people were not given to great concern over social injustices, but Channing apparently reached them. Catharine Sedgwick, who had heard him frequently in the past, described in a letter to Fanny Kemble "the inspired expression" with which he transfixed the congregation for an hour and a quarter.[147] Every element of Channing's peculiar genius was present, as if deliberately orchestrated for his last, great effort as preacher and proclaimer of the liberating word — the distinctive voice, the integrity of feeling, the unusual consistency of perspective, the response to crisis in the human condition by inflaming the moral instincts and appealing to the good hidden deep in the human heart. He stood before his Berkshire following as the person that sixty-two years had made him, an honest soul capable of looking into the abyss of evil without vertigo, an honest *gentleman,* upstanding, decorous, fervent, and inspirational, who genuinely wanted for every human being the freeing faith and hope which he experienced.

". . . There are certain truths," he said, "which I can no more doubt than my own existence. That God is just and good, and that justice and goodness are his laws, and are at once the safety and glory of his creatures. . . . When I am told that society can only subsist by robbing men of their dearest rights, my reason is as much insulted as if I were gravely taught that effects require no cause. . . . The doctrine that violence, oppression, inhumanity, is an essential element of society, is so revolting, that, did I believe it, I would say, let society perish, let man and his works be swept away. . . . No! it is safe to be just, to respect men's rights, to treat our neighbors as ourselves."[148]

Having spilled out the essence of his life on the antislavery theme which had brought that essence to its greatest heights of emotional ardor, Channing languished at the Lenox Inn for a few days like "a broken wave."[149] As on so many earlier occasions, he pulled himself together, and he and Ruth finished out the month of August thoroughly caught up in the Berkshire patterns of natural beauty and human companionship.

Early in September, they packed their traveling bags and headed north toward the Green Mountains of Vermont, the long way round to Boston. Arriving at Bennington's Walloomsac Inn, Channing was decidedly ill and went at once to bed. Dr. Walter Channing was summoned from Boston to associate himself with local physicians who had diagnosed typhoid fever. Channing, aware of the gravity of his condition, was happier "than ever before" to see his distinguished brother.[150] There seemed for a time to be an improvement, sufficient to make Walter think of returning to Boston. The brothers sat together for hours, gazing out an east window across the Bennington green and the East Bennington valley to the mountain range, talking of family affairs and politics, of slavery and poverty, of religion and medicine. Walter became more convinced than ever that his brother was a man of awesome proportions. To their absent brother George, he confided by mail that while William was necessarily "a frail being" like all others, he was also a most remarkable "manifestation of the Supreme . . . to me an object of reverence and love."[151]

Improvement in Channing's condition was fleeting, and from day to day he wasted, causing Walter to prescribe less and less weighty conversation with those taking turns at the bedside. For this Channing was grateful. The activity of his brain was pushed beyond endurance by fever. Several times he asked those who came into his room if they could help him direct his thoughts to "common things" and away from "these crowds of images, these visions of immensity, and rushing thoughts." Moral teacher to the end, he spelled out an ordinance for calm thoughts. "We must beware," he murmured, "of overexcited feelings, of vague sentiment, of mingling our theoretical views or our favorite imaginations with the truth. We need to feel the *reality*, the REALITY of the spiritual life."[152]

Ernest Renan, in his critical assessment of Channing, wrote of the "extraordinary spectacle" in European eyes of a genuine apostle and saint living his life "like anybody else" in the domestic and private realm. Before writing, Renan had read in William Henry Channing's *Memoirs* how the great man, dying and aware of it, was invariably cheerful to those attending him, complimenting them as "most admirable bed-makers," drolly warning them not to strain themselves as they lifted his gossamer body, and urging them to spend more time in the fresh air and less in the wearying confinement of his room.[153]

On the night of September 30, Daniel Webster rose before a packed audience at Faneuil Hall to rationalize his retention of a place in Tyler's cabinet. Almost as if hearing the thunder of his old friend's booming voice, Channing spent a night of sleepless misery. Earlier that day he told Dr. Swift, the attending Bennington physician, that he longed to be back in Boston, "to die there," but quickly added: "It will all be well; it *is* all well."[154]

When the steeple bells rang on Sunday morning, October 2, he advised everyone to go to church. Reminded that visiting the sick was also biblically recommended as true religion, he good-naturedly agreed, asking only that someone read the Sermon on the Mount. By afternoon he periodically drifted into stupor, rousing to whisper, "I have received many messages from the spirit," and indicating a wish to be turned toward the window, where he might look out at the hills warming themselves in the sun. No one present knew precisely the moment. Without struggle or sigh, he died.

His body was borne by a Western Railroad Company car to Boston, where on Friday, October 7, Ezra Stiles Gannett preached a funeral eulogy from the Federal Street pulpit. As the coffin lid closed over the waxen face framed by the still soft, dark brown hair, and the procession moved from the church, the bell that tolled was the bell of the Catholic cathedral.[155]

Source Notes

Works, in the following notes, refers to the one-volume edition of *The Works of William Ellery Channing* published in 1901 by the American Unitarian Association. For the convenience of readers who may not have access to this edition, the titles of particular works are also indicated in parentheses. The following abbreviations are used:

AUA: Archives of the American Unitarian Association (now Unitarian Universalist Association), Boston, Massachusetts

Meadville: Library of the Meadville Theological School of Lombard College, Chicago, Illinois

MHS: Massachusetts Historical Society, Boston, Massachusetts

RIHS: Rhode Island Historical Society, Providence, Rhode Island

WEC: William Ellery Channing

WHC: William Henry Channing

Prologue

1. Conrad Wright, "The Rediscovery of Channing: Some Comments on Recent Scholarship," *Proceedings of the Unitarian Historical Society* 12, no. 2 (1959): 8.
2. John Pierpont, *A Discourse Occasioned by the Death of the Rev. William Ellery Channing* (Boston: Oliver Johnson, 1842); Abe C. Ravitz, "The Return of William Ellery Channing," *American Quarterly* 13, no. 1 (Spring 1961): 70; article on John Pierpont by George Harvey Genzmer in Dumas Malone, ed., *Dictionary of American Biography*, vol. 7, part 1 (New York: Charles Scribner's Sons, 1962), p. 586.
3. Ravitz, "William Ellery Channing."
4. Max Weber, *Jugendbriefe*, ed. Marianne Weber (Tübingen, 1936), pp. 120–121. (Translations here and elsewhere prepared by Richard E. Myers.)
5. Channing Centenary Volume (Boston: American Unitarian Association, 1881), p. 22.
6. Sydney E. Ahlstrom, "The Interpretation of Channing," *New England Quarterly* 30 (September 1957): 99.
7. Alexander Cowie, "Still a Good Light to Guide by," *New York Times Book Review*, September 1, 1963.
8. Ibid.
9. *Works*, p. 609 ("A Discourse Occasioned by the Death of the Rev. Dr. Follen").

10. Ibid., p. 1 ("Introductory Remarks").
11. Ibid.
12. Ibid., p. 3.
13. Elizabeth Palmer Peabody, *Reminiscences of Rev. Wm. Ellery Channing, D.D.* (Boston: Roberts Brothers, 1880), p. 388.
14. Ibid., p. 389.
15. *Works,* p. 4 ("Introductory Remarks").
16. Ibid.
17. Ibid., p. 469 ("Letter on Catholicism").
18. Peabody, *Reminiscences,* p. 3.
19. *Works,* p. 11 ("Introductory Remarks").
20. Ibid., p. 7.
21. Herbert W. Schneider, "The Intellectual Background of William Ellery Channing," *Church History* 7 (1938): 3; also the same author's *History of American Philosophy* (New York: Columbia University Press, 1946), pp. 61–67.
22. Anne Holt, *William Ellery Channing (1780–1842): His Religious and Social Thought* (London: Lindsey Press, 1942).
23. Robert Leet Patterson, *The Philosophy of William Ellery Channing* (New York: Bookman Associates, 1952).
24. David P. Edgell, *William Ellery Channing: Apostle of the Free Mind* (Boston: Beacon Press, 1955).
25. Arthur W. Brown, *Always Young for Liberty* (Syracuse, N.Y.: Syracuse University Press, 1956).
26. Madeleine Hooke Rice, *Federal Street Pastor* (New York: Bookman Associates, 1961).
27. Ahlstrom, "Interpretation of Channing," p. 104.

Chapter 1

1. Bertram Lippincott, *Indians, Privateers, and High Society* (Philadelphia: J. B. Lippincott Co., 1961), pp. 9, 155.
2. Edward Peterson, *History of Rhode Island and Newport* (New York: J. S. Taylor, 1853).
3. *Works,* p. 421 ("Christian Worship: Discourse at the Dedication of the Unitarian Congregational Church, Newport, Rhode Island, July 27, 1836").
4. WHC, *Memoir of William Ellery Channing, with Extracts from his Correspondence and Manuscripts,* 3 vols. (Boston: Wm. Crosby and H. P. Nichols, 1848), 1: 13–14.
5. Ibid., p. 14.
6. Ibid., pp. 16, 17.
7. Ibid., p. 20.
8. *Works,* p. 421.
9. Elizabeth Palmer Peabody, *Reminiscences of Rev. Wm. Ellery Channing, D.D.* (Boston: Roberts Brothers, 1880), pp. 61–63.
10. John W. Chadwick, *William Ellery Channing: Minister of Religion* (Boston: Houghton Mifflin Co., 1903), p. 24.
11. Samuel Eliot Morison, *The Oxford History of the American People* (New York: Oxford University Press, 1965), p. 302.
12. WHC, *Memoir,* 1: 33.
13. *Works,* p. 425 ("Christian Worship").

286

14. WHC, *Memoir,* 1: 31.
15. Ibid., p. 33.
16. George G. Channing, *Early Recollections of Newport, R.I., from the Year 1793 to 1811* (Newport: A. J. Ward and C. E. Hammett, 1868).
17. WHC, *Memoir,* 1: 43.
18. Chadwick, *William Ellery Channing,* p. 31.
19. Harvard College Archives, Cambridge, Mass.: College Records (unpublished), vol. 4, entry for April 14, 1797.
20. Arthur Train, *Puritan's Progress* (New York: Charles Scribner's Sons, 1931), p. 96.
21. WHC, *Memoir,* 1: 43.
22. Samuel Eliot Morison, *Three Centuries of Harvard* (Cambridge, Mass.: Harvard University Press, 1936), p. 185.
23. WHC, *Memoir,* 1: 60.
24. Morison, *Three Centuries,* pp. 185, 186.
25. Conrad Wright, "The Rediscovery of Channing," pp. 11–12.
26. WHC, *Memoir,* 1: 63.
27. Ibid., p. 64.
28. Peabody, *Reminiscences,* pp. 367–368. Price, Channing said, "opened my mind to transcendental depths."
29. WHC, *Memoir,* 1: 52.
30. Ibid., p. 50.
31. Ibid., p. 73.
32. Ibid., p. 71.
33. Ibid., p. 72.
34. Ibid., p. 77.
35. Ibid., p. 78.
36. Ibid., p. 79.
37. Ibid., p. 80.
38. Ibid., p. 82.
39. Ibid., pp. 82–83.
40. Ibid., pp. 88–89.
41. Ibid., p. 92.
42. Ibid., p 93.
43. Ibid., p. 90.
44. Ibid., p. 83.
45. Ibid., p. 85.
46. Gerda Lerner, *The Grimké Sisters from South Carolina* (Boston: Houghton Mifflin Co., 1967), p. 102.
47. WHC, *Memoir,* 1: 100.
48. Ibid., p. 101.
49. Adam Ferguson, *An Essay on the History of Civil Society* (London: A. Millar and T. Cadell, 1768). See especially pp. 28–34 ("Of the Principles of Union Among Mankind"). This doubtless influenced Channing's "Remarks on Associations."
50. Chadwick, *William Ellery Channing,* p. 49.
51. WHC, *Memoir,* 1: 115.
52. Ibid., p. 130.
53. Ibid., p. 126.
54. *Works,* p. 422 ("Christian Worship").
55. WHC, *Memoir,* 1: 138.
56. Ibid., p. 139.
57. *Works,* p. 422.

58. WHC, *Memoir*, 1: 156.
59. Morison, *Three Centuries*, pp. 34–35.
60. WHC, *Memoir*, 1: 143.
61. Ibid., p. 126.
62. Ibid., pp. 154–158.
63. Ibid., p. 158.
64. Ibid., p. 161.
65. Charles T. Brooks, *William Ellery Channing: A Centennial Memory* (Boston: Roberts Brothers, 1880), p. 90.
66. MS letter, MHS.
67. WHC, *Memoir*, 1: 168. A manuscript copy of Channing's formal letter of acceptance is framed and hangs in the Memorial Room of the Arlington Street Church, Boston, Mass.

Chapter 2

1. WHC, *Memoir*, 1: 175.
2. Ibid., p. 176.
3. Ibid., p. 177.
4. Ibid., p. 179.
5. Ibid., pp. 194, 195.
6. John W. Chadwick, *William Ellery Channing: Minister of Religion* (Boston: Houghton Mifflin Co., 1903), p. 67.
7. Van Wyck Brooks, *The Flowering of New England* (New York: E. P. Dutton and Co., 1936), p. 9.
8. George Hillard, *The Dangers and Duties of the Mercantile Professions* (Boston: Ticknor, Reed, and Fields, 1850), pp. 43–45.
9. Cleveland Amory, *The Proper Bostonians* (New York: E. P. Dutton and Co., 1947), p. 81.
10. WHC, *Memoir*, 1: 210.
11. Brooks, *Flowering of New England*, p. 9.
12. Quoted in Chadwick, *William Ellery Channing*, p. 381.
13. WHC, *Memoir*, 3: 313.
14. Ibid., 1: 229.
15. Quoted in Paul Goodman, "Ethics and Enterprise: The Values of a Boston Elite, 1800–1860," *American Quarterly* 18, no. 3 (Fall 1966): 439.
16. Ibid., p. 442.
17. Brooks, *Flowering of New England*, p. 34.
18. Goodman, "Ethics and Enterprise," p. 446.
19. WHC, *Memoir*, 1: 232, 233.
20. Goodman, "Ethics and Enterprise," p. 448.
21. Ibid., p. 449.
22. Conrad Wright, *The Beginnings of Unitarianism in America* (Boston: Beacon Press, 1955), p. 252.
23. Ibid., pp. 261–263.
24. Quoted in Wright, *Beginnings of Unitarianism*, pp. 265, 266, from Joseph H. Jones, ed., *The Life of Ashbel Green* (New York, 1849), p. 225.
25. Wright, *Beginnings of Unitarianism*, pp. 269f.
26. Ibid., p. 270.
27. Ibid., p. 272; J. F. Freeman, *Remarks on the American Universal Geography* (Boston: Belknap and Hall, 1793).
28. *Columbian Sentinel*, November 24, 1804.

288

29. Ibid., January 16, 1805.
30. Wright, *Beginnings of Unitarianism*, p. 280.
31. Daniel T. McColgan, *Joseph Tuckerman: Pioneer in American Social Work* (Washington, D.C.: Catholic University of America Press, 1940), pp. 71–74.
32. WHC, *Memoir*, 1: 206.
33. Ibid., p. 188.
34. Ibid., p. 189.
35. Ibid., pp. 203, 204.
36. Ibid., p. 211.
37. Henry R. Viets, "Walter Channing," in Allen Johnson and Dumas Malone, eds., *Dictionary of American Biography*, vol. 2, part 2 (New York: Charles Scribner's Sons, 1957–58); James Freeman Clarke, *Memorial and Biographical Sketches* (Boston: Houghton, Osgood and Co., 1878), pp. 171–178.
38. WHC, *Memoir*, 1: 392.
39. Hosea Ballou, *A Treatise on Atonement* (1805, reissued Boston: Beacon Press, 1959). Ballou published critical reviews of Channing's sermons, but there seems to be no record of their having provoked any response from Channing. Cf. Ballou's *Strictures on a Sermon Entitled "Religion a Social Principle," Delivered in the Church in Federal Street, Boston, December 10, 1820, by William Ellery Channing* (Boston: Henry Bowen, 1820). Ballou was invited to, and probably attended (along with other Boston clergymen), the ordination of Ezra Stiles Gannett as colleague pastor of the Federal Street Church on June 30, 1824. (Records of the Arlington Street Church, MHS.)
40. For a sympathetic contemporary portrait of Codman, see William Allen, *Memoir of John Codman, D.D.* (Boston: T. R. Marvin and S. K. Whipple and Co., 1853).
41. WEC, *A Sermon Delivered at the Ordination of the Rev. John Codman to the Pastoral Care of the Second Church of Christ in Dorchester, on December 7, 1808* (Boston: J. Belcher, 1808).
42. Ibid.
43. Chadwick, *William Ellery Channing*, p. 119.
44. Quoted in Chadwick, *William Ellery Channing*, p. 119.
45. Ibid., p. 120.

Chapter 3

1. Walter Muir Whitehill, *Boston: A Topographical History* (Cambridge, Mass.: Harvard University Press, 1959), p. 69; Harold and James Kirker, *Bulfinch's Boston, 1787–1817* (New York: Oxford University Press, 1964), p. 231.
2. WHC, *Memoir*, 1: 205.
3. Ibid., p. 209.
4. Ibid., p. 210.
5. Ibid., p. 212.
6. *Monthly Anthology* 1, no. 2 (December 1830): 81–82.
7. Ibid., 1, no. 3 (January 1804): 99–103. The authority for ascribing the poem and articles referred to here to Channing is Mark A. deWolfe Howe, ed., *Journal of the Proceedings of the Society Which Conducts the Monthly Anthology and Boston Review* (Boston, 1910), pp. 317 ff. A rare edition of

the *Monthly Anthology,* containing the names of many of the contributors of the articles written into the manuscript is in the possession of the Boston Athenaeum. This edition attributes to Channing a different set of articles.

8. George G. Channing, *Early Recollections of Newport, R.I., from the Year 1793 to 1811* (Newport: A. J. Ward and C. E. Hammett, 1868), pp. 62–63.
9. WEC to Eloïse Payne, AUA.
10. WHC, *Memoir,* 2: 168, 169.
11. Ibid., 1: 215.
12. Elizabeth Palmer Peabody, *Reminiscences of Rev. Wm. Ellery Channing, D.D.* (Boston: Roberts Brothers, 1880), p. 17.
13. WHC, *Memoir,* 1: 216.
14. Ibid., pp. 216, 217.
15. Peabody, *Reminiscences,* p. 103.
16. WHC, *Memoir,* 2: 150, 151.
17. Samuel A. Eliot, ed., *Heralds of a Liberal Faith* (Boston: American Unitarian Association, 1910), 2: 149, 150.
18. WHC, *Memoir,* 1: 217.
19. Eliot, *Heralds,* 2: 143, 144.
20. Ibid., pp. 135, 136.
21. Van Wyck Brooks, *The Flowering of New England* (New York: E. P. Dutton and Co., 1936), p. 13.
22. Edmund Quincy, *Life of Josiah Quincy* (Boston: Ticknor and Fields, 1867), pp. 256, 258.
23. Josiah Quincy, *A Municipal History of the Town and City of Boston* (Boston: C. C. Little and J. Brown, 1852), pp. 21, 22.
24. Quoted in Samuel Eliot Morison, *The Oxford History of the American People* (New York: Oxford University Press, 1965), p. 382.
25. WEC, *A Sermon Preached in Boston, July 23, 1812, the Day of the Publick Fast Appointed by the Executive of the Commonwealth of Massachusetts in Consequence of the Declaration of War Against Great Britain* (Boston: J. Eliot, 1812).
26. WEC, *A Sermon Preached in Boston, April 5, 1810, the Day of the Public Fast* (Boston, 1810).
27. WEC, *A Sermon Preached in Boston, July 23, 1812.*
28. *Works,* pp. 679–684 ("Duties of the Citizen in Times of Trial or Danger").
29. Ibid., pp. 682–683.
30. Max Weber, *Jugendbriefe,* ed. Marianne Weber (Tübingen, 1936), p. 192.
31. WHC, *Memoir,* 2: 98, 99.
32. Ibid., p. 100.
33. *Works,* pp. 684–688 ("Duties of the Citizen in Times of Trial or Danger").
34. See, for example, James Truslow Adams, *The Epic of America* (Boston: Little, Brown and Co., 1931), p. 144.
35. Messala [pseud.], *Remarks on the Rev. Mr. Channing's Sermon, and the Religious Festival at Boston in Commemoration of the Conquest of France by the Allies* (Boston: Rowe and Hooper, 1814).
36. *Works,* pp. 629–642 ("The Union").
37. Eliza Susan Quincy's journal entry for February 23, 1815, gives a lively account of this ball. See Mark A. deWolfe Howe, ed., *The Articulate Sisters* (Cambridge, Mass.: Harvard University Press, 1946), pp. 14–16.
38. Edward T. Channing, *Life of William Ellery,* in Jared Sparks, ed., *The Library of American Biography,* vol. 6 (Boston: Hilliard, Gray and Co., 1836), pp. 138–139.
39. Printed in *The Friend of Peace* 1, no. 2: 39.

40. Merle Curti, *The American Peace Crusade* (Durham, N.C.: Duke University Press, 1929), pp. 3–20.
41. *Works,* pp. 642–652 (1816 Discourse on War).
42. Ibid., pp. 667–669 ("Lecture on War").
43. John W. Chadwick, *William Ellery Channing: Minister of Religion* (Boston: Houghton Mifflin Co., 1903), p. 300.
44. Harvard College Archives, Cambridge, Mass.: Corporation Records (unpublished), vol. 5, pp. 112, 126, 134, 148, 228.
45. Peabody, *Reminiscences,* p. 82.
46. Ibid., p. 87.
47. Ibid., p. 88.
48. WHC, *Memoir,* 2: 178.
49. Ibid., pp. 178–182.
50. See Harriet Martineau, *Society in America,* 3 vols. (London: Saunders and Otley, 1937), and Frances Trollope, *Domestic Manners of the Americans,* 2 vols. (London: Whittaker, Treacher and Co., 1832).
51. E. T. Channing, *William Ellery,* pp. 92–93.
52. G. G. Channing, *Early Recollections,* p. 134.
53. George Gibbs, *The Gibbs Family of Rhode Island and Some Related Families* (New York: privately printed, 1933), pp. 16–17, 104–108, 184.
54. Susan Higginson Channing to Mrs. Stephen Higginson, November 6, 1816, MHS.

Chapter 4

1. Elizabeth Palmer Peabody, *Reminiscences of Rev. Wm. Ellery Channing, D.D.* (Boston: Roberts Brothers, 1880), p. 22.
2. John W. Chadwick, *William Ellery Channing: Minister of Religion* (Boston: Houghton Mifflin Co., 1903), p. 149.
3. MS letter, Everett collection, MHS.
4. Cf., e.g., Williston Walker, *The Creeds and Platforms of Congregationalism* (New York: Charles Scribner's Sons, 1893), pp. 119–122.
5. William C. Gannett, *Ezra Stiles Gannett: A Memoir* (Boston: Roberts Brothers, 1875), p. 37
6. Thomas Belsham, *Memoirs of the Life of the Reverend Theophilus Lindsey, M.A.* (London: J. Johnson and Co., 1812), pp. 238–243.
7. Gannet, *Ezra Stiles Gannett,* p. 48.
8. [Samuel C. Thacher], "[Review of] *The Constitution and Associate Statutes of the Theological Seminary in Andover, . . .*" *Monthly Anthology* 5, no. 11 (November 1808): 602–614; and "Defence of the Review," *Monthly Anthology* 6, no. 3 (March 1809): 195–205.
9. Chadwick, *William Ellery Channing,* pp. 127–128.
10. John Adams to Jedidiah Morse, May 15, 1815, RIHS.
11. W. H. Howard Knott, "Jeremiah Evarts," in Allen Johnson and Dumas Malone, eds., *Dictionary of American Biography,* vol. 3, part 1 (New York: Charles Scribner's Sons, 1959), p. 215.
12. Earl Morse Wilbur, *A History of Unitarianism,* vol. 2 (Cambridge, Mass.: Harvard University Press, 1945), p. 418.
13. WHC, *Memoir,* 1: 377.
14. Ibid., pp. 380–396.
15. Ibid., pp. 396–410.

16. *Works,* pp. 478–486 ("The System of Exclusion and Denunciation in Religion Considered").
17. WEC to Susan A. Channing, August 24, 1812, Pierpont Morgan Library, New York City.
18. Peabody, *Reminiscences,* p. 19.
19. Ibid., p. 13.
20. Ibid.
21. Ibid., p. 14.
22. *Works,* pp. 328–336 ("Preaching Christ: Discourse at the Ordination of the Rev. John Emery Abbot, Salem, 1815").
23. Ibid. The phrase, and the ideas contained in the sermon, may have provided Emerson with some of the inspiration for the essay *Solitude and Society.*
24. Peabody, *Reminiscences,* p. 19.
25. Journal of Eliza Susan Quincy, April 1815, in Mark A. DeWolfe Howe, ed., *The Articulate Sisters* (Cambridge, Mass.: Harvard University Press, 1946), pp. 16, 17.
26. WHC, *Memoir,* 2: 139–142.
27. Howe, *Articulate Sisters,* pp. 20, 21.
28. *Columbian Sentinel,* July 12, 1817.
29. MS letter, September 15, 1817, AUA.
30. Samuel A. Eliot, ed., *Heralds of a Liberal Faith* (Boston: American Unitarian Association, 1910), 2: 146.
31. WHC, *Memoir,* 2: 187–189.
32. Ibid., pp. 116, 117.
33. Rebecca Funk, *A Heritage to Hold in Fee, 1817–1917, First Unitarian Church of Baltimore* (Baltimore, 1962).
34. Jared Sparks, Diary (1819–1823), Archives of the First Unitarian Church of Baltimore.
35. Funk, *Heritage,* p. 14.
36. Chadwick, *William Ellery Channing,* p. 145.
37. *Works,* p. 462 ("The Moral Argument Against Calvinism").
38. Funk, *Heritage,* p. 41.
39. Annabelle M. Melville, *Jean Lefebvre de Cheverus, 1768–1836* (Milwaukee: Bruce Publishing Co., 1958), p. 209.
40. WHC, *Memoir,* 2: 75–80.
41. *Works,* p. 462.
42. Moses Stuart, *Letters to the Rev. Wm. Ellery Channing, Containing Remarks on His Sermon Recently Preached and Published in Baltimore* (Andover, Mass.: Flagg and Gould, 1819), p. 108.
43. Eliot, *Heralds,* 2: 206–209.
44. Quoted in Wilbur, *History of Unitarianism,* 2: 432.
45. Ibid., p. 433.
46. Joseph Henry Allen, *Our Liberal Movement in Theology* (Boston: American Unitarian Association, 1882), p. 28.
47. Wilbur, *History of Unitarianism,* p. 441.

Chapter 5

1. Edward T. Channing, *Life of William Ellery,* in Jared Sparks, ed., *The Library of American Biography,* vol. 6 (Boston: Hilliard, Gray and Co., 1836), p. 147.

2. WHC, *Memoir*, 1: 419.
3. Harvard College Archives, Cambridge, Mass.: Corporation Records (unpublished), vol. 6, pp. 24, 32.
4. *Boston Town Records, 1814–1822* (document 128–1906) (Boston, 1906), pp. 161–164.
5. Jacob C. Meyer, *Church and State in Massachusetts from 1740 to 1833* (Cleveland: Western Reserve University Press, 1930), chapters 7–9.
6. Daniel T. McColgan, *Joseph Tuckerman: Pioneer in American Social Work* (Washington, D.C.: Catholic University of America Press, 1940), p. 56.
7. Ibid., p. 58.
8. WEC, *Religion a Social Principle: A Sermon Delivered in the Church in Federal Street, Boston, December 10, 1820* (Boston: Russell and Gardner, 1820).
9. Hosea Ballou, *Strictures on a Sermon Entitled "Religion a Social Principle," Delivered in the Church in Federal Street, Boston, December 10, 1820, by William Ellery Channing* (Boston: Henry Bowen, 1820); see also Ernest Cassara, *Hosea Ballou* (Boston: Universalist Historical Society, 1961), p. 145.
10. *Works*, p. 182 ("Spiritual Freedom").
11. Ibid., pp. 618–625 ("Memoir of John Gallison, Esq.").
12. Ibid., pp. 220–232 ("The Evidences of Revealed Religion").
13. WHC, *Memoir*, 2: 96, 97.
14. Quoted in Arthur W. Brown, *Always Young for Liberty* (Syracuse, N.Y.: Syracuse University Press, 1956), p. 140.
15. Ibid.
16. Perry Miller, *Life of the Mind in America* (New York: Harcourt, Brace and World, 1965), p. 45.
17. WEC to Susan Higginson Channing, August 27, 1820, Pierpont Morgan Library, New York City
18. WHC, *Memoir*, 2: 194.
19. Ibid., p. 199.
20. Ibid., p. 343.
21. Josiah Quincy, Jr., *Figures of the Past: From the Leaves of Old Journals* (Boston: Roberts Brothers, 1883), pp. 305–307.
22. WHC, *Memoir*, 3: 17.
23. Elizabeth Palmer Peabody, *Reminiscences of Rev. Wm. Ellery Channing, D.D.* (Boston: Roberts Brothers, 1880), p. 41.
24. MS letter, Meadville.
25. WHC, *Memoir*, 2: 190.
26. Ibid., p. 191.
27. Ibid.
28. WEC to Susan Higginson Channing, May 27, 1822, Pierpont Morgan Library, New York City.
29. WHC, *Memoir*, 2: 201.
30. Ibid., p. 205.
31. Peabody, *Reminiscences*, p. 76.
32. WHC, *Memoir*, 2: 220.
33. Ibid., pp. 217, 218.
34. Ibid., p. 218.
35. Peabody, *Reminiscences*, p. 98.
36. Ibid., pp. 98, 99.
37. *Works*, p. 473 ("Letter on Catholicism").

38. Ibid., p. 474.
39. WHC, *Memoir,* 2: 224.
40. Ibid., pp. 224–228.
41. Ibid., p. 230.
42. Ibid., pp. 230–232.
43. Ibid., p. 233.
44. Ibid., p. 235.
45. Ibid., p. 239.
46. Anna Letitia LeBreton, ed., *Correspondence of William Ellery Channing, D.D., and Lucy Aikin, from 1826 to 1842* (Boston: Roberts Brothers, 1874), p. 5.
47. James Martineau, "Memoirs and Papers of Dr. Channing," *Essays, Reviews, and Addresses* (London and New York, 1890–91), 1: 121. Martineau (1805–1900) was the brother of Harriet Martineau.
48. WHC, *Memoir,* 2: 248–250.
49. Channing autographs 17, 18, RIHS.
50. *Works,* pp. 563–564 ("Remarks on the Character and Writings of Fénelon").
51. WHC, *Memoir,* 2: 295–296.
52. Ibid., 3: 3, 4.
53. William B. Sprague, *Annals of the American Unitarian Pulpit* (New York: R. Carter and Brothers, 1865), pp. 372–375.
54. *Works,* p. 58 ("On the Elevation of the Laboring Classes").
55. Ibid., p. 60.
56. WHC, *Memoir,* 3: 15, 16.
57. Ibid., p. 17.
58. *Works,* p. 276 ("The Demands of the Age on the Ministry: Discourse at the Ordination of the Rev. E. S. Gannett, Boston, 1824").
59. Letter dated July 18, 1824, quoted in Octavius Brooks Frothingham, *George Ripley* (Boston: Houghton, Mifflin and Co., 1882), p. 28.
60. Charles Crowe, *George Ripley* (Athens, Ga.: University of Georgia Press, 1967), p. 36.
61. William C. Gannett, *Ezra Stiles Gannett: A Memoir* (Boston: Roberts Brothers, 1875), p. 75.
62. Quoted in Brown, *Always Young for Liberty,* p. 160.
63. WHC, *Memoir,* 3: 124.
64. Ralph Waldo Emerson, *Works* (Boston: Houghton, Mifflin and Co., 1883), 10: 352; David P. Edgell, *William Ellery Channing: Apostle of the Free Mind* (Boston: Beacon Press, 1955), p. 151.
65. WHC, *Memoir,* 3: 124.
66. Peabody, *Reminiscences,* p. 8.
67. WHC, *Memoir,* 3: 124.
68. Ibid., p. 131.
69. Samuel Eliot Morison, *The Oxford History of the American People* (New York: Oxford University Press, 1965), p. 438.
70. WHC, *Memoir,* 3: 111.
71. Ibid., p. 172.
72. *Works,* pp. 73–74 ("Ministry for the Poor: Discourse Delivered Before the Benevolent Fraternity of Churches, Boston, April 9, 1835").
73. Peabody, *Reminiscences,* p. 277.
74. WHC, *Memoir,* 3: 53.
75. *Boston Quarterly Review* 1 (January 1838): 127; see also Arthur M. Schlesinger, Jr., *A Pilgrim's Progress: Orestes A. Brownson* (1939, reissued New York: Octagon Books, 1966), p. 78.

76. John W. Chadwick, *William Ellery Channing: Minister of Religion* (Boston: Houghton Mifflin Co., 1903), pp. 320, 321.
77. *Works,* p. 103 ("Address on Temperance").
78. Ibid., p. 104.
79. WHC, *Memoir,* 3: 73, 74.
80. Ibid., p. 25.
81. Ibid., p. 29.
82. Ibid., p. 70.
83. MS dated November 17, 1831, Channing papers, MHS.
84. Arthur M. Schlesinger, Jr., *The Age of Jackson* (Boston: Little, Brown and Co., 1946), p. 134
85. Ibid., p. 135.
86. Thomas Whittemore, *Life of Hosea Ballou,* 4 vols. (Boston: J. M. Usher, 1854–55), 3: 62; Cassara, *Hosea Ballou,* p. 153.
87. Henry S. Commager, "The Blasphemy of Abner Kneeland," *New England Quarterly* 8 (March 1935): 29–41.
88. Whittemore, *Life of Hosea Ballou,* 3: 180. To Ballou's credit, even though he seemed to desert his earlier contention to Channing that the state should not involve itself in the determination of acceptable religious views, he often visited Kneeland in prison and treated him with great personal kindness.
89. WHC, *Memoir,* 3: 101–108.
90. Ibid., p. 107.
91. Robert H. Lord, John E. Sexton, and Edward T. Harrington, *History of the Archdiocese of Boston in the Various Stages of Its Development, 1604 to 1943,* 3 vols. (New York: Sheed, 1944), 2: 205–239.
92. WEC to Jonathan Phillips, July 24, 1834, Phillips papers, MHS.
93. WHC, *Memoir,* 3: 159–160.
94. Ibid., pp. 245–250.
95. LeBreton, *Correspondence,* pp. 203–204.
96. WEC to William Rathbone, August 10, 1842, Channing papers, MHS.
97. *Works,* p. 32 ("Self-Culture").
98. Ibid., p. 56 ("On the Elevation of the Laboring Classes").
99. Ibid., p. 57.
100. McColgan, *Joseph Tuckerman,* pp. 166–167.
101. WHC, *Memoir,* 3: 159.
102. Schlesinger, *Age of Jackson,* p. 164.
103. *Works,* pp. 135–158 ("Remarks on Associations").
104. Edgell, *William Ellery Channing,* p. 200.
105. WHC, *Memoir,* 3: 120.
106. LeBreton, *Correspondence,* pp. 251, 253.
107. *Works,* pp. 577–578 ("Remarks on the Character and Writings of Fénelon").
108. Ibid., p. 579.
109. Ibid., p. 86 ("Ministry for the Poor").
110. Schlesinger, *Pilgrim's Progress,* p. 81.

Chapter 6

1. Harriet Martineau, *Retrospect of Western Travel,* 2 vols. (New York: Harper and Brothers, 1838), 2: 121.
2. *Works,* p. 909 ("Emancipation in the British West Indies").
3. WHC, *Memoir,* 3: 148–150.

4. *Works,* pp. 907–924 ("An Address . . . on the . . . Anniversary of Emancipation in the British West Indies").

5. Edwards A. Park, *Memoir of the Life and Character of Samuel Hopkins, D.D.* (Boston, 1854), pp. 131–138. Hopkins wished to educate the two black men to become missionaries to Africa.

6. George G. Channing, *Early Recollections of Newport, R. I., from the Year 1793 to 1811* (Newport: A. J. Ward and C. E. Hammett, 1868), pp. 91, 92.

7. Walter Channing, *My Own Times, or 'Tis Fifty Years Since* (reprinted from the *Monthly Miscellany and Journal of Health*) (Boston, 1845), p. 14; G. G. Channing, *Early Recollections,* pp. 46–47, 142; Elizabeth Palmer Peabody, *Reminiscences of Rev. Wm. Ellery Channing D.D.* (Boston: Roberts Brothers, 1880), p. 388.

8. G. G. Channing, *Early Recollections,* p. 7.

9. Ibid., p. 171.

10. WHC, *Memoir,* 1: 85.

11. Samuel Eliot Morison, *The Oxford History of the American People* (New York: Oxford University Press, 1965), p. 405; Harrison Gray Otis to WEC, March 3, 1820, autograph no. 45, RIHS.

12. Mrs. S. P. Hale to Edward Everett, March 28, 1826, Everett papers, MHS.

13. WHC, *Memoir,* 3: 135.

14. WEC to Daniel Webster, May 14, 1828, in Daniel Webster, *Works,* 18 vols. (Boston, 1877), 5: 366–367.

15. WEC, MS sermon, Meadville. The MS is dated November 1830.

16. Van Wyck Brooks, *The Flowering of New England* (New York: E. P. Dutton and Co., 1936), p. 192.

17. WEC, MS sermon, Meadville.

18. WHC, *Memoir,* 3: 136–137.

19. Ibid., pp. 137–139.

20. WEC to Joseph Tuckerman, January 15, 1831, Channing papers, MHS; WHC, *Memoir,* 3: 140.

21. WHC, *Memoir,* 3: 142–146.

22. *Works,* pp. 916–917, 921–922 ("Emancipation in the British West Indies").

23. Elizabeth Palmer Peabody, *Reminiscences of Rev. Wm. Ellery Channing, D.D.* (Boston: Roberts Brothers, 1880), p. 358.

24. Ibid.

25. John W. Chadwick, *William Ellery Channing: Minister of Religion* (Boston: Houghton Mifflin Co., 1903), p. 263.

26. Harriet Martineau, *Autobiography,* ed. Maria Chapman (Boston: J. R. Osgood and Co., 1877), vol. 2, appendix.

27. William Lloyd Garrison to WEC, January 20, 1834, Antislavery Collection, Boston Public Library.

28. WEC to E. S. Gannett, August 6, 1833, Gannett papers, MHS.

29. E. S. Gannett to WEC, August 23, 1833, Gannett papers, MHS.

30. E. S. Gannett to WEC, September 4, 1833, Gannet papers, MHS.

31. Peabody, *Reminiscences,* p. 359.

32. WHC, *Memoir,* 3: 154.

33. John Greenleaf Whittier, ed., *Letters of Lydia Maria Child* (Boston: Houghton, Mifflin and Co., 1883), pp. 24–25, 44–48.

34. WHC, *Memoir,* 3: 154–155.

35. Thomas J. Mumford, ed., *Memoir of Samuel Joseph May* (Boston: Roberts Brothers, 1873).

36. Ibid., pp. 156–157.
37. WHC, *Memoir*, 3: 157–158.
38. Ibid., pp. 438–442.
39. Anna Letitia LeBreton, ed., *Correspondence of William Ellery Channing, D.D., and Lucy Aikin, from 1826 to 1842* (Boston: Roberts Brothers, 1874), p. 193.
40. WHC, *Memoir*, 3: 159–160.
41. Edward Strutt Abdy, *Journal of a Residence and Tour in the United States of North America, from April, 1833, to October, 1834*, 3 vols. (London: J. Murray, 1835), 3: 217–238 (Abdy's account of his interview with Channing). Cf. p. 219: "I was assured that all those colored persons who had come under the notice of the Doctor were men of indifferent character; that the whole race were remarkable for want of sympathy with one another's misfortunes: and that, according to the evidence of a correspondent in Philadelphia, the generality of those of African descent in that city were degraded to the lowest state." See also Thomas F. Harwood, "Prejudice and Antislavery: The Colloquy Between William Ellery Channing and Edward Strutt Abdy, 1834," *American Quarterly* (Winter 1966), pp. 696–700. Harwood regards the interview as "another example of the important British stimulus to the revived antislavery impulse of the 1830's" and as illustrating the predominance of the theme of prejudice in British abolitionists' descriptions of America.
42. Martineau, *Retrospect*, 2:120.
43. Mary B. Slade, "Prince Saunders," in Allen Johnson and Dumas Malone, eds., *Dictionary of American Biography*, vol. 8, part 2 (New York: Charles Scribner's Sons, 1963), p. 382. Opinions about Saunders have not always been favorable. The *Emancipator*, of July 4, 1839, announcing his death, called him a "humbug, fathered and flattered by none in America except the Colonizationists." Vernon Loggins, in *The Negro Author: His Development in America* (New York: Columbia University Press, 1931), states: "Saunders was an opportunist, and his experiences at Christophe's court had made him a sycophant. He was far remote in character from men of the sincerity of Allen and Forten and Purvis. . . . But the obstacles he overcame in following up his career, however unworthy it might have been, prove that he was a man of extraordinary ability" (p. 72). A reading of Saunders's own addresses conveys a more positive impression of the man. Cf. his *Memoir Presented to the American Convention for Promoting the Abolition of Slavery* (Philadelphia, 1818).
44. WHC, *Memoir*, 1: 201.
45. Abdy, *Journal*, 3: 220–221.
46. Ibid., p. 228.
47. Harriet Martineau, "The Martyr Age in the United States," *London and Westminster Review* 31 (December 1838–April 1939): 8.
48. WHC, *Memoir*, 3: 162–164.
49. Chadwick, *William Ellery Channing*, p. 271.
50. WHC, *Memoir*, 3: 165, 166.
51. Ibid., pp. 167, 168.
52. Ibid., p. 169.
53. Martineau, *Retrospect*, 2: 118.
54. Ibid., p. 121.
55. Morison, *Oxford History*, p. 508f. See also Arna Bontemps, *Black Thunder: Gabriel's Revolt* (1936, new edition Boston: Beacon Press, 1968).
56. WHC, *Memoir*, 3: 171.

57. Ibid., p. 172.
58. *Works*, p. 691 ("Slavery").
59. Ibid., pp. 695–696.
60. Ibid., pp. 697–704.
61. Ibid., pp. 704–707.
62. Ibid., pp. 707–722.
63. Ibid., pp. 723, 724.
64. Ibid., pp. 725–731.
65. Ibid., pp. 737–739.
66. Martineau, *Retrospect*, 2: 121.
67. *Liberator*, December 12, 1835.
68. Ibid., December 19, 1835; December 26, 1835; January 2, 1836.
69. WHC, *Memoir*, 3: 173, 174.
70. Chadwick, *William Ellery Channing*, p. 276.
71. *Anti-Slavery Magazine*, ed. Elizur Wright, vol. 1, no. 4 (July 1836).
72. Charles F. Adams, ed., *Memoirs of John Quincy Adams*, 12 vols. (Philadelphia, J. B. Lippincott and Co., 1876), 9: 266.
73. William Francis Channing to William Lloyd Garrison, December 7, 1879, Antislavery Collection, Boston Public Library.
74. *Congressional Globe*, appendix (2nd session, Twenty-fourth Congress), p. 266.
75. James T. Austin, *Remarks on Dr. Channing's "Slavery" by a Citizen of Massachusetts* (Boston: Russell, Shattuck and Co., 1835), p. 14; Chadwick, *William Ellery Channing*, p. 279.
76. WHC, *Memoir*, 3: 174, 175.
77. Samuel J. May, *Some Recollections of Our Antislavery Conflict* (Boston: Fields, Osgood and Co., 1869), pp. 177–185.
78. Harriet Martineau, *Society in America*, 3 vols. (London: Saunders and Otley, 1837), 2: 161–162; abridged by Seymour Martin Lipset (Garden City, N.Y.: Doubleday, 1962), p. 254.
79. Martineau, "Martyr Age," pp. 30–31.
80. Martineau, *Retrospect*, 2: 219.
81. WHC, *Memoir*, 3: 176–182.
82. Lerone Bennett, Jr., *Before the Mayflower: A History of the Negro in America, 1619–1964* (rev. ed. Baltimore: Penguin Books, 1966), pp. 130–136.
83. WHC, *Memoir*, 3: 179.
84. Ibid.
85. Ibid., p. 180.
86. Ibid., pp. 180–181.
87. See William Birney, *James G. Birney and His Times* (New York: D. Appleton and Co., 1890).
88. *Works*, p. 743 ("Slavery").
89. Ibid., p. 744.
90. WHC, *Memoir*, 3: 188.
91. Ibid., p. 189.
92. Ibid.
93. *Works*, pp. 752–789 ("A Letter to the Hon. Henry Clay on the Annexation of Texas to the United States").
94. Ibid.
95. WHC, *Memoir*, 3: 201.
96. Ibid., pp. 203, 204.
97. Ibid., p. 207.

98. Ibid., p. 208.
99. Ibid.. pp. 212–213.
100. Ibid., pp. 214–215.
101. *Liberator*, December 22, 1837.
102. Ibid.; see also January 5, 1838, and February 23, 1838.
103. WHC, *Memoir*, 3: 229.
104. Ibid.
105. Ibid., p. 231.
106. WEC to Levi Lincoln, February 7, 1837, MHS.
107. J. Q. Adams to WEC, August 11, 1837, RIHS.
108. WEC to Joseph Tuckerman, August 2, 1838, AUA.
109. Peabody, *Reminiscences*, pp. 360–363.
110. *Works*, pp. 782–820 ("Remarks on the Slavery Question in a Letter to Jonathan Phillips, Esq.").
111. WHC, *Memoir*, 2: 394.
112. Henry Ware, Jr., in the *Christian Examiner*, May 1839, p. 272.
113. James T. Austin, *Review of the Rev. Dr. Channing's Letter to Jonathan Phillips, Esq., on the Slavery Question* (Boston: J. H. Eastburn, 1839).
114. Chadwick, *William Ellery Channing*, p. 291.
115. C. F. Adams, *John Quincy Adams*, 10: 39–40, 40–42.
116. *Works*, p. 93 ("Charge for the Ordination of Mr. Robert C. Waterston, as Minister at Large"). A note at the beginning of the sermon explains that it was not delivered "on account of the Author's state of health."
117. S. T. Pickard, *The Life and Letters of John Greenleaf Whittier* (Boston: Houghton, Mifflin and Co. 1894), 2: 642, 643; the MS letter is at AUA.
118. *Works*, p. 615 ("A Discourse Occasioned by the Death of the Rev. Dr. Follen").
119. WHC, *Memoir*, 2: 310.
120. *Works*, pp. 434–436 ("The Church").
121. WHC, *Memoir*, 3: 233–234.
122. *Works*, pp. 844f. ("Emancipation").
123. WHC, *Memoir*, 2: 324.
124. Francis J. Grund, *Aristocracy in America. From the Sketch-Book of a German Nobleman*, 2 vols. (London: R. Bentley, 1839), 2: 132–150.
125. James Freeman Clarke, *The Church as It Was, as It Is, as It Ought to Be: A Discourse Delivered . . . March 15, 1845* (Boston, 1909), p. 17.
126. Chadwick, *William Ellery Channing*, p. 355.
127. *Works*, p. 164 ("The Present Age").
128. W. H. Furness to WEC, June 5, 1841, Channing papers, Meadville.
129. W. F. Channing to T. W. Higginson, January 24, 1879; T. W. Higginson, "Two New England Heretics: Channing and Parker," *Independent* (May 22, 1902), pp. 1235, 1236.
130. Peabody, *Reminiscences*, p. 263.
131. Ibid.
132. WHC, *Memoir*, 3: 477.
133. Granville Hicks, "Dr. Channing and the *Creole* Case," *American Historical Review* 37 (1931–32): 516, 517.
134. *Works*, p. 906 ("Duty of the Free States, Part II").
135. Ibid., p. 858 ("Duty of the Free States, Part I").
136. WEC to Robert C. Winthrop, December 30, 1841, Winthrop papers, MHS.
137. Charles Sumner to George Sumner, quoted in Edward L. Pierce, *Memoir and Letters of Charles Sumner*, 4 vols. (Boston: Roberts Brothers, 1877–93), 2: 223.

138. WEC to Jonathan Phillips, dated May 3 and May 12, 1842, Phillips papers, MHS.
139. WHC, *Memoir,* 3: 471.
140. WEC to Charles Sumner, June 4, 1842, Harvard College.
141. WEC to Jonathan Phillips, July 26, 1842, Phillips papers, MHS.
142. Mary E. Dewey, ed., *Life and Letters of Catharine M. Sedgwick* (New York: Harper and Brothers, 1871), p. 283.
143. WHC, *Memoir,* 3: 476.
144. WEC to Catharine M. Sedgwick, Sedgwick papers, MHS. It is marked, "My last letter from Dr. Channing."
145. LeBreton, *Correspondence,* pp. 418, 419.
146. Ibid., pp. 420–424.
147. C. M. Sedgwick to Fanny Kemble, in Frances A. Kemble, *Records of Later Life* (New York: H. Holt and Co., 1882), pp. 273, 274.
148. *Works,* p. 922 ("An Address Delivered at Lenox . . .").
149. Chadwick, *William Ellery Channing,* p. 419.
150. Dr. Walter Channing to George G. Channing, September 26, 1842, Channing papers, MHS.
151. Ibid.
152. WHC, *Memoir,* 3: 481–482.
153. Ibid., p. 484.
154. Ibid., p. 485.
155. Ibid., p. 488.

Index

The following abbreviation is used: WEC: William Ellery Channing

307